Southern Religion, Southern Culture

Southern Religion, Southern Culture

Essays Honoring Charles Reagan Wilson

Edited by
Darren E. Grem, Ted Ownby,
and James G. Thomas, Jr.

University Press of Mississippi / Jackson

The University Press of Mississippi is the scholarly publishing agency of
the Mississippi Institutions of Higher Learning: Alcorn State University,
Delta State University, Jackson State University, Mississippi State University,
Mississippi University for Women, Mississippi Valley State University,
University of Mississippi, and University of Southern Mississippi.

Chancellor Porter L. Fortune Symposium in Southern History Series

www.upress.state.ms.us

The University Press of Mississippi is a member of
the Association of University Presses.

Copyright © 2019 by University Press of Mississippi
All rights reserved

First printing 2019
∞

Library of Congress Cataloging-in-Publication Data

Names: Grem, Darren E., editor. | Ownby, Ted, editor. | Wilson, Charles
Reagan, honoree. | Thomas, James G., Jr., editor.
Title: Southern religion, Southern culture: essays honoring Charles Reagan
Wilson / edited by Darren E. Grem, Ted Ownby, and James G. Thomas, Jr.
Description: Jackson: University Press of Mississippi, [2018] | Series:
Chancellor Porter L. Fortune Symposium in Southern history series | "First
printing 2019." | Includes bibliographical references and index. |
Identifiers: LCCN 2018021907 (print) | LCCN 2018033400 (ebook) | ISBN
9781496820488 (epub single) | ISBN 9781496820495 (epub institutional) |
ISBN 9781496820501 (pdf single) | ISBN 9781496820518 (pdf institutional)
| ISBN 9781496820471 (cloth)
Subjects: LCSH: Southern States—Church history. | Wilson, Charles Reagan. |
Church historians—Southern States.
Classification: LCC BR535 (ebook) | LCC BR535 .S685 2018 (print) | DDC
277.5—dc22
LC record available at https://lccn.loc.gov/2018021907

British Library Cataloging-in-Publication Data available

Contents

vii Introduction
    DARREN E. GREM

3   Judgment, Grace, Race, and the Transcendental Blues: The Study of Religion in the South in the Era of Charles Reagan Wilson
    PAUL HARVEY

Religious History and Church History

19 The Riverbank Politics of Uncommon Prayers in Antebellum Arkansas
    RYAN L. FLETCHER

47 Race and the Visions of John Lafayette Girardeau
    OTIS W. PICKETT

63 Having Our Own: The Colored Methodist Episcopal Church and the Struggle for Black Autonomy in Education
    ALICIA JACKSON

Religious History beyond Institutions

79 Spirit in the Air: Pentecostal and Holiness Media Innovation in the Twentieth-Century South
    RANDALL STEPHENS

102 "The Pure of Body Are Pure of Soul": Religion and
the Emerging Sports Culture of the New South
ARTHUR REMILLARD

113 The Land of Misfit Relics: Southern Protestants and the Sacred Play
of Cultural Objects
CHAD SEALES

121 Afterword: Charles Reagan Wilson as Scholar, Editor, Innovator,
and Resonator
TED OWNBY

131 Contributors

133 Index

Introduction

DARREN E. GREM

A saint lingers in the Tupelo Room at the University of Mississippi's Barnard Observatory. At the back of the room, within full view of anyone who walks in, hangs an oversized linen sheet. Painted on the sheet is a depiction of a handsome young man, dead now for four decades. His hair is groomed and jet black. His expression is blank. His skin is pale. His chest peeks out from a black jacket. A pink aura surrounds his head. He neither smiles nor scowls. His lips are pursed. Black paint, suggestive of blood, drips from his jacket. His grayish blue eyes meet the eyes of anyone who looks at him. He holds a relaxed, fixed gaze. It is the eternal gaze of a saint. It is the gaze of Elvis Presley.

Stenciled at the top of the sheet is a declaration: "THE SHROUD OF MEMPHIS." Of course, it is not really a shroud. It did not cover Elvis's bloated, drug-addled body after his death in 1977. Moreover, the word "shroud" is struck through. The shroud is *really* "THE KING SIZE SHEET OF MEMPHIS." It is an ordinary object, albeit one that suggests Elvis *was* a certain kind of saint. To be sure, he was not a saint in accordance with, say, Roman Catholic standards. And he certainly was no saint in the iconoclastic, Pentecostal faith in which he and other rock and rollers (from Little Richard to Jerry Lee Lewis to Johnny Cash) were raised. Rather, Elvis was a saint of another kind of faith (see Figure 1).

Elvis was a saint of rock and roll.[1] He was a saint of ostentation and gaudiness, at least according to mid-century norms of middle-class decorum. He was a saint of gold necklaces, jungle rooms, pink Cadillacs, and private jets with "TCB" ("Taking Care of Business") slapped on the tail wing. He was a saint of sex, of one-night stands, of shaking hips, of kissable lips, and of sweat left on jumpsuits and bed sheets. He was a saint of racial license. In his younger

The Shroud of Memphis, by William Dunlap. Photo by James G. Thomas, Jr.

years, Elvis's hair and dress mimicked a fashionable African American man about town on a Saturday night in Jim Crow Memphis. He was cool. He was hip. He was a stylish, charismatic saint, exuding sexual and racial danger. For such reasons, Elvis excited his audiences, especially millions of teenage white women. They flocked to his performances. They rushed to buy his records. They fantasized about him and gushed about him in letters to their girlfriends. They ran to his side after gigs and tore at his clothes.[2] They kept the "TLC" ("tender loving care") necklaces he gave them. They lusted after him when he appeared on primetime television. They loved to see him shake it—as songwriter Gillian Welch later put it—"like a holy roller, baby, with his soul at stake."[3]

Onstage, writes historian Joel Williamson, "it was as if [Elvis] and the teenage girls in his audience existed in a huge and protective bubble, alone, ecstatic, and away from the stultifying world."[4] Elvis's aura captured his fans' attention and drew out their desires in a manner akin to how Jesus Christ *should* have drawn them to chaste thinking, upright living, and regular church attendance. He made teenage women—as well as millions of others—feel what pastors and parents across the South proclaimed as the source of true religious feeling. They felt free, alive, reborn, and thirsting for more. Therein lay his holy-unholy appeal. Therein lay his potential for sainthood.

Years of drug abuse set the stage for Elvis's pitiable death in an upstairs bathroom at an estate named after grace (Graceland in Memphis, Tennessee). But the feelings he invoked did not die out, even as his addictions hounded him, his weight ballooned, and his audiences aged, settled down, or otherwise moved on. When he died, his fans, old and new, thronged at Graceland's gates and mourned his passing.[5]

Then they canonized him with culture. They bought figurines *in memoriam*, which they placed on mantles and coffee tables. They sought out and collected relics: snippets of clothing, signed pictures, sweat-stained handkerchiefs. They pilgrimaged, not only to Memphis but to Tupelo, where he was born. They held yearly music festivals in his honor. They celebrated his birthday. They impersonated him. They drove to their nearby post office and bought commemorative stamps. They made folk art.[6]

They also felt drawn to Holly Springs, Mississippi, where, sometime around 1990, a Detroit-born autoworker and ex-convict named Paul MacLeod opened a makeshift shrine to Elvis. MacLeod refurbished his two-story home to mimic the exterior façade of Graceland and stuffed it with anything and everything Elvis-related he could acquire. He christened it "Graceland Too." "Jesus has his missionaries," MacLeod believed. "God is taken care of. I'm Elvis'[s] missionary." Unlike most missionaries, MacLeod did not seek out those of little faith; rather, he enticed the faithful and curious to come to him.

MacLeod's shrine was open to the public twenty-four hours a day, seven days a week. Hundreds, perhaps thousands, made the pilgrimage to Graceland Too each year. Some wanted to meet and have their pictures taken with the eccentric MacLeod, who claimed to drink dozens of Coca-Cola's every day and reportedly once sued the company "over a contaminated soda, settling for a shed full of more Coca-Cola." Others wanted to witness MacLeod's massive collection of Elvis relics and icons, which covered the rooms from floor to ceiling. A reporter from the *New York Times* observed "Elvis posters, Elvis candy wrappers, and Elvis postage stamps, photographs of famous people with Elvis and photographs of famous people who did not know Elvis but who had been in the same city at some point, a homemade electric chair meant to evoke 'Jailhouse Rock' and scraps of carpet that came (he told visitors) from Graceland, and which you could buy for $20 a square inch." MacLeod also had a bank of televisions constantly on, using them to "carefully mark down every mention of Elvis and store each note in a growing library of binders." An onsite collection of firearms included a pink shotgun, which matched a Cadillac that MacLeod had painted pink and peppered with "TLC" and "TCB" stickers.

Attendance ebbed and flowed over the years, but MacLeod's faith held firm, and Graceland Too stayed open until the day he died. Like Elvis, MacLeod passed away under peculiar circumstances. On July 15, 2014, he had an "altercation" with David Dwight Taylor, Jr., a black handyman to whom MacLeod probably owed money. According to reports, Taylor barged into Graceland Too late at night, demanding payment. After a brief struggle, MacLeod ran to get a gun and shot Taylor in the heart with a .45 Colt. Taylor bled out and died just inside Graceland Too's front door. Police interviewed MacLeod but did not file charges, largely due to Mississippi's "castle doctrine." (In brief, the state allows homeowners to use deadly force if deemed under "imminent danger" in their home.) Less than forty-eight hours later, someone driving past MacLeod's shrine saw his body slumped in a rocking chair on his front porch. At his funeral, it was clear that MacLeod's zeal for Elvis had come at a cost. Local friends, a few Elvis aficionados, and MacLeod's estranged daughters attended; however, a son, whom MacLeod had named Elvis Aaron Presley MacLeod and whom he had allegedly forced to dress like Elvis well into high school, wanted nothing to do with his father or Graceland Too. The next year, MacLeod's massive collection of Elvis memorabilia went up for auction. One could make a last-ditch effort to keep MacLeod's mission alive with the purchase of a "GRACELAND TOO FOREVER!" T-shirt. But, in truth, the spirit of Elvis had already left the building.[7]

Elvis's cultural afterlife, whether quaint or quizzical, conveys a basic fact. Elvis was more than the "King of Rock and Roll," edging out other black and white rockers who no doubt had rightful claims to the crown.[8] Through his faithful's efforts, Elvis became a saint of rock and roll, venerated and enduring like no other musician before or since. His music endured. His face endured. His hips endured. His spirit endured. His aura endured. His gaze endured.

The Shroud of Memphis is a work of art by Mississippi artist William Dunlap. It trades in Dunlap's trademark "hypothetical realism"; that is, his art seeks to capture the "realities" of southern life more usually conveyed through the region's music, literature, folk art, and landscape. *The Shroud of Memphis* also reveals Dunlap's artistic inspiration. "Read the Bible," he has suggested for anyone seeking to understand his work. "Genesis and the Book of Revelation might hold a clue."[9] Certainly, themes of creation, death, resurrection, and glorification make *The Shroud of Memphis* intelligible. But it can also be interpreted via the interdisciplinary methodology of southern studies and, more specifically, the critical framework that Charles Reagan Wilson used during his scholarly career for understanding the intersection of religion and culture in the American South.

Wilson taught southern studies courses in the Tupelo Room for over three decades (and, for about twenty-five years, under Elvis's saintly gaze). At some point during a class or lecture, Wilson showed off photos of unexpectedly "religious" objects: a hand-stitched quilt, a used-car dealer's leaflet, a late-model truck painted with biblical scenes. Or, he would talk about places and spaces marked by unexpectedly "religious" symbolism: roadside crosses urging drivers to "Get Right with God," heavenly imagery chiseled into Hank Williams's grave, a weekend beauty pageant representing a feminine "cult of beauty." His private collection of handheld church fans was of particular interest. Church fans represented, as Wilson termed it, southern "popular religion." This religion had "its own material artifacts" and was "especially prone to using the ordinary to apprehend the holy." According to Wilson, Elvis was another means to apprehend the holy. Elvis was not merely "music, sound, the voice, [and] words." Elvis was "also a look and an image." Hence, though dead and gone, Elvis's spirit lingered "in an amazing variety of material artifacts" that included "posters, banners, postcards, magazine covers, comic books, bubblegum cards, dolls, caps, jackets, T-shirts, scarfs, sunglasses, shoes, socks, shoestrings, slippers, ties, mittens, bracelets, earrings, watches, rings, keychains, necklaces, pins, magnets, and many more objects."[10]

Wilson is fascinated by objects. Until recently, Barnard Observatory's display cases housed dozens of souvenirs, trinkets, oddities, and memorabilia that he has snagged in his travels or that fellow fans of the southern sacred (and silly) have sent to him. (A "vial" of Elvis's sweat was a notable curiosity, at least until an unknown relic-robber stole away with it, perhaps enchanted by its "sacred" power or, more likely, its pawnshop value.) Not quite every item featured religious themes, but each certainly traded in reverence through material means. Wilson understood such items as in line with the southern search for ultimate meaning. The ordinary and mundane were hardly ordinary or mundane. Southern material culture evidenced a wide-ranging effort to adhere high-minded concepts or even sacred meaning to race, gender, class, sexuality, social status, and politics.[11]

As a work of art, *The Shroud of Memphis* unmistakably considers the regional and the religious. Dunlap seems to be saying that Elvis remains a sacred figure in southern popular religion. Dunlap, however, does not trade in simplistic nostalgia or rose-colored hagiography. His art is frank regarding Elvis's death. His death was not a saintly death. It was not a martyr's death. It was, in many ways, an ordinary, almost meaningless death only made meaningful by the fact that the man who died was Elvis. Hence, what covered his body afterwards was what could have covered anyone's body after they died. It was just a "king size sheet," probably taken from the same bed his failing health and obese frame had confined him to for months before his death. But Dunlap is no didactic moralist. He lets the viewer wrestle with that fact and even pokes fun at Elvis. Tongue firmly in cheek, Dunlap's "shroud" was also a sheet fit for a cultural king who died thanks to the rock and roll lifestyle that made him a king in the first place. As a king, he indulged his appetites. He indulged his God as well, loving and performing gospel music throughout his career.[12] But God did not save him. Gospel music did not save him. And when he faced a kind of judgment for a life of unmet and unmitigated desire, he faced it face down on a cold bathroom floor. Dunlap's pun tugs at the heartstrings. It also might draw a judgmental, condescending, or knowing laugh.

Another subtle theme orients Dunlap's piece. The whiteness of the sheet, backgrounding a white man deeply shaped by the South's interracial musical, religious, and cultural exchanges, suggests the dominance of white supremacy as more than a political system or cultural norm. It was the sacred social canvas on which southerners, deemed "white" or "black," or "colored," or "other," painted their lives.[13]

Wilson began his scholarly career before whiteness studies or critical race theory became formalized methodologies. Yet his early work clearly understood that white southerners constructed whiteness and gave it social and political power through religion. Wilson's insight, however, was to draw the scholar's eye outside the doors of religious institutions and denominations and into the landscape of southern popular religion: fields, streets, homes, public squares, recreational venues, roadsides, and stages, all of which constituted other arenas of racial construction and religious expression. Wilson's groundbreaking first book, *Baptized in Blood: The Religion of the Lost Cause, 1865–1920*, demonstrated how white southerners forged whiteness and white supremacy not merely through institutional means and politics but also through a religion of memorialization and social ritual that constructed "southernness" and fixed that identity to whiteness, nostalgia, regional pride, and reverence for a dead Confederacy. The white South's religion of the "Lost Cause," Wilson argued, sought to whitewash the southern present with the past by telling the story "of the afterlife of a Redeemer Nation that died." The Lost Cause thus became a "sacred presence" and "holy ghost haunting the spirits and actions of post–Civil War Southerners." "Religion," Wilson argued, "was at the heart of this dream, and the history of the attitude known as the Lost Cause was the story of the use of the past as the basis for a Southern religious-moral identity, an identity as a chosen people."[14]

The white South's "religious-moral identity" was hardly innocuous. The canonization and veneration of Confederate saints like Robert E. Lee, Jefferson Davis, and Stonewall Jackson legitimized militarized white power over southern society. Emancipated "blackness" became linked with marginality and danger. As per the Lost Cause's cultural framework and as worked out in the Jim Crow South, blackness was in need of infantilization, ridicule, "mammyfication," and limitation. Thus, in the late nineteenth century and well into the twentieth, black suppression came not only through voter restriction and segregation but through a white-supremacist public religion, meted out through pro-Confederate Memorial Days, monuments, public rituals, educational programs, memorabilia, and, of course, flags. The Lost Cause, as scholars building off Wilson's work further demonstrated, became a powerful means for propping up the racist political arrangements, economic programs, and social manners of the New South (even in states like Kentucky, which never left the Union over slavery).[15] Postbellum Christians dressed whiteness and white supremacy in sacred garments and armed it with sacred swords. In the decades after the death of the Confederacy, death without due process became an acceptable punishment for crimes against sacred whiteness. Lynching, according to historian Donald Mathews, became a "sacred rite." Thousands of African Americans, shot, tortured, or otherwise "swaying in the southern breeze"—to cite Billie Holiday's haunting rendition of the lynching song "Strange Fruit"—were clear evidence of the power of religion to not merely uplift, enrich, and inspire but to maim, torture, and kill. This legacy continues. The death of David Dwight Taylor, Jr., at Graceland Too, though framed by a social, political, and racial context different than the Mississippi of a century ago, nevertheless happened in accordance with a Jim Crow–era religious and legal logic. Vigilante "defense" of hearth and home, whether an ordinary domicile or a shrine to Elvis, has the protection and endorsement of a state that interprets the "right" to home protection, even to the point of stockpiling weapons and shooting on site, as a "sacred rite," especially for whites. Intrusion on white persons and property still begets "sacred" violence, often with the tacit or explicit assurance of social or political pardon.[16]

Grace, however, was also a crucial part of the South's sacred landscape before, and after, the Civil War. As Wilson explored in his second book, *Judgment and Grace in Dixie: Southern Faiths from Faulkner to Elvis*, graciousness unfolded behind and across the region's color lines. This made possible other cultural exchanges and sites of sacred conception, whether found in the best of southern literature and folk art or in the bravery of organized, sacrificial activism against the sacralized status quo of white supremacy and segregation. Along with gospel music, the blues, and jazz before it, rock and roll was a midcentury exercise in moving back and forth and within the boundaries of the South and nation's sacred supremacies, a cultural (and commercial) crossing and dwelling.[17] Through rock and roll, performers and audiences played with racial boundaries and sexual "norms." They crafted a musical form that turned "sinful" desires into a new form of dwelling. To have faith in rock and roll was to belong to a musical moment and immediate spiritual experience more often felt by the South's religious "others" and social sojourners, whether southern African American and Latino communities, poor whites, or certain religious minorities (such as the Pentecostal faithful who shaped Elvis and numerous other early rockers).[18]

Whether speaking to or for the status quo or sojourners, southern faiths unfolded in a society that, to paraphrase James C. Cobb and William Stueck, was always more a part of the world than a world apart.[19] Certain figures, such as revered University of Alabama football coach Bear Bryant, usually had state or regional boundaries surrounding their sacred spirits. But Elvis's spirit proved unbounded. In this way, he joined the likes of, for instance, Scarlett O'Hara and Martin Luther King, Jr. Fans from all over visited Graceland as a sacred site each year, much as others—mostly white women—revered and memorialized Margaret Mitchell's fictional world through material culture and iconography. Reverence for *Gone with the Wind* was primarily a feminine conceit, but it also showed up among anyone who imagined Mitchell's story as a fitting symbol of an admirable South now lost. As journalist Tony Horwitz discovered in his tour through the South in the 1990s, Japanese tourists, many of them men, also viewed Mitchell's novel or Vivien Leigh's iconic silver screen performance as affirmative of their forebears' material struggle to survive after a military defeat—or a mannerly culture they wished to maintain. Hence, they pilgrimaged across the Pacific to Atlanta in search of a Tara that never existed in the real world. The Lorraine Motel, best read as the most public of sites made meaningful by King's sacrificial life and the vigilante violence of white supremacy, similarly became a pilgrimage site for visitors from around the region, nation, and world. It was also a contested site for those who considered the National Civil Rights Museum's memorial or educational mission an unfortunate, or even unholy, departure from the civil rights movement's more radical vision of fuller economic and political equality. ("The best monument to Dr. Martin Luther King, Jr.," protestor Jacqueline Smith told geographer Derek H. Alderman in 1995, "would be a center at the Lorraine offering housing, job training, free community college, health clinic or other services for the poor.") Today, King's legacy in deeds and words continue to be used and misused for a wide array of political and cultural purposes, granting sacred meaning to contemporary struggles from both the left and the right.[20]

As Wilson would see it, continuing and contested interest in southern religious figures and sites are to be expected and reflect the region's long history of religious activity unfolding in a national and global context. As Wilson concluded in his 2006 lecture for the Charles Edmonson Historical Lectures at Baylor University, "The South, from one perspective, is part of the postcolonial world, exploited historically by the economic and political forces of Western Europe and the northern industrial structure." Conservative, white southern Protestantism, as well as other religious groups and identities in the region, thus worked to tie "the South to far-flung places resisting Western secularization and modernization."[21] Resistance is not the only role for religion, of course, and the felt experience of the "real" via an individualized or communal "spirit" does not necessarily have within it the means to slow or stop secularization and modernization. If anything, religion has encouraged further secularization or modernization, as a newer generation of scholars are detailing. From the "Christian" pursuits of Walmart or Chick-fil-A to the political aspirations of the Christian Right, southern religious forms have advanced secular ends and ideals. This has provided new opportunities for non-Protestants, LGBTQ activists, and religious progressives to exude social or public influence. Simultaneously, conservatives often justified the legal and cultural restriction of their social or political opponents under the guise of secular tropes like democracy, rationality, or "religious freedom."[22]

Resilience, however, does seem to capture, at least in part, what Wilson has suggested about non-institutional religion, especially in his latest book, *Flashes of a Southern Spirit: Meanings of the Spirit in the US South*. Just as there was no fixed or unitary "mind" of the South, Wilson argued there were many spiritualities of the South, each working to affirm traditionalist social arrangements and inspire flashes of creative musical and artistic expression. Such creativity "resulted from the long dominance of a traditional culture and the stimulus the southern environment and social [and racial] system have provided to individuals who have generated creative sparks." A "final spark that galvanized the creative spirit of numerous artists" was modernization, "expressed in a commercial mass culture."[23] This commercial enabler of southern religious spirits went abroad, crossing regional and national boundaries to dwell in contexts outside the South as well as taking on new auspices as migrants—from across the US or from Asia and Latin America—diversified the evangelical South with new spiritual forms, arenas, and expressions.[24] In a transnational, globalized present, with nationalist or racist overtures remaining powerful, it remains critical to understand how forms of "the religious" or "the spiritual" shape individual and collective imaginings of the holy or unholy. For this reason, among many other reasons, Wilson's work remains relevant and revelatory.

This volume honors the methodological and scholarly groundwork laid by Charles Reagan Wilson. It began as papers presented in 2015 at the Porter Fortune History Symposium on "Southern Religion and Southern Culture," and it uses certain episodes and moments in southern religious history to expand the horizons that Wilson's work traced out. The essays that follow focus first on churches and ministers among various religious groups, starting with Ryan L. Fletcher's investigation of slavery and finance among Episcopalians in Arkansas. Otis W. Pickett's piece is a case study of a Presbyterian leader who, after the Civil War, simultaneously worked to shape churchly reform and Lost Cause religiosity. The educational institutions and efforts of the African Methodist Episcopal Church orient Alicia Jackson's essay while Randall Stephens traces out the long and complex relationship between Holiness-Pentecostals and technology, innovation, and mass media. The volume then considers religious and cultural constructions outside formalized religious bodies and institutions. Arthur Remillard delves into "the religious" in sports culture while, last but not least, Chad Seales considers the fascinations of Protestants with certain "relics" of racial, political, and communal violence.

As historian Paul Harvey notes in the essay that opens and frames the volume, "The present and future of [southern religious] history is about incorporating a diversity of southern religious stories." This volume is a step toward doing so, but it is also "a case of back to the future." It follows in Wilson's footsteps and emulates his model, featuring both majoritarian and minority voices from the archives and deploying various interpretive schema to understand the South's remarkable religious diversity and the many arenas of private and public life where faith did more than merely linger. Southern religion and culture played with one another, at times with deadly results. At other times, southern religion and culture exhibited facets as ordinary as they were extraordinary. Southern faiths, however expressed, drew both southerners and non-southerners to find meaning in paradoxical feelings: freedom and censure, inspiration and oppression, continuity and change, laughter and heartbreak. Such faiths endure, and they endure in unexpected places and spaces today. They endure like a man millions venerate as St. Elvis of Rock and Roll.

Notes

1. I use here Françoise Meltzer and Jaś Elsner's conception of what constitutes a "saint." A saint, they argue, is "a figure of mediation who by definition enacts or suggests 'vertical' access to a supernatural power or a higher dimension of being." Saints like Elvis did not necessarily serve as mediators with a named, divine being or essence but rather served as "a point of intensification," or, more accurately, "a source of seduction even within a rigidly secularist perspective." Meltzer and Elsner, eds., *Saints: Faith without Borders* (Chicago: University of Chicago Press, 2011), ix.

2. On one teenager's brush with Elvis and sexual ecstasy, see Eugenia Dettelbach Wicker and Marcie Cohen Ferris, "The KISS Letter: An Encounter with Elvis," *Southern Cultures* 14:4 (Winter 2011), 116–20; on Elvis, rock and roll, and sexual and racial danger, see Glenn C. Altschuler, *All Shook Up: How Rock 'n' Roll Changed America* (New York: Oxford University Press, 2003), 35–98.

3. Gillian Welch, "Elvis Presley Blues," *Time (The Revelator)*, Acony Records, 2001.

4. Joel Williamson, *Elvis Presley: A Southern Life* (New York: Oxford University Press, 2012), xx.

5. Ibid., 3–21; on the last years of Elvis's life and career and their immediate impact, see Peter Guralnick, *Careless Love: The Unmaking of Elvis Presley* (New York: Little, Brown, and Company, 1999).

6. On the social, racial, sexual, and cultural dynamics at play in Elvis remembrance, see Erika Doss, *Elvis Culture: Fans, Faith, and Image* (Lawrence: University Press of Kansas, 1999).

7. Elise Jordan, "The Last Days of Graceland Too," *Buzzfeed*, January 8, 2015, https://www.buzzfeed.com/elisejordan/the-last-days-of-graceland-too-the-worlds-most-notorious-elv?utm_term=.ly1699pB2#.nj7XDDy21; Campbell Robertson, "Two Lives Collide, and End, at an Elvis Shrine," *New York Times*, July 17, 2014, https://www.nytimes.com/2014/07/18/us/two-lives-collide-and-end-at-an-elvis-shrine.html; J. B. Clark, "Deadly Force Permissible Under Castle Doctrine in Mississippi," *Daily Journal*, June 8, 2013, http://www.djournal.com/news/deadly-force-permissible-under-castle-doctrine-in-mississippi/article_5387c241-e566-5d3d-a981-59f638cd3e2c.html; *Mississippi Code*, 97-3-15, Chapter 3 (2010), http://law.justia.com/codes/mississippi/2010/title-97/3/97-3-15; Therese Apel, "Graceland Too Owner Paul McLeod Dies," *Clarion-Ledger*, July 17, 2014, http://www.clarionledger.com/story/news/local/2014/07/17/graceland-too-owner-paul-mcleod-dies/12775231/; J. B. Clark, "Man Killed at Graceland Too by Owner," *Daily-Journal*, July 17, 2014, http://www.djournal.com/news/crime-law-enforcement/man-killed-at-graceland-too-by-owner/article_2d98f678-a4ba-5886-b35a-fab523fb1758.html; "Weapons Grade Elvis," *Bitter Southerner*, http://bittersoutherner.com/weapons-grade-elvis/#.WTxaUuvyvIU; Eileen Townsend, "The King and I," *Paris Review*, February 3, 2015, https://www.theparisreview.org/blog/2015/02/03/the-king-and-i/; "Elvis Memorabilia Sells at 2nd 'Graceland Too' Auction," *Clarion-Ledger*, May 4, 2015, http://www.clarionledger.com/story/news/2015/05/04/second-graceland-too-auction/26860413/.

8. On the marginalization of black artists and the remembered roots and legacy of rock and roll, see Jack Hamilton, *Just Around Midnight: Rock and Roll and the Racial Imagination* (Cambridge: Harvard University Press, 2016).

9. Jill R. Chancey, "Dunlap, William," in *Mississippi Encyclopedia*, eds. Ted Ownby, Charles Reagan Wilson, Ann J. Abadie, Odie Lindsey, and James G. Thomas, Jr. (Jackson: University Press of Mississippi, 2017), 369.

10. Charles Reagan Wilson, *Judgment and Grace in Dixie: Southern Faiths from Faulkner to Elvis* (Athens: University of Georgia Press, 1995), 84, 129–30, 132.

11. Wilson's Southern Tacky Collection is now housed at the Mississippi Department of Archives and History.

12. Charles Reagan Wilson, "'Just a Little Talk with Jesus': Elvis Presley, Religious Music, and Southern Spirituality," *Southern Cultures* 12:4 (2006), 74–91.

13. On race as the primary cultural framework for religion in the South, see Paul Harvey, *Freedom's Coming: Religious Culture and the Shaping of the South from the Civil War through the Civil Rights Era* (Chapel Hill: University of North Carolina Press, 2005).

14. Charles Reagan Wilson, *Baptized in Blood: The Religion of the Lost Cause, 1865–1920* (Athens: University of Georgia Press, 1980), 1.

15. Gaines M. Foster, *Ghosts of the Confederacy: Defeat, the Lost Cause, and the Emergence of the New South, 1865–1913* (New York: Oxford University Press, 1987); Grace Elizabeth Hale, *Making Whiteness: The Culture of Segregation in the South, 1890–1940* (New York: Vintage Books, 1995); David W. Blight, *Race and Reunion: The Civil War in American Memory* (Cambridge: Harvard University Press, 2001); Anne Marshall, *Creating a Confederate Kentucky: The Lost Cause and Civil War Memory in a Border State* (Chapel Hill: University of North Carolina Press, 2010); Luke E. Harlow, *Religion, Race, and the Making of Confederate Kentucky, 1830–1880* (Cambridge: Cambridge University Press, 2014).

16. Donald G. Mathews, "The Southern Rite of Human Sacrifice," *Journal of Southern Religion* (August 22, 2000), http://jsr.fsu.edu/mathews.htm. For broader context, see Edward J. Blum, *Reforging the White Republic: Race, Religion, and American Nationalism, 1865–1898* (Baton Rouge: Louisiana State University Press, 2005); on Holiday's rendition, see David Margolick, *Strange Fruit: The Biography of a Song* (New York: HarperCollins, 2001).

17. Thomas A. Tweed, *Crossing and Dwelling: A Theory of Religion* (Cambridge: Harvard University Press, 2006).

18. Paul Harvey, *Christianity and Race in the American South: A History* (Chicago: University of Chicago Press, 2016); Julie M. Weise, *Corazón de Dixie: Mexicanos in the US South since 1910* (Chapel Hill: University of North Carolina Press, 2015); Andrew H. M. Stern, *Southern Crucifix, Southern Cross: Catholic-Protestant Relations in the Old South* (Tuscaloosa: University of Alabama Press, 2015); Jarod Roll, *Spirit of Rebellion: Labor and Religion in the New Cotton South* (Urbana: University of Illinois Press, 2010); John Hayes, *Hard, Hard Religion: Interracial Faith in the Poor South* (Chapel Hill: University of North Carolina Press, 2017); Patrick Mason, *The Mormon Menace: Violence and Anti-Mormonism in the Postbellum South* (New York: Oxford University Press, 2011); Randall J. Stephens, *The Fire Spreads: Holiness and Pentecostalism in the American South* (Cambridge: Harvard University Press, 2008). On Pentecostalism's influence on Elvis and other early rock and rollers, see Randall J. Stephens, "'Where Else Did They Copy Their Styles But from Church Groups?': Rock 'n' Roll and Pentecostalism in the 1950s South," *Church History* 85:1 (March 2016): 97–131.

19. James C. Cobb and William Stueck, eds., *Globalization and the American South* (Athens: University of Georgia Press, 2005), xi.

20. Helen Taylor, *Scarlett's Women: Gone with the Wind and Its Female Fans* (New Brunswick: Rutgers University Press, 1989), 1–6; Tony Horwitz, *Confederates in the Attic: Dispatches from the Unfinished Civil War* (New York: Vintage, 1998), 282–311; Derek H. Alderman, "Street Names as Memorial Arenas: The Reputational Politics of Commemorating Martin Luther King Jr. in a Georgia County," in *The Civil Rights Movement in American Memory*, ed. Renee C. Romano and Leigh Raiford (Athens: University of Georgia Press, 2006), 74. On the redeployment of King and "civil rights" language on the right, see David John Marley, "Riding in the Back of the Bus: The Christian Right's Adoption of Civil Rights Movement Rhetoric," in *Civil Rights Movement in American Memory*, eds. Romano and Raiford, 346–62.

21. Charles Reagan Wilson, *Southern Missions: The Religion of the American South in Global Perspective* (Waco: Baylor University Press, 2006), 52.

22. Bethany E. Moreton, *To Serve God and Wal-Mart: The Making of Christian Free Enterprise* (Cambridge: Harvard University Press, 2009); Darren Dochuk, *From Bible Belt to Sunbelt: Plain-Folk Religion, Grassroots Politics, and the Rise of Evangelical Conservatism* (New York: W. W. Norton, 2010); Daniel K. Williams, *God's Own Party: The Making of the Christian Right* (New York: Oxford University Press, 2010); Chad Seales, *The Secular Spectacle: Performing Religion in a Southern Town* (New York: Oxford University Press, 2013); Darren E. Grem, *The Blessings of Business: How Corporations Shaped Conservative Christianity* (New York: Oxford University Press, 2016).

23. Charles Reagan Wilson, *Flashes of a Southern Spirit: Meanings of the Spirit in the U.S. South* (Athens: University of Georgia Press, 2011), 119.

24. Wilson, *Southern Missions*, 33–53.

Southern Religion, Southern Culture

Judgment, Grace, Race, and the Transcendental Blues

The Study of Religion in the South in the Era of Charles Reagan Wilson

PAUL HARVEY

Southern religious history from the age of European colonization begins with water, tragedy, and survival. It opens at St. Augustine, on Florida's Atlantic Coast, and at the swampy mire of Jamestown. Early Virginians planted a colony in a microenvironment that virtually guaranteed death for the great majority of early migrants to a land that eventually became the American South. Early Virginians set a pattern, too, for the combustible mix of piety and avarice that powered much of southern history from the seventeenth century forward—what the brilliant journalist and writer Wilbur J. Cash outlined as the southern archetypes of "the Puritan" and "the hedonist."[1] From Jamestown grew the wealthy and powerful slave society that would lead a nation into its bloodiest war.

Almost four hundred years later, in 2005, floodwaters nearly destroyed the city of New Orleans. The disaster was long foretold and well predicted by those who knew anything about the city's inadequately constructed system of levees and water diversion canals. Hurricane Katrina is a tale in which largely manmade forces (interacting with environmental conditions and economic realities) created a society that could produce incredible wealth and an intellectual and a cultural life that defined a nation's sensibility alongside a level of racial and social inequality that belied the myths upon which the society rested.

In the region's origins in the swamplands of early Virginia, and in the destructive path of Katrina, determination, resistance, survival, and sometimes even transcendence mark the story. In both cases, religious institutions, beliefs, and faith played a key role in defining the differences between people in those societies. Over the last two hundred years or so, a broadly shared Christianity in the region could not transcend the deep social hierarchies that defined people's lives, their hopes, expectations, and daily realities.

C. Vann Woodward wrote about the ironies of southern history. Here, the focus is more on the *paradoxes* of southern religious history. Here is one: namely, the region's central role in fashioning a globalized world economy (including a circulation of people, as well as goods), along with the region's tribal provincialism, marked by hostility to outside ideas and agitators. In few other places did such a diverse mixture of religious ideas and expressions result in a dominant establishment at once so internally focused and so productive of extraordinary cruelty and astonishing creativity. This was true especially in music, art, and all forms of oral artistry. Indeed, the "solid South" was religiously riven. In those cracks arose spiritually charged expressions that came to define American culture.

Charles Reagan Wilson has made a career of exploring the paradoxes and flashes of the southern spirit. Barbara Mandrell sang about being country when country wasn't cool. Charles Reagan Wilson *was* cultural history before cultural history was cool. Wilson wove music, literature, art, and all forms of culture into a broad, sympathetic, empathetic, but not uncritical understanding of southern history. This essay will consider the past, present, and future of southern religious history and suggest how much of Charles Reagan Wilson's academic lifetime of work has foreshadowed, shaped, and developed work in the field over the last generation.[2]

Scholars of Wilson's generation tried to understand the origins and dominance of evangelicalism. They examined what seemed to hold white southern churches in so-called cultural captivity. After that came the explosion of studies on slavery and African American religion, making the African American experience a central part of the dominant paradigms of southern history. Such work continues, particularly in the recent studies of slavery, Jim Crow, and capitalism.[3] The present and future of historical writing in this field is about incorporating a diversity of southern religious stories, ranging from the Powhatan Confederacy in early Virginia, to Moravians in North Carolina, Spiritualists in New Orleans and elsewhere, and Catholics throughout the region. In the more recent South, too, immigrants have made cities and even smaller southern regional centers such as Dalton, Georgia, places where Latino

Catholics, Hindus, Buddhists, and Muslims vie for attention alongside the better-known Southern Baptists and Methodists.[4]

The current emphasis on pluralism is a case of back to the future. The American South began with a polyglot, diverse set of religious traditions and interactions between people from Europe, Africa, and indigenous peoples from North America. Native religious practices, Christian and Islamic traditions of widely varying origins and belief systems, West- and Central African-based spiritual worlds, and irreligion and indifference coexisted. They competed with each other in colonies like Virginia (which resembled start-up enterprises from hell), in Spanish colonial outposts such as Florida, and in precarious French experiments that attempted to create some semblance of what they conceived as "civilization" in the bayous and swamplands of Louisiana. Seriously examining the long legacies of the region's religious history foregrounds, for example, periods in which Native religious practices, French and Spanish Catholicism, and African-Islamic religious influences were central rather than peripheral.

In recent work on the pre-Evangelical South, scholars have learned to place evangelicalism within its proper historic context. Evangelicalism was a religious upstart in the eighteenth century and a rising movement by the time of the Revolution. It was a growing presence in the antebellum era, seemingly culturally dominant from the Civil War era to the mid-twentieth century, and it now exists as an important tradition within a region that still demographically has been an "evangelical belt" but is rapidly diversifying—and even losing ground—in major southern metropolitan areas.

Another major theme of southern religious history is the centrality and constant interplay of the revolutionary and the revivalist traditions in southern history, and a parallel interplay between racialized particularity and Christian universalism in southern religious thought and practice. The dislocations and movements spurred by the age of revolutions sparked an African American religiosity and spread a black evangelical diaspora. At the same time, the post-revolutionary years also saw a tightening of controls, culminating in the repression following real and abortive slave rebellions of the 1820s and 1830s. The dual revolutions of the South—the revolutionary and the revivalist—gradually gave way to the dual power brokers in the region: the evangelical movement and the pro-slavery complex. For slaveholders, the disturbing implications of political and religious revolutions compelled the intellectual birth of southern conservatism (with its emphasis on hierarchy, order, and obedience). Another powerful connection through southern history from the late eighteenth century to the civil rights era is the connection between evangelical and conservative thought among white southerners, leading from the intellectual enterprise of pro-slavery thought to contemporary religio-conservative movements. During the same years, a nascent liberation theology applied radical evangelicalism to political questions of human rights in a society defined by racialized hierarchies. Since the mid-eighteenth century, these two religious visions have shaped the most fundamental philosophical concerns, social struggles, and spiritual expressions of southerners.

If these previous themes were about the forging (and challenging) of the "solid South," the next is about the ever-present cracks and fissures in the "solid South," and the longevity of undercurrents of southern dissent against the dominant regional establishment. This theme arose especially from the "lived religion" approach borrowed from religious studies, as well as the black diaspora emphasis drawn from Africana studies. While evangelical Protestantism ostensibly emphasizes doctrine, religious practices expressed through art, music, folklore, and products of material culture expand the field of the sacred, expanding the bounds of what typically has been regarded as "southern religion." Here, I would point to the importance of music and art in iconoclastic and anti-ritualist traditions. Charles Reagan Wilson's work helped us to see the meaning of artists such as Howard Finster, artifacts such as church fans, and why Elvis had a little talk with Jesus. If intellectual history is properly seen not as the history of thought but of the history of humans *thinking* creatively, then here especially is where the influence of Wilson's academic lifetime of work may be felt most keenly.

Terms such as "community" have long defined southern culture. And in a recent survey of what (if any) generalizations still hold true for "the South," journalist and author Tracy Thompson's *The New Mind of the South* concludes that a particular tribalized form of community and an emotional religiosity still characterizes regional culture. Thompson writes that the "box" of southern identity has two "constants," the "two great institutions that have defined the limits of the available contents: evangelical religion and slavery." Yet the part of the box of southern identity represented by those two is shrinking. While the past is never dead, sometimes it does seem "past," or amenable to change.[5]

Indeed, the sharp-edged political culture wars between a relatively declining but still powerful evangelical South and a rising pluralist (and freethinking or religiously indifferent) South appears in conflicts over electoral politics, public prayers, and fights over the continued persistence of evangelical mores in public life. Much depends on location and context. The urbanity of Charleston or the high-tech and higher educational nirvana of the Research Triangle contrasts sharply with many small and medium-sized towns throughout the region. In those places, the Bible remains a central part of public discourse and political life.

If the South won't be defined by the Confederacy, then what will define the region? The "most important," Thompson suggests, is "a sense of community forged under the conditions that obtained in the South." She goes on to say that despite the Americanization of the region, its being "urbanized, suburbanized,

[and] strip-malled," the region still "bears the imprint of that deep sense of community and an almost tribal definition of kin."[6]

That may be the case. Yet, from Jamestown to Katrina, wrenching, sweeping, community-altering change is a central theme of southern history. Wilbur J. Cash, William Faulkner, C. Vann Woodward, Lillian Smith, Loretta Lynn, Johnny Cash, and generations of black southerners who went through any number of forced and voluntary migrations all understood this. And so, if not community, then what defines the new mind of the South? Perhaps religiosity does. It is not quite the same religiosity as before, and it is being altered by immigrants and also by the rise of a more vocal class of "nones." Still, evangelicalism remains far more characteristic of southern life than for any other region. The new mind of the South, then, still has a fair portion of the old mind of the South.

Immigration Patterns and Southern Religion

Looking toward studies of the contemporary South, a necessary focus of religious history will be to narrate the rise of Latinos, both Catholics and Protestants, as a significant force in southern religious life throughout the region. A quick look at the demographic statistics of recent southern history will demonstrate the ethnic, racial, and religious transformation of the region since the 1960s. In many respects, it mirrors that which has occurred nationally after the 1965 reforms created a new era of American immigration history.

Historically, the South has been noted for its overwhelming predominance of a biracial culture, with relatively few "white ethnics" or other groups to complicate the mix. Until recently, Catholics have been concentrated primarily in particular sub-regions (Louisiana, Texas, Maryland, and Florida). Jews have never made it even to one percent of the population base; Latinos were scarce outside of Texas. Asians represented the tiniest minority of all. As a result, scholars have been able to speak of a "solid South" in religion, one that has room for High Church Christianity for the elite and for Catholics in particular regions, but one that is fundamentally defined by Southern Baptists, Methodists, Presbyterians, and (more recently) Pentecostals. This is a far remove from the United States as a whole, where, for example, Catholics form the single largest religious grouping.

Like the rest of the country, the South has undergone radical demographic changes over the last few decades, and this has reshaped the religious landscape. One may start the discussion of minority religions in the South, and the diversification of southern religion itself, with the Catholics. Over 15 percent of southerners polled in 1999 claimed a Catholic identity. As one may expect, the majority are still comprised of historic Louisiana Catholics, Mexican Americans in Texas, and Cuban Americans in Florida. But Catholicism has found its way into the Deep South as well, mixing in unobtrusively with the familiar landscape of evangelical Protestant churches. In recent years, several southern parishes count in the top ten of fastest-growing parishes in the United States. Atlanta's 322,000 Catholic parishioners in 2002 grew to one million by 2012, and Atlanta now has the largest Eucharistic Congress in the country. Catholics in Charleston, Charlotte, and Little Rock have grown in substantial numbers over the last decade. Immigration accounts for part of this. More significant, however, is migration, as national firms draw in increasing numbers of workers from other parts of the country. In particular urban regions—Atlanta, Charlotte, the Research Triangle, and even in the evangelical Vatican of Nashville—Catholics have assumed a regularized presence in the southern landscape, such that to be southern and Catholic no longer means being the "tolerable alien," but instead just another religious southerner. "Our Protestant brothers and sisters have done us a great favor. Talking about faith here in the South is like eating, breathing, and sleeping," said the cofounder of an online Catholic magazine. "There's an openness about faith here, which makes it easier to be open about your faith if you're Catholic." Plus, all those questions your Protestant friends are constantly tossing in your direction forces southern Catholics to defend their faith consciously, more so than when Catholicism is "just there."[7]

One of the most notable trends in southern demography is the recent and rapid growth of traditions historically identified as Asian religions (meaning mostly Buddhism and Hinduism, along with a sprinkling of South and Southeast Asian Islam). In the 2000 census, immigrants to the South numbered just over eight million people. Comparing census data from 1960 and 2000, one sees a quadrupling of the South's foreign-born population. The largest percentage consists of Latino immigrants, but they have increasingly been joined by Asian immigrants to southern cities. Evidence for the impact of Asian in-migration to the region could be seen in Hindu statues, Thai temples, Cambodian wats, and Vietnamese Catholic shrines that were popping up even in the most unexpected parts of the southern landscape, including an entire section of Oklahoma City now dominated by a Southeast Asian (mostly Vietnamese) community. Unless trends change dramatically, ongoing immigration to the region will make the southern future look much more like the polyglot past of the early South.

In the Evangelical Mode

For all of the pluralization of the contemporary South, it should be clear that the South is still called the "Bible Belt" for good reason.[8] Some years ago, Wilson joined with the religious historian and sociologist Mark Silk to produce a volume entitled *Religion and Public Life in the South: In the Evangelical Mode*.[9] The book surveyed the strikingly continued dominance of evangelical Protestantism within the region despite the recent trends towards diversification. Some recent events in the Southern Baptist Convention (SBC), the nation's largest Protestant denomination, suggest much about the stability of the "evangelical mode" and its recent evolution in the post–civil rights movement South.

In 2012, the Southern Baptist Convention elected the Rev. Fred Luter, a black pastor of a successful Southern Baptist church in New Orleans, as its president. Leaders of the convention have portrayed this as a "historic" moment for a denomination that until the civil rights movement had remained lily-white. Historically, the very term "Southern Baptist" evoked a particular kind of white southerner: a working-class or middle-class evangelical volubly open about his or her faith, strictly conservative in personal morals, likely to be a rural or small-town resident, and by political affiliation historically a conservative Democrat but, since the 1960s, disproportionately counted in the Republican column. In addition, the SBC for decade after decade experienced rapid, exponential growth, reaching at one point a high of about eighteen million members.

Several trends converged to help bring about the election of Luter. The first is a plateauing, and more recently a pronounced decline, in SBC membership. The second is a demographic shift from a largely rural and small-town SBC constituency to one more concentrated in metropolitan areas. The third is an effort on the part of the denominational leadership to "own up" to its slaveholding and Jim Crow-supporting past and to engage in public gestures of racial apology and "reconciliation." The fourth, and related, trend has been a rapid rise in ethnic minority membership and participation in the SBC, which currently counts about 20 percent of its membership as black, Latino, or Asian.

One other factor has been an attempt to bring together social and moral conservatives, who historically might have been divided into racially defined congregations but could come together on issues such as opposing abortion or gay marriage. Luter is a cultural conservative in that sense, as are a sizable proportion of black evangelical Protestants.

Like many other southern denominations in the decades following the civil rights era, the Southern Baptists staged rituals of racial reconciliation and have promoted African Americans from within the convention's ranks to positions of authority. Yet while white and black evangelicals may express the same faith commitments—and some of the same moral conclusions arising from those commitments—they nonetheless often see the social and political world differently. The historical white evangelical emphasis on individual salvation and acts of kindness, for example, ill-fits an African American experience that suggests that there are times when only governmental power is adequate to bring justice to a fallen world. Most black evangelicals, in short, espouse conservative moral positions but retain a strong emphasis on the very themes of social justice that arouse white evangelicals' deepest suspicions. In that sense, southern evangelicals remain divided by faith, a fact much in evidence in reactions to issues of police-community relations that have risen to prominence in the last few years.[10]

The Future of Southern Religious History: Thoughts on Methods

One of the major scholarly developments of the last generation has been the rise of the field of religious studies, a field premised in part on the never-ceasing and ever-evolving quest to define the term "religion" and to historicize that term. And when the term is historicized, we also end up discussing its ostensible, but not actual, opposite: secularism. But these two terms are not in a binary; instead, each defines itself in its relationship to the other.

What might a marriage of methods derived from history and religious studies (as well as, of course, anthropology and other fields) mean for the study of southern religious history? My thinking here is influenced by Manuel Vasquez's *More Than Belief*, a book that simultaneously serves as a history of methods in the study of religion and charts an intellectual program for its future. As Vasquez writes, "The task of the scholar of religion is to study how embodiment and embeddedness in time and place enable and constrain diverse, flexible, yet patterned subjective experiences that come to be understood as religious."[11]

One key point of religious studies scholarship is to suggest that the very term "religion" was invented in the eighteenth and nineteenth centuries by scholars seeking to delimit its practices to the world of the private, thereby creating a secular public world. So "religion" came to imply interiority. It was about belief. That is why our students today say, "Christians believe that..." or "Muslims believe that..." when we ask them to free associate with the term "Christian" or "Muslim." They assume that religion means, in effect, a set of doctrinal beliefs to which one subscribes. They have no sense of historicizing how that concept came into being.

And, in truth, one may ask: Could there be a worse subject to pick than Protestants in the American South on which to experiment with the ideas about "religion" coming from religious studies? These are the people who conceived of religion in precisely the way that this field tells us not to; "religion" for them was a matter of the private conscience, was disembodied, full of doctrine and ratiocination, and as deeply individualistic (at least in theory) as one could possibly conceive.

At the same time, perhaps Vasquez's program and ideas perfectly fit a properly historicized view of the South. For example, religion in the American South emerged as part of a globalized, transnational movement of peoples from the seventeenth through the nineteenth centuries. Prior to about 1820, the largest single number of migrants arriving to American shores came from Africa, and they were not coming by choice. African slaves employed a variety of strategies and developed new forms of religious expressions in acculturating to their lives on the new continent. At the same time, they were at the very bottom of an international globalized economic order that empowered some of the greatest wealth-producing machines—sugar plantations, for example—that had existed in human history up to that point.

Africans brought religion expressed as bodily movement, communal rituals, and emplaced interactions with the natural world. Over the course of the evangelical revolution, southern religious expressions grew embodied and ritually enacted. And thus it is clear that Africans exerted an immense influence even over those who conceived of their subjects as lacking in honor.

Africans invoked ancestral spirits through ritual music, dancing, and chanting. Their practices involved beseeching and appeasing the lesser deities who were responsible for the world of matter and spirit. Religious or ritual specialists (priests) divined messages from the *Orishas,* who communicated to humans via natural objects and whose power might be manipulated through material "fetishes" such as *gris-gris.*

Many Europeans, too, came quasi-involuntarily, as indentured servants. Recent work on the religion of ordinary and poorer early modern Europeans has shown how much of a world of wonder and a sense of embodied practices that they shared with Africans who were ostensibly heathens while they were so-called Christians. This became clearer even as the Great Awakening reached the South in the late eighteenth century, when Scots-Irish communal rituals of immanent transcendence merged with African notions and practices of bodily expressions. In a sense, they helped teach an entire culture a different way of experiencing religion in and through the body. Through this process, religious seekers adopted, if unconsciously and insensibly, ways of enacting relationships with transcendent beings. These invoked ritually powerful emotions that were patterned after a synthesis of learned motor behaviors from vastly disparate parts of the world.

This development worried the colonial power elite, who exclaimed unhappily that white evangelicals were filling the heads of slaves with "a Parcel of Cant-Phrases, Trances, Dreams, Visions, and Revelations," including visions of the "Deliverance of the Negroes from servitude."[12] The elites had their own embodied religious practices, too, repeated through the Anglican annual calendar that prescribed prayers, recipes for feast days, knitting patterns for women's material creations, and numerous other forms of prescribed religio-social behavior. In short, even in a historically Protestant, text-centric, doctrinal region as the American South, religious expression has been embedded, embodied, and environmentally patterned, whether we are talking about scattered Anglican churches in nineteenth-century Virginia, praise houses in the nineteenth-century Low Country, or suburban megachurches in contemporary Tennessee.

One also sees there both power and resistance, including the central role of religious behaviors and visions in slave revolts. One sees globalizing forces fundamentally shaping the realities of the region. One sees as well material-biological constraints (including high mortality rates in particular regions) and material adaptations of natural materials into sacred frameworks. One sees, to invoke Thomas Tweed, both "dwelling" and "crossing."[13] There is "dwelling" in the sense of a heavy sense of place that grew up around rural communities. This shows in the post–Civil War nostalgia about "place" that empowered southern popular culture, including country music lyrics that valorized the "old home place" even while singing about proletarian, displaced work lives with honky-tonk angels there to help them drink away the pain. And one sees "crossing"—the crossing of religious traditions that emerged from transnational globalized economic networks and that came together in micro-local contexts, which, ironically, made them appear as provincial and narrow as could be found in any American region. Further, these southern religious practices emerged in the highly charged power context of a historical transformation, developing from a "society with slaves" to become a "slave society."

Much recent religious studies scholarship focuses on local worlds, with heavy emphasis on micro-descriptions and self-reflections. Much can be gained from such micro-ethnographies. The pitfall of such an approach is a failure to connect localized practices to the larger contexts in which they are embedded, including transnational and global economic, political, cultural, and environmental processes. For example, in the first half of the nineteenth century a large number of whites and nearly one million Africans migrated from the eastern seaboard to the inland territories and states that became the Upland South and Deep South, one of the largest migrations per capita in all of American history. Moreover, those migrations, of course, were made possible only through a series of imperial wars and colonial displacements that "cleared" the land for white settlers, and through conflicts seen by their Native participants (especially the Muskogees of Alabama) as religious ones.

Religious culture in the American South almost perfectly exemplifies both the Cartesian mind/body dualism that has dominated thought about religion, and the kinds of complex "emplacement" and "embodiment" Vasquez calls for in the study of religion. In other words, part of the story of religion as more than belief in the American South is the struggle to contain religious experience within right belief. It is the constant pushing of religious experience beyond those boundaries into embodiment and *through* embodiment into the larger channels of American popular culture. For example, to the extent that American popular music derives from southern music, and to the extent that that music has its roots in varied religious traditions (from the cries of African griots to the field hollers of slaves to the gritty ballads of the Ulster Scots who settled the upcountry and Appalachian regions), then American popular music may be seen as a kind of secularized religious embodiment.

For much of the twentieth century, if southern churches slumbered in "cultural captivity," southern culture held the nation captive. People responded to the elemental force of its blues, country, and gospel music, its evocation of the most fundamental emotions of human life, and its literary grapplings with the most profound questions of race and American history. The literature, poetry, music, and other cultural products of those grapplings drew from many sources, of course, but were always deeply imbibed in biblical history and lore. That was true not only of the gospel tradition but also of the bawdier tunes and the blues.

The biblically literalist culture of the American South both inspired and was ultimately overcome by the spectacularly imaginative readings given to biblical passages by southern musicians, from the spirituals of collectively anonymous authors to the carefully rendered character sketches, ribald parodies, or angry manifestoes of contemporary artists. In other words, by taking seriously the idea of the Bible as a literal and historical document, southern musicians extrapolated tales that wove their way into deeply American histories of struggle, injustice, triumph, backsliding, and visionary experiences.

Much of the scholarship in southern religious history, like American religious history in general, is bound by belief and doctrine in ways critiqued by religious studies scholars. But here is the paradox: it is difficult to conceive of another place, and another set of religious expressions, that are more about embodiment and emplacement in American religious history than those of the American South, which produced the culture of the transcendental blues and many other forms of American popular religion, art, letters, and music. Thus, marrying history and religious studies approaches within the contexts of the American South, the exciting project is to determine how, exactly, to translate religious studies theories into the gritty world of southerners who worshipped lustily at camp meetings even as they bought and sold slaves at the market; who invented much of American popular culture even as their dominant religious institutions were among the most vociferous critics of that popular culture, precisely because it was so bodily expressive; whose black Christians carried on their own tug-of-war between an extra-institutional set of religious practices carried on through bodily movements in particular embedded spaces obscured or hidden from dominant powers, even as black

Christian institutional leaders preached a politics and personal behavior of respectability that attempted to root out and shame those engaged in those bodily expressions; and whose poorer residents, white and black, gave voice to apocalyptic visions far removed from the gospel of progress preached by the major denominations. Southerners embodied, as it were, the Cartesian split.

The work of Charles Reagan Wilson has straddled the Cartesian split, and thus given us some models for doing what best can be done with a marriage of history, religious studies, anthropology, and related fields. From *Baptized in Blood* to *Flashes of a Southern Spirit*, Wilson's work has explored theology and doctrine alongside practice and cultural expression. He has been equally at home invoking Clifford Geertz, Elvis Presley, Bear Bryant, Richard Wright, McKendree Long, Cherokee folktales, Tom T. Hall, Martin Luther King, Jr., and Gertrude Morgan. In showing us how to appreciate, explore, and critique the products of the southern religious mind and body, he has prepared for us a path, one that we can be grateful to follow as the next generation of scholarship in southern cultural and religious history takes these methods onto new topics and eras.

Notes

1. Wilbur J. Cash, *Mind of the South* (New York: Alfred A. Knopf, 1941).

2. Works referenced here include Beth Barton Schweiger, *The Gospel Working Up: Progress and the Pulpit in Nineteenth-Century Virginia* (New York: Oxford University Press, 2000); Beth Barton Schweiger, "The Literate South: Reading before Emancipation," *Journal of the Civil War Era* 3 (2013): 331–59; Darren E. Grem, *The Blessings of Business: How Corporations Shaped Conservative Christianity* (New York: Oxford University Press, 2016); Randall Stephens, *The Fire Spreads: Holiness and Pentecostalism in the American South* (Cambridge, MA: Harvard University Press, 2008); Carolyn Dupont, *Mississippi Praying: White Southern Evangelicals and the Civil Rights Movement, 1945–1975* (New York: New York University Press, 2013); Art Remillard, "God and Games in Dixieland: Religion and the Making of the South's Modern Sports World, 1865–1930" (unpublished manuscript), Microsoft Word file; Art Remillard, *Southern Civil Religions: Imagining the Good Society in the Post-Reconstruction Era* (Athens: University of Georgia Press, 2011); Jeff Wilson, *Dixie Dharma: Inside a Buddhist Temple in the American South* (Chapel Hill: University of North Carolina Press, 2014).

3. For example, see Edward Baptist, *The Half Has Never Been Told: Slavery and American Capitalism* (New York: Basic Books, 2014), which also contains a short but penetrating analysis of slave religion among those caught up in the international networks of slavery.

4. Mary E. Odem and Elaine Lacy, eds., *Latino Immigrants and the Transformation of the US South* (Athens: University of Georgia Press, 2009).

5. Tracy Thompson, *The New Mind of the South* (New York: Simon & Schuster, 2013), 7–8.

6. Ibid., 234–35.

7. Stephen Beale, "Protestant South Becoming a New Catholic Stronghold," *National Catholic Register*, May 11, 2013, http://www.ncregister.com/daily-news/protestant-south-becoming-a-new-catholic-stronghold.

8. See this map, for example, drawn from the 2010 Religious Congregations and Membership Study documented in the Association of Religion Data Archives: http://www.rcms2010.org/images/001.jpg.

9. Charles Reagan Wilson and Mark Silk, eds., *Religion and Public Life in the South: In the Evangelical Mode* (Lanham, MD: AltaMira Press, 2005).

10. An interesting recent exploration of evangelical "racial reconcilers" trying to overcome being "divided by faith" is Nancy Wadsworth, *Ambivalent Miracles: Evangelicals and the Politics of Racial Healing* (Charlottesville: University Press of Virginia, 2013). My thoughts on this work, and on the larger issues, are discussed here: "Divided by Faith," Marginalia, http://marginalia.lareviewofbooks.org/divided-by-faith-paul-harvey/ (accessed March 30, 2016).

11. Manuel Vasquez, *More Than Belief: A Materialist Theory of Religion* (New York: Oxford University Press, 2011).

12. *South Carolina Gazette*, April 24, 1742; see Paul Harvey, *Moses, Jesus, and the Trickster in the Evangelical South* (Athens: University of Georgia Press, 2012), 68.

13. Thomas Tweed, *Crossing and Dwelling: A Theory of Religion* (Cambridge, MA: Harvard University Press, 2008).

Religious History and Church History

The Riverbank Politics of Uncommon Prayers in Antebellum Arkansas

Ryan L. Fletcher

This is no time for noisy disputants to lead us. We should ask counsel of the experienced, the sober, the God-fearing men among us.
—Bishop Henry C. Lay, "Pastoral Letter," *Arkansas State Gazette*, December 22, 1860.

The ecstasies of frontier revivals supplied the introit for the processional to the constitutional convention of Arkansas in 1836. The convention seated Anthony H. Davies of Chicot County on the committees on banking and "on miscellaneous subjects" and the committee "on banking." Those committees enjoyed jurisdiction over Article VII of the draft constitution. Article VII, entitled "General Provisions," annulled the supposed democracy inherit in the constitution with an anti-labor litany that included: granting a slaveholding minority in Arkansas veto power over antislavery legislation, allowing for the imprisonment of a debtor who committed "fraud" or refused to "deliver [. . .] up his estate," envisioning a regressive framework of taxation, ordering the legislature to "make provisions" for "improvements in relation to roads, canals, and navigable waters," and encouraging the incorporation of two banks.

The committee on miscellaneous subjects dropped the distractions of religion clauses into Article VII, too. A 4-3 majority of the committee on miscellaneous subjects recommended the imposition of religious constraints on the political system. Section five of the committee's language required

Arkansans to affirm "the being of God" and "a future state of rewards and punishments" before either holding an elected office in the state or avowing an oath in court. Davies, an Episcopalian, voiced the disagreement of the three dissenters. All three dissenters represented plantation counties in the Delta. The committee's minority, Davies pressed, envisioned an Arkansas in which "no religious test shall ever be required as a qualification to any office of public trust." Davies propounded two separate motions to strike the totality of the religious examinations from the miscellany of the proposed constitution. The convention defeated both of Davies's attempted erasures. Recognizing that the convention preferred the maintenance of a religious test, Davies shifted strategies by furnishing his colleagues with an amendment to limit Arkansas's theological criterion. The delegate from Chicot County managed to persuade the convention to eliminate the "future state of rewards and punishments" tenet from the constitution's religious assessment. Davies uncovered more support on the floor of the convention to delete section six, which barred "Ministers of the Gospel" from "the office of Governor, or . . . a seat in either branch of the General Assembly." Davies won a 38-12 vote of the convention to expunge section six. Davies, therefore, notched impressive—albeit incomplete—victories in a planter-class campaign to ratify an anti-labor constitution by utilizing the veils of religious identities to polarize Arkansans.[1]

Davies contested the evangelical propagandists who endeavored to conceal the Episcopalians of the southern frontier. One Presbyterian observed in the 1840s, for example, that the Episcopal Church's "whole system of worship is incongruous to the genius of the people of Arkansas." Historian S. Charles Bolton contends that in Arkansas the "greatest monument of antebellum Episcopalianism seems to have been architectural in nature" because "Episcopal formalism . . . was a difficult sell in an environment nurtured by evangelicalism."[2] Bolton is correct that Episcopalians in the antebellum South did not master the art of selling their version of Christianity to the masses of small farmers, squatters, wage laborers, and slaves. Instead, Episcopalians fixated on mastering the political architecture of slavery. The Episcopal Church did not need entertaining sermons, water immersions, camp meetings, or the legalities of establishment to thrive in the antebellum South. Labor power—which households of Episcopalians controlled in massive quantities—embodied the one and only prerequisite for the westward migration of *The Book of Common Prayer.*

This essay reconsiders the historiographical paradigm that pairs the flourishing of evangelicalism with the declension of the Episcopal Church in the antebellum South. Evangelicalism's ascendancy neither caused nor signified the vanishing of Episcopalians in the antebellum South. Historians must remember that the Episcopal Church inherited centuries of Anglican expertise in imposing "supremacy" and "uniformity" upon dissenters. The southern frontier pitted disciplined Episcopalians united around slaveholding conservatism against antebellum evangelicalisms that suffered from spasms of classless consciousness, denominational cannibalism, emotional incontinence, and doctrinal dementia.³ Rather than impeding the Episcopal Church in the nineteenth-century South, the haphazard "organizing process" of revivalism factionalized a slipshod opposition.⁴

Arkansans reached for the political melatonin of antebellum evangelicalism to alleviate the tangible pains of economic hardship. Drowsiness, however, emerged as a side effect of southern evangelicalism that limited the "democratic implications" of the religious "mobilization of people." The "denominational bureaucracies" and rhetorical "populism" of evangelicalism nurtured an identity politics that oiled the machinery of the Episcopal Church in the antebellum South.⁵ That assertion, hopefully, venerates Barbara J. Fields's admonition to historians "inclined to romanticize, sentimentalize, or take vicarious comfort in the flowering of cultural forms among the oppressed which challenge their subordination," like those forms associated with evangelicalism. In the realm of politics, evangelicalism conformed to Fields's assessment of "the slogan" of white supremacy, in that a born-again message "never led to consensus on a single program." Transcribing Fields's analysis of white supremacy onto religious ideology reminds historians that "the slogans and ritual" of southern evangelicalism "offered no material solution" to the converted so the movement "grew larger the more it was fed" by the persistence of exploitation.⁶

Revivalists equipped poor souls with impotent weapons. As a consequence, democratizing muscles atrophied.⁷ The limp swords of shouting, jerking, crying, signing, praying, and denominational bureaucracies did not scare Episcopalians in the South—quite the contrary. Camp meetings exhausted the revolutionary energies of marginalized people all across the antebellum South. Then, bureaucracies and identities associated with evangelical denominations engendered a false consciousness of institutional organization that profoundly disorganized laboring people. On that less-romantic frontier characterized by hierarchy-reinforcing piety, Episcopalians in Arkansas weathered the flood by sandbagging their fiefdoms with the rural fortifications of land, slaves, and uncommon prayers.

The Episcopal Church and the Whig Party shared a coterminous geography in Arkansas during the 1830s and 1840s: the slaveholders in the river counties of the state. The state party operated as a vessel for the slaveholding conservatism and "conscious planning" of Arkansas's Episcopalians.⁸ In Arkansas, the politics of banking attracted a sizeable ensemble of planter-class Episcopalians to the Whig Party. Anthony H. Davies and the committee of banking mandated that one of the constitutionalized banks envisioned by Article VII had to "promote the great agricultural interests of the country."

The general assembly exercised that agricultural prerogative by concocting the Real Estate Bank (REB). Following the constitutional convention, voters in Chicot County elected Davies to Arkansas's House of Representatives. In the general assembly, Davies sired the enabling legislation that birthed the REB in 1836. According to historian Ted Worley, the Davies Bill designed the REB "for the benefit of planters" by assigning most of the branch offices to the "cotton producing areas" of the state.[9]

Baptists and Methodists, masquerading as populists, generated some of the brassiest invective against the Episcopalian-backed REB in the state legislature. Mark W. Izard of St. Francis County whipped the opposition to the Davies Bill in the Arkansas Senate. Izard's roots in evangelicalism stretched back to the territorial era when born-again people elected him "the founding moderator" of the St. Francis Baptist Association. Baptists who subsequently formed the General Association of Eastern Arkansas in the 1850s elevated Izard to the vice presidency of that organization. The state senator, thus, regularly pastored churches in the state until 1855. In the Arkansas Senate, the Baptist deemed the REB to be "unequal, unfair, and unjust and is calculated from its nature, to enrich the few at the expense of the many." The state senator personified the spirit of Jacksonian Democrats by introducing amendments to the bill that automatically terminated the REB if the institution ever refused "to pay in specie" and codified in law that the "General Assembly shall have power, at all times . . . to regulate the operations of the said institution." The state senate killed both of the Izard amendments prior to approving the Davies Bill.[10]

As a pressure valve for class tensions, the bank war in Arkansas enriched both Episcopalians and evangelicals. Evangelicalism and anti-bank warfare credentialed Izard as a Baptist Democrat, which bestowed upon him a sizeable base of support. Izard's popularity as a Baptist Democrat secured the pastor multiple re-elections to the state legislature enabling him to even win the presidency of the Arkansas Senate. Populist costumes, however, must not obscure Izard's support for legislation that carved up the laboring majority of his state, thereby cementing the rule of a planter-class minority. The Izard-backed leadership of the state senate invoked the mantras of evangelical-white supremacy to transform alcohol and card playing on the Sabbath into wedges that segregated working-class culture. The populist bluster of the Baptist Democrat, hence, entrenched him in the legislature where he divided laborers in Arkansas and allowed slaveholders to conquer.[11]

As evangelicals gained adherents by denouncing the Davies Bill, the passage of the law evidenced the competence of Episcopalians in implementing their legislative priorities. Davies ascended to become the financial institution's chief executive. President Davies openly confessed that the REB functioned as an appendage of the planter class. The bank's blessings, Davies assured, manifested themselves in "the extension of . . . plantations and villages" and in "the increase of . . . cultivation and exports." Davies and other administrators demanded that Arkansans subordinate their democratic sensations to the supremacy of the REB. "THE PUBLIC," Davies and the bank's trustees admonished, invited a reign of economic terror if the people wielded their sovereignty by passing a law in the general assembly that "violently" seized the property owned by the bank. Davies and his colleagues pledged to deny their "assent to any bill" that removed funds beyond the bank's control, because such legislation promised the "total ruin of their private fortunes." That dismissal of majoritarian control over banks and a willingness of bankers to execute antagonists unleashed an impressive backlash against the REB.[12]

Archibald Yell channeled both the simmering hostility directed towards the REB and the saving grace of his state's revivalism into incredible political success during the 1840s. Yell mimicked Andrew Jackson, his counterpart at the national level, because the Arkansan marshaled a coalition of common people while possessing eight hundred acres of land and eight slaves in Washington County. Voters in Arkansas elected Yell as the state's governor in 1840. An evangelical gloss shrouded Yell's inauguration. Inaugural planners noticed that Arkansans associated with the Methodist Episcopal Church had descended upon Little Rock for an annual conference presided over by Bishop Beverly Waugh. Committeemen invited the Methodist bishop to participate in the inaugural festivities. Waugh joined the processional and opened the ceremony by summoning "the blessings of Divine mercy upon the assembled multitude in a most excellent, impressive and appropriate prayer." The words of that evangelical bishop, however, should not overshadow the centrality of Episcopalian Daniel W. Ringo. Chief Justice Ringo of the Arkansas Supreme Court "administered" the oath of office to Yell. The Episcopalian's recitations transmitted more power to the governor than the supplications of the Methodist prelate.[13]

Governor Yell dedicated his inaugural address to sermonizing against the sins of banks. The governor accused banks of the "most odious and unjust oppression" in his inaugural address. Banks, the Jacksonian scoffed, had the power to raise or depress "the price of all . . . staple products." The "heartless tyranny" of the banks, Yell continued, elevated the rights of "corporations" over the prosperity of the state's residents. Arkansas's governor summoned the legislature to restore specie and "lay the axe at the root of the evil." The general assembly, Yell demanded, must "teach brokers and stockjobbers a salutary lesson" by empowering "the producing part" of the state. A successful bank war, the governor maintained, promised to ensure that "the laboring classes receive a just compensation as the reward of their industry." In a subsequent message to the general assembly, Yell thundered that Arkansans were "in the midst of a great revolution" against banks. Banking, the governor decided, needed "a radical reform" because financial institutions voraciously devoured "the hard earnings of the laboring classes." Governor Yell proclaimed banking in the 1840s to be nothing more than "legalized swindling." Unfazed Episcopalians, however, turned their ignoring ears away from the aimless populism of the governor and toward the systematic prayers of James H. Otey, the acting bishop of the southwest. Otey visited Little Rock to consecrate Christ Church in 1842. The general assembly of the state happened to be in session during the bishop's stopover. State legislators "'waited upon'" the bishop and invited him to address the general assembly "'on education.'" Otey accepted and "'delivered an address on education . . . Well received'" inside of the House of Representatives.[14]

Bishop Otey's confirmations stiffened the faith of legislators in the banking initiatives of Episcopalians. Lawmakers in the general assembly swung at the governor by passing the Pay Act in 1843, which required the state to distribute the salaries of legislators in specie rather than the vaunted paper money of the state's banks. Governor Yell vetoed the legislation because the Pay Act threatened to "depreciate the paper in the hands of the people." He claimed the legislation presumed to coin "one currency for members of the Legislature and another for the people." The general assembly overrode the governor's veto, which incited the livid residents of Lawrence County to amass for agitation. A caucus of the county's citizens nominated David Orr to preside as the meeting's president. Lawrence County had previously elected Orr to serve in the territorial legislature prior to Arkansas's statehood. In addition to his political résumé, Orr's accomplishments as a Baptist preacher assisted his election too. Orr recalled that, upon his arrival in Arkansas in 1828, "mourners were brought to a knowledge of their sins forgiven." Seven years later, nine Baptist churches in the territory and the Spring River Baptist Association all honored Orr as their initiator. In addition to church planting, Orr utilized the ever-popular camp-meeting revivals on Arkansas's frontier for "preaching Christ and him crucified." Orr's evangelism throughout northern Arkansas appealed to the popular masculinity of the frontier. Critics of Orr satirized the pastor's reputation for utilizing both "*profanity*" and "the exhilarating glass . . . of the inspiring draught."[15]

The muscular evangelicalism of Orr endeared him to a county dedicated to the "dearest rights of the people." In 1843, the Baptist-tinged summit considered the Pay Act to be unassailable evidence of the "unprecedented strides of Aristocracy" in the state. Delegates at the Lawrence County rally praised the commander of the bank war for vetoing the legislation. The governor's actions verified that he was "in favor of the whole people" and "against the strides for power." Legislators, the resolves insisted, had "disregarded" the "voice of the sovereign people." The pronouncements reached their crescendo with Lawrence County's most militant demand. Pastor Orr's associates ordered lawmakers in the Episcopalian-heavy legislature to "resign their offices to the hands of the people." The Baptist pastor's countenance of an extralegal impeachment of the elected general assembly exhibited unthreatening populism by prodding action on compensation policies for aristocratic wages while neglecting to address the pervasive exploitation of labor.[16]

The religious polarization of the bank war crested in the pivotal year of 1844. Governor Yell mobilized his evangelical base in Lawrence County and around the state by seeking the sole seat held by Arkansas in the United States House of Representatives. Two men associated with the Episcopal Church steered the Whig Party's campaign to stymie Yell's dreams. Thomas W. Newton partnered with Vestryman Frederick W. Trapnall to crush Governor Yell because they hoped to decapitate the booming voice of anti-banking Arkansans. Trapnall animated Whigs with a gospel of "prosperity, peace, and happiness" that gushed from banking institutions. The Episcopalian cautioned his audiences that the Democrats offered "the laborers and mechanics" nothing but "broken bank promises." The Whig Party nominated David Walker to oppose the bank-war governor. Yell's electioneering "resorted to his favorite hobby—his opposition to State Banks." Alongside bank bashing, however, Yell's strategy brandished religion, too. The governor exemplified his mastery over evangelical voters during a joint campaign appearance on Kings River in northern Arkansas. Yell and Walker both attended a camp-meeting revival. Walker reacted with disgust when Yell began "leading the old class-leaders in the amen corner, and singing with musical voice on a key above all others that old hymn 'How Happy Are They Who Their Savior Obey.'" The Wesleyan hymn sung by the governor celebrated a "sweet comfort" in heaven tendered to the people in "the blood of the Lamb." The warm reception extended by the camp meeting to the governor illustrated how the pseudo-populisms of the bank war and evangelicalism inhabited the same social geography in Arkansas.[17]

The governor's opposition received assistance from John Drennen, the president of the REB's branch in Van Buren. Drennen exhibited a clear religious allegiance. Prior to his intervention in the Yell-Walker race, Drennen developed a hearty relationship with the Episcopal Church. The banker authenticated his commitment to the denomination by donating two lots in Van Buren for the construction of Trinity Church, and he opened his home for services of bishop-led worship. The Episcopalian attempted to undermine Yell's reputation as the candidate standing with the people against the banks. Drennen composed a letter in September of the congressional campaign announcing that the governor, in contradiction to his speechmaking, had procured stock in the REB. Newton, a cashier for the REB's branch in Little Rock, provided the Walker campaign with a second letter citing the REB's official books as evidence that Yell had indeed purchased fifty-one shares.[18]

Unmasking the imaginary populisms of Arkansas, apparently, required more than one scandalous disclosure of hypocrisy. The hymn-singing patron saint of the camp-meeting common folk trounced Walker by winning thirty-six of the state's forty-six counties and over 59 percent of the popular vote statewide. Pulaski County's legislative races emerged as consolation prizes for Whig-supporting Episcopalians. Newton and Trapnall both landed seats in the general assembly of Arkansas. The exploits of Newton and Trapnall, however, did not restrain their colleagues in the general assembly from giving voice to the decree of the voters regarding banks. Following Yell's landslide victory in the congressional election, the Arkansas general assembly penned an amendment to the state's constitution that declared: "No bank or banking institution shall be hereafter incorporated, or established in this State." Two years later, the amendment was officially ratified. Ironically, the meaningless deconstitutionalizing of banks shifted the religious politics of Arkansas to more favorable terrain for Episcopalians.[19]

Episcopalians in Arkansas recognized that the crassness of banks was superfluous to the "domestic system" of labor. Episcopalians in the state depicted "Plantation life" as "genial and pleasant" with "little need for coercion" because of "the attachments which bind together master and his dependents." The paternalistic dependency of "domestic ties" in Arkansas, churchmen asserted, allowed masters to govern slaves with "moral influence" instead of resorting to "physical force." Arkansas's commitment to slavery after the bank war permitted Episcopalians to return home and peacefully aggrandize their kingdoms in the late 1840s and throughout the 1850s. The Episcopal Church assisted its communicants by deploying bishops and priests to bolster the localized dominion of the lords of river fiefdoms.[20]

In 1844, the Episcopal Church appointed George W. Freeman to serve as the bishop of the southwest. Bishop Freeman promptly reignited his church's concord with Arkansas's slaveholders by disbursing a program of paternalism to reinforce plantation-based hierarchies. The bishop did "not dispute the *rights* of masters," but argued that he had an obligation to "show [slaveholders] that they have sacred duties to perform toward those under their control." Colossians 4:1 enshrined in the Bible, from Freeman's exegetical perspective, the marrow of the church's paternalistic mission in the Arkansas wilderness. Bishop Freeman's ownership of a slave in Pulaski County in 1850 undoubtedly aided in his fraternization with fellow slaveholders.[21]

As camp meetings transitioned into denominational bureaucracies, the evangelical churches of Arkansas joined Bishop Freeman in centralizing the issue of labor. The Arkansas Annual Conference of the Methodist Episcopal Church-South adopted a series of resolutions in 1845 that proclaimed for "the public" that the relationship between master and slave was "not of itself necessarily sinful, or a moral evil." Methodists in the state agreed to collaborate with slaveholders to ameliorate the "spiritual welfare" of slaves. Baptists mirrored their Methodist neighbors. In October 1847, the Mountain Spring campground in Dallas County hosted a revival in which Baptists, Methodists, and Presbyterians each participated. The evangelical denominations brushed aside their theological differences for "the conversion of sinners." The *Arkansas State Gazette* estimated that "upwards of a thousand souls" attended. Attendees listened to the stylings of Baptist William H. Bayliss, among others. Following the revival, the Saline County Baptist Association proposed the formation of a state convention. The Arkansas Baptist State Convention (ABSC) assembled in 1848 and elected camp-meeting evangelist Bayliss as the body's president. The ABSC recommended that local churches construct "some apartment for [slaves] to hear the preaching" and that biracial congregations elect a committee to supervise the instruction of slaves. In addition, the ABSC subsequently sanctioned the concept of Baptists working with slaveholders in the southern counties of the state to establish a regime of slave missions.[22]

John T. Johnson's revivalism in Arkansas incarnated the emptiness of religious populism on questions of labor. Johnson hailed from an esteemed family of elected officials in Kentucky. The people of the bluegrass had elected Johnson as a Jacksonian Democrat to two terms in the United States House of Representatives, while his brother was serving a concurrent term in the United States Senate. Johnson exited politics, "much to the regret of the people," to become an evangelist for a frontier form of Christianity inspired by Alexander Campbell. In February 1845, the congressman emeritus and his co-evangelist, R. C. Ricketts, traveled from Kentucky to Arkansas to proclaim the Campbellite version of restoration theology. Campbell's evangelists in Arkansas emphasized the New Testament's plainness by describing the sequencing of salvation as: "*Faith,* Repentance, Reformation, Confession, and Immersion." Calling themselves simply Christians, Campbell's disciples openly scorned what they deemed to be the unscriptural traditions of denominationalism. In Little Rock, Johnson and Ricketts preached "day and night without intermission." Crowds "thronged" to listen to the Kentucky preachers. The *Arkansas State Gazette* designated the revival as an event like "we have never had among us." The evangelists both saved the unconverted and persuaded people belonging to other denominations to join their identity politics of claiming to reject identity politics. During Little Rock's festival of grace, the revivalists scheduled baptisms in the Arkansas River every other day. "Crowds of people stood on the banks" of the river to witness the Kentuckians administer the poignant rite of immersion baptism during what they described as their "siege" of Little Rock. The newly saved emerged from the waters with a liberating dislike of being "dictated to." The Campbell Movement attracted Arkansans who by humbly studying the

Bible "renounced . . . contradictory creeds" long imposed upon ordinary people by denominational elites. Arkansas's Christians, however, zealously accepted the pro-slavery creed of Alexander Campbell. Frontier upstarts, therefore, aligned with the more established denominations of evangelicalism in propping up a once-despised aristocracy of bankers by shielding the unremitting lashing of slave labor from moral scrutiny.[23]

Episcopalians profited as the religious politics of the state transitioned from derogating banks to defending slavery. In 1846, Archibald Yell challenged the reappointment of Chester Ashley to the United States Senate. Senator Ashley, with clear linkages to both the REB and the Episcopal Church, clobbered the hero of anti-banking evangelicals. Similarly, Newton entered a special election as one of his party's nominees to occupy Arkansas's seat in the United States House of Representatives. Democrat George W. Paschal gained traction as the bank cashier's toughest competitor by describing banks as institutions "calculated to . . . establish the aristocracy of a 'monied power.'" The literature of Paschal's campaign applauded the dawning of a new era as many states in the "the great west" had moved to either "prohibit the establishment of banks" or at a minimum impose strict "restrictions" upon financial institutions. Anti-banking incitement, however, no longer guaranteed landslides. The fractured ballot of five candidates—a fitting metaphor for southern evangelicalism—allowed the Episcopalian to win the seat with less than 29 percent of the statewide vote. Newton, however, tallied over 48 percent of the combined votes from the five river counties abutting the Mississippi.[24]

The Whiggish Episcopalian dedicated his ephemeral tenure in Congress to a bank-free agenda of protecting the western expansion of slavery by opposing the Wilmot Proviso and securing federal dollars for improvements to the state's rivers. In a speech to the House of Representatives, Newton declared that he did "not apprehend the great danger in the permanency of our Union, by the addition of a few more slave States." Press agents for Newton back in Arkansas announced that the congressman "is opposed to the 'Wilmot Proviso,' utterly, totally, at all times, and under all circumstances—opposed to it root and branch." Extending slavery required transportation, so Newton voted for the Wisconsin Appropriations Bill (WAB) of 1847. The WAB earmarked $550,500 for transportation projects. Despite the camouflaging name of the legislation, the WAB allocated at least 48 percent of that handsome sum to ventures designed to benefit slaveholding states. Whiggish Episcopalians maintained that river improvements had the capacity to "vastly" increase the value of "plantations and other property" throughout Arkansas. Newton, therefore, embodied how Episcopalians in the late 1840s and throughout the 1850s resuscitated their public images by openly associating with the planter class rather than the profession of banking. The congressman and other Whigs noticed that evangelicalism in

Arkansas had stamped the stealing of labor with the Bible's seal of approval, while denying that same endorsement to the stealing of capital.[25]

The commandeering of high offices by slaveholding Episcopalians, however, stirred the "Associated Mechanics of Little Rock" (AMLR) in 1846. The AMLR condemned the state's politicians for "taxing [mechanics] to support . . . unfair competition." Mechanics demanded a "home market" with economic alternatives to the "culture of cotton." The AMLR challenged Newton and other Episcopalians who presumed to earmark tax dollars for legislation that enriched riverbank planters. The state government, the AMLR insisted, needed to implement a jobs program subsidized by "direct taxation" for the mechanical folk. Mechanics, therefore, concurred with Newton's commitment to government stimulation of the economy. The AMLR and the congressman, however, sharply diverged on the question of which social class governmental intervention needed to prioritize. As the AMLR indicted the state for treating unfettered laborers "worse than slaves," Newton and Whiggish Episcopalians retreated to the identity politics of evangelicalism to subdue the masses.[26]

In 1848, Newton chaired the organizational seminar of the Little Rock Bible Society (LRBS) inside of a Methodist meetinghouse. The LRBS mined identity politics by appealing to the "the congregations of the Evangelical churches of the city." Attendees committed themselves to "the circulation of the Scriptures among those families in the city and neighborhood who are without a copy of the Scriptures and are destitute of the means . . . to procure it." Like toothless populism, the LRBS advocated a mushy benevolence that treated a minor symptom of social inequality rather than eradicating the systemic disease. Bible-welfare for the poor did not save Newton later that year when he earned less than 40 percent of the popular vote statewide in a quixotic bid to reclaim his old seat in the United States House of Representatives.[27] Clearly, Whiggish Episcopalians needed actual evangelicals to score in evangelicalism's game of identity politics.

Despite Newton's thrashing at the ballot box in 1848, Episcopalians heard a divine voice in the wilderness emanating from a contest for a seat in the state senate. Whiggish Episcopalians had backed Cyrus W. Wilson in a senatorial district that encompassed the counties of Pulaski and Prairie. Wilson's advocates hammered the identity politics of evangelicalism. Campaign literature depicted Wilson as "a clear expounder of the Scriptures . . . a consistent christian and a Whig." Wilson's campaign portrayed his physical appearance in sappy terms because his hands had been "hardened by the handle of the plough" and his "cheek . . . bronzed from *labor* in the summer's heat." The allusion to a bronze cheek amounted to a frontier precursor of redneck politics. Appeals to the cultural imagery of plebian voters, however, obscured the fine print of the campaign literature which clearly announced that, unlike subsistence farmers,

Wilson considered himself to be an "industrious farmer." Vapid, yet evocative, sloganeering resulted in Wilson cruising to victory. Episcopalians learned a valuable lesson from the election of 1848. Wilson outperformed Newton in both of the senatorial district's counties, or to translate: voters in Arkansas preferred a Whiggish evangelical to a Whiggish Episcopalian even though both men pledged allegiance to the same platform of the planter class.[28]

Whigs chained planter-class policies to the wonder-working power of evangelicalism in Arkansas's gubernatorial election of 1849, thereby fomenting a watershed in the state's religious politics. Episcopalians like Newton and Trapnall concocted the most efficacious political strategy of their careers. Newton, Trapnall, and other Whig-supporting Episcopalians nominated State Senator Cyrus W. Wilson as the gubernatorial nominee of their party in 1849. The Whig Party simply transmitted the messages of Wilson's senatorial campaign to a statewide audience. Wilson's backers plagiarized the poetry of Jacksonian democracy by describing their nominee as "the *People's Candidate.*" Southern foodways helped license the Whig Party's nominee as an everyman. Wilson's promoters headlined that the aspirant had happily "eaten corn bread and bacon." Whiggish Episcopalians trumpeted the identity politics of rural Arkansas by painting Wilson as "the *plain old FARMER.*"[29]

As Wilson's election to the state senate corroborated: religion had the capacity to obfuscate the glaring disconnect between planter-class policies and a commoner façade. Wilson trained for electoral politics by graciously expounding upon the Good News of Christ's redemption as a preacher for the Cumberland Presbyterian Church. The Whiggish Episcopalians who endorsed Wilson had selected an evangelist from a denomination that typified the very essence of the faux-populism of frontier evangelicalism. Cumberland Presbyterians had seceded from the other species of Presbyterians during the early decades of the nineteenth century. Cumberland theologians jettisoned the predestination of "extreme" Calvinism and instead announced that God's grace "is available to all." All of the people, Cumberland Presbyterians proselytized, had "the freedom" to respond to the loving salvation offered by God. The denomination prioritized the "plain" doctrines generated in revivalism over the legalistic writings of "scholastics." Cumberland Presbyterians seduced sympathetic audiences in Arkansas by scorning the "Blue stockings" throughout the 1830s and 1840s. Cephas Washburn of Benton County sneered at the members of the denomination as "the strong champions" of camp meetings and producers of the "strong excitement of animal passions, shoutings, noise & disorder." As a Presbyterian who obviously loathed Cumberland Presbyterians, Washburn derided the frontier denomination for an inability to "believe it possible for a revival of religion to exist where there was not much noise & confusion or that a sinner could be converted but at a campmeeting [sic]."[30]

The Cumberland Presbyterian Church, however, bottled that egalitarianism in the safe confines of camp meetings and denominational bureaucracies. Cumberland Presbyterians, like other evangelicals, did not offer the converted a true populism capable of bringing a kingdom of justice to Arkansas. Instead, a committee of the Cumberland Presbyterian Church's general assembly rejected excluding slaveholders from membership and declared that political agitation over slavery "can be productive of no real benefit to master and slave." Arkansas's Cumberland Presbyterians followed the example of their general assembly. The White River Presbytery in northeastern Arkansas adopted a resolution divining slavery to be "a political question, and that we are opposed to its introduction into the Church . . . we do not feel at liberty to interrogate one another on that subject." Whiggish Episcopalians cloaked themselves in the illusory populism of the Cumberland Presbyterian Church by nominating State Senator Wilson. That decision highlighted how pro-slavery evangelicalisms immunized southern Episcopalians.[31]

Wilson's abettors viewed his pastoral career as evidence of a democratic ethos because the Cumberland Presbyterian's "life ha[d] been spent among the people, and a large portion of it devoted to their Eternal welfare." Given that the People's Candidate had demonstrated such fervency for ushering the plain folk of Arkansas to heaven, Whiggery's logicians extrapolated that voters should invest their confidence in Wilson's fidelity to their earthly prosperity. Whigs gleefully welcomed references to the People's Candidate with the alias "Parson Wilson" since in their calculation that moniker conveyed an equivalent connotation. The Whig Party's allies postulated that any criticism of Wilson amounted to an assault upon religion. Whiggish cleverness spawned an associative property that denounced Democratic attacks as demeaning to all Bible-believing Arkansans. Wilson's supporters attempted to formulate camaraderie with ordinary Arkansans by claiming that "genteel society" disdained their candidate because of his occupation as a "preacher of the gospel." Whigs explicitly accused Democrats of detesting Wilson simply "because he is a Christian and a minister." Democrats, Whiggery's partisans bellowed during the campaign, exhibited an "overt hatred of ministers and religion." Political hacks aspired to use a phantom prejudice against frontier evangelicalism to implement aristocratic economics.[32]

The People's Candidate also recited the bank-war script by promising to usher in an "equalized" system of taxation that both allayed the burdens of the "poor working man" and required more from "the money changer." Wilson distanced himself from discredited capital by declaring that Arkansas's "miserable Banking establishments should be wound up." After tiptoeing around the banking landmine, the People's Candidate revealed the unvarnished designs of his sponsors. Wilson echoed Newton by pledging to use the levers of government for "the improvement of [Arkansas's] Roads and Rivers" that knitted together the planter class. Dressed up in the homespun clothes of a pastor-farmer, the agenda of Episcopalians like Newton gained more traction statewide under the hypnotic banner of a Cumberland Presbyterian.[33]

State Senator Wilson and his Episcopalian handlers manufactured the closest gubernatorial election in Arkansas during the entirety of the nineteenth century. Abysmal voter turnout likewise contributed to the narrow margin of the final tabulation. Democrat John S. Roane—notably an alumnus of a college operated by the Cumberland Presbyterian Church—defeated Parson Wilson. Roane earned 50 percent of the popular vote, while the People's Candidate secured, by Whiggery's standards in Arkansas, an impressive 49 percent. The People's Candidate racked up an eye-catching 62 percent of the aggregate vote in the river counties of Chicot, Crittenden, Desha, and Phillips. The tightness of the statewide results, however, did not portend a new age of ascendancy for the Whigs. Instead, the election confirmed the deracination of the bank war's bright line among Arkansas's political parties. Arkansans in the 1850s decided that the "old issues," including that of banking, had become "obsolete." As slavery increasingly "occupied center stage" in the state's politics in the 1850s, the old partisan breakdowns rapidly wilted. Parson Wilson's campaign elucidated how the fictitious populisms of redneckism and evangelicalism engendered an identity politics that suffocated the viability of leveling solidarity in the antebellum South.[34]

As an increasing number of evangelicals and slaves populated Arkansas, kneelers multiplied at the Holy Table of Episcopalians. Indeed, the Episcopal Church's aggregate number of communicants in Arkansas swelled by approximately 167 percent between 1850 and 1860. Bishop Freeman and his missionaries scattered to every corner of the state in the 1850s, discovering that Episcopalians had avenues to power that circumvented the electoral system of Arkansas. As Parson Wilson conceded his loss of the governorship in 1849, a Whig administration in the nation's capital doled out patronage to Arkansas's Episcopalians. Zachary Taylor, for example, elevated Daniel W. Ringo to the federal bench by appointing the ex-chief justice of Arkansas as the district judge for the entire state. Likewise, Millard Fillmore tapped John Drennen to serve as a Choctaw agent before promoting the Episcopalian to a superintendent position in the Bureau of Indian Affairs. In 1850, Bishop Freeman visited the "frontier stations" in western Arkansas, where he "baptized George Holden, infant son of [his] friend Colonel John Drennen of the Choctaw agency." Slaveholding Episcopalians, like Ringo and Drennen, helped the peculiar institution by staffing the federal bureaucracy inside of Arkansas.[35]

Judge Ringo, while on the federal bench, co-owned slaves in Chicot County in a partnership with Frederick W. Trapnall. Control over labor power on a river plantation was a fitting reimbursement for Trapnall's career as a longtime elder of the Whig Party, state representative for Pulaski County, vestryman, and benefactor of Parson Wilson's campaign in 1849. The two Episcopalians joined a planter class in Chicot County that already included an astonishing number of their coreligionists. Bishop Freeman obsessed over Chicot County because he considered "wealthy planters" desirous of religious instruction for their slaves to be the backbone of the county's free population. Chicot County provided Freeman with warm memories of paternalism. For instance, the prelate vacationed on the county's plantations during one Christmas season. Freeman recounted how the "ladies from the several plantations" engaged in purchasing Christmas presents for their slaves. The bishop of the southwest traveled with one plantation baroness to Columbia and observed her loading a wagon with gifts. That "benevolent errand" of planter-class women, Freeman exclaimed, guaranteed the diffusion of gladness throughout the "plantations in Chicot when Christmas-day arrived."[36]

In January 1850, Freeman performed the Episcopal Church's liturgy in Chicot County. Anthony H. Davies—opponent of religious discrimination and longtime tycoon of the Real Estate Bank—hosted Freeman by offering his home as a sanctuary for services. The bishop baptized five children and administered Holy Communion to five people during his visit to the region encircling Lake Chicot. Freeman marveled at the lake-crusted landscape as "a beautiful clear sheet of water, bordered by valuable cotton plantations, in a high state of cultivation." Davies's planter-class neighborhood in the Arkansas Delta was small, Freeman recorded, yet "substantially united in favor of the Episcopal Church." Bishop Freeman returned to Chicot County later in 1850 because of a summons issued to him by a vanquished grandee of the Whig Party. Thomas W. Newton directed his attention to matters of the heart following his inability to propel Parson Wilson into the governor's office. Newton, despite residing in Little Rock, decided to marry Amelia Cordell in the Arkansas Delta. As Freeman traveled to the wedding, he stopped at Sandford C. Faulkner's plantation. Faulkner's connection with the Real Estate Bank included a stint as the president of the branch at Columbia. In the Delta, Faulkner controlled over 940 acres of cotton-producing land. Bishop Freeman submitted adorations to God with twenty whites and "the same number of slaves" on Faulkner's plantation. The vicar eventually reached Newton's marital-abode on the plantation of John Llwellyn. *The Book of Common Prayer*'s presence on plantation sediment drenched in the sweat of slave labor demonstrated the undiminished hegemony of the miter in antebellum Arkansas. The distant noise of "anxious hearers" attending evangelical revivals, in which the people "thronged" to "the altar of prayer" for conversions and "the moralizing" of towns, serenaded Episcopalians while they sipped from a chalice in the serenity of a Delta wedding.[37]

In the Arkansas of the 1850s, Episcopalians touted themselves to the planter class as conservative defenders of patriarchal households. Reverend Otis Hackett partnered with Bishop Freeman to propagate Davies's vision of an Arkansas in which "families of all religious denominations will be readily received and treated with equal kindness and attention; but equal conformity to the rules and discipline of [Episcopalians] will be required of all." Hackett transferred to the Delta heartland of his denomination in 1856 to serve the plantations in the vicinities of Helena, Chicot County, and Marianna. In 1858, four Episcopalians from Phillips County dispatched a letter to Hackett beseeching him to publish one of his sermons that had triggered Presbyterians to level "injurious reproaches." Planters John T. Jones and Jamison W. Rice headed the list of four requestors. Hackett replied to his slaveholding patrons by vowing to defend the "the Church we love."[38]

Reverend Hackett viewed the "violent assault upon the Episcopal Church" by the Protestant churches invented during the "last few hundred" years as an attempt to arouse a "popular clamor" against his denomination. The priest rapturously proclaimed that his theological opponents in the late 1850s had "mistaken ... the temper of the day." Hackett proceeded to annunciate the deferential strictures that southern Episcopalians expected of evangelicalism by criticizing "the clergy of other denominations" for plunging "into the maddening vortex of politics." Episcopalians had witnessed other denominations "lose the parson in the partizan [sic]." Hackett thumped evangelicalism for demonstrating "vastly greater zeal—even Calvinists—in reference to an election to some petty secular office, than an election to eternal life." The Delta priest, without a hint of irony, boasted that "[no] man fears, in entering an Episcopal Church, that he shall be compelled to listen to a political harangue or a partizan [sic] prayer." Unlike the "prostituted" denominations of evangelicalism, Hackett concluded, the Episcopalians accorded their parishioners "a sober, conservative, and purely religious Church." Hackett emphasized the Episcopal Church's dominion over evangelicalism by delivering his confrontational sermon at an aging monument that memorized how affluent Episcopalians had both incited and smashed mock populism. The verses of the Delta priest reverberated throughout a campground.[39]

Hackett's anti-populism infused the hierarchy-building episcopate of Henry C. Lay. The Episcopal Church elected Lay to the see of the southwest following the death of Bishop Freeman in 1858. Lay's relocation from Huntsville, Alabama to Fort Smith dramatized the weight of labor power to the church's presence in Arkansas at every level of the denomination. The bishop accompanied his slaveholding household—which consisted of a "wife, children, servants, and furniture"—as it navigated the Arkansas River in the spring and summer of 1860. Low water levels stranded the Lay household "200 miles below Fort Smith."

Lay occupied "a vacant plantation house on the river bank" owned by Reverend William C. Stout—one of the church's priests in Arkansas. The slaveholding bishop admitted his class anxieties on the Stout plantation because "there [was] no white person about the premises," which Lay explained "obliged" him "to stay and protect [his] household." Lay eventually reached Fort Smith, which he portrayed as both a "trading point with the Indians" and "the point of departure for the far West." In such a borderland town, Lay emitted the slogans of white supremacy by sensationalizing the daily occurrence of "red men coming in on their little ponies" speaking "their strange discourse" with the assistance of interpreters. Episcopalians documented how the identity politics of evangelical-white supremacy crossed the open border between Arkansans and Indian Territory. A Presbyterian facility in the territory, for instance, aspired to teach "Indian boys . . . to raise sufficient cotton to keep them in groceries and clothing." Likewise, the Methodist Manual Labor School consisted of "Carpenter and wheel-wright and blacksmith shops, a brick yard, loom, dairies—in short every facility for imparting instruction, not only in letters, but in the mechanical arts." The training grounds of evangelicalism that operated west of the state's border amplified the labor power of the planter class back in Arkansas.[40]

Arkansans, the rookie bishop observed, had "been born in a land where servitude is recognized . . . benign and pleasant." Lay echoed his predecessor by defining slavery in the paternalistic terminology of the spiritual household. The bishop insisted that the Bible protected the right of planters to "order . . . households" of "children and the servants born in the house." The Bible, Lay assured, codified a household architecture with "a law of marriage," "the duty of filial subordination," and "the legality of slavery." Arkansas's Episcopalians supported their bishop when he declared that on matters related to slaveholding households: "We cannot permit free speech in the sense of unrestrained popular discussion of existing institutions, for the agitation would be infinitely mischievous."[41]

A cadre of laborers in Little Rock resisted the dissent-suppressing sentiments of the bishop by organizing themselves for a session of collective bargaining with Episcopalians. The "direct competition" generated by the employment of "*free* and *slave* negroes with that of convict's labor" spurred a "movement of mechanics" (MM) in Little Rock. A detachment of the city's mechanics unfurled a southern-style strike by refusing "to instruct free and slave negroes in the mechanic arts." That MM also announced a boycott against both "work on any building with [African Americans] as mechanics" and jobs "for any mechanic that gives [African Americans] employment to the exclusion of whites." The MM pledged to enter the political domain of Episcopalians by endeavoring "to urge the passage of a certain act or acts by [Arkansas's] Legislature . . . for the suppression or removal of these evils."[42]

Mechanics zeroed in on the Episcopalians who controlled the governmental infrastructure of Little Rock. Appointed by President James Buchanan, the postmaster, Thomas J. Churchill, regulated the correspondence of the MM. Outside of the post office, the slaveholding postmaster gave as gifts copies of *The Book of Common Prayer* to the priests and deacons of his church. In January 1858, voters in Little Rock re-elected William E. Ashley, a devout Episcopalian and energetic singer in the choir of Christ Church. A healthy contingent of Episcopalians reinforced the Ashley Administration as city aldermen during the 1850s. The MM scolded the reigning Episcopalians and reminded the sovereigns that laboring people had the capacity "to form a society of mechanics before the election and vote for no man who would not carry out their wishes."[43] Supporters of the ruling Episcopalians snapped back that "[so] long as our city continues to improve as it is now doing [mechanics] will all get as much employment as they can desire" assuring that "[they] will never have idleness forced upon them."[44]

Unlike the banality of the bank war, the MM touched the vital nerve of the ruling class. Arkansas's planters launched a swift and aggressive response to dissemble the MM. Opponents of the MM mocked "the *association of labor*" as a "useless" exercise on the subsistence-rich frontier. In "the great west," the gentry calculated, "a few hours of labor in each day would suffice to procure food." As the city digested the declaration of the MM, apologists for slaveholders injected the s-word of American politics into the debate: socialism. The establishment of Little Rock mused that if a "socialistic community" was "not disposed to interfere with the subject of slavery or to advance such odious doctrines as free-love or an abrogation of the marriage tie, but simply to associate together for agricultural or mechanical purposes, we could not well object to their coming." That sexualized socialism-bashing tickled the patriarchal moralizing of evangelicalism. As Christine Leigh Heyrman underscores, southern evangelicals "tailored their teachings to uphold, ever more unequivocally, the authority of male heads of household, particularly over godly women." Alongside undermining patriarchy, the slaveholder-controlled press of Little Rock pronounced that should those socialists "be found to be abolitionists ... they will find Arkansas too warm to hold them." Elites in Little Rock sounded the alarm, because in their opinion "associated labor," like the MM, threatened to "abolish slavery in the south." Since the MM justified their demands on the basis of unfair "competition," affluent urbanites warned that such a limitless critique opened the door to anti-competition insurrections in rural Arkansas too in relation to "the negro upon the farm."[45]

Alongside socialist-baiting, the identity politics of evangelicalism aided Episcopalians in undermining the labor association. As the MM bristled, Bishop John Early of the Methodist Episcopal Church-South assembled the Arkansas

Annual Conference for "a most harmonious session of five days" that concluded with the appointment of preachers to "African Mission[s]" segregated from circuits of free Methodists. Presbyterians sainted their politicians like Edwin M. Williams because, as a "member of the Presbyterian church," the state representative from Prairie County "had lived, trusting for salvation in the merits of a crucified Redeemer." The Arkansas Senate massaged the identity politics of evangelicalism too by engineering a chaplaincy election that occurred during the uprising of the MM. Senators wrangled over the triviality of deciding between a "Methodist and a Democrat" or a "Baptists, and . . . a Democrat." For the record, the Methodist Democrat from Fort Smith prevailed over the Baptist Democrat from Prairie County—and nothing materially changed for mechanics or slaves. Outside of the capital, evangelical revivalists manufactured "protracted meetings . . . exciting a deep interest in the minds of the people." An interlocking directory of Baptists, Methodists, and Presbyterians had the "deign to protract" gatherings in Arkansas to increase "professions" in 1858. As a "new era in religious matters . . . dawned," Episcopalians smiled. Decades of canvasses in Arkansas validated for Episcopalians the motto that evangelicalism "makes men better friends, better neighbors, better citizens."[46]

Indeed, the "better citizens" of evangelicalism anointed a new mayor in the election following the disturbances connected to the MM. That slaveholding mayor-elect affiliated with the Episcopal Church. Little Rock inaugurated Vestryman Gordon N. Peay to the office of mayor in 1859. Voters did not exile Ashley from city government, because the Episcopalian and outgoing mayor simply rotated to a seat on the board of aldermen—alias, the board of slaveholders.[47] Episcopalians armed with labor power, therefore, remained ascendant in Arkansas until the Civil War because the identity politics of evangelicalism and white supremacy fragmented the common prayers of laboring people. Evangelicalism composted the southern frontier with the blood of exploitation, and that potent fertilizer nourished a bumper crop of Episcopalians.[48]

A Historiographical Prayer, 1853

Bishop Freeman insisted to his church (and his historians) that the "general excitement . . . produced" by evangelical wolves did not devour the "general steadfastness of the little flock" that methodically pastured on the "green spots" that silhouetted Arkansas's rivers:

> My visits to parish and missionary stations, where there are clergymen, are usually occasions of much interest. People assemble from the country around, a series of religious services are held, and we have all the benefit without the

confusion and wild excitement of what is styled outside of the church, the protracted meeting. Not unfrequently, the result is a larger number confirmed than had been anticipated.[49]

Notes

1. "Methodist Appointments," *Arkansas Gazette*, June 27, 1832; *Journal of the Proceedings of the Convention Met to Form a Constitution and System of State Government for the People of Arkansas—At the Session of the Said Convention Held at Little Rock, in the Territory of Arkansas, Which Commenced on the Fourth Day of January, and Ended on the Thirtieth Day of January, One Thousand Eight Hundred and Thirty-Six* (Little Rock: Albert Pike, 1836), 3, 18, 22–26, 36–37, 47; *Revised Statutes of the State of Arkansas, Adopted at the October Session of the General Assembly of Said State, A.D. 1837, in the Year of Our Independence the Sixty Second, and of the State the Second Year* (Boston: Weeks, Jordan, and Company, 1838), 36–41; Margaret Simms McDonald, *White Already to Harvest: The Episcopal Church in Arkansas, 1838-1971* (Sewanee, TN: University Press of Sewanee, 1975), 47; James S. Kabala, *Church-State Relations in the Early American Republic, 1787–1846* (London: Pickering & Chatto, 2013), 118–19.

2. C[ephas] Washburn to A. H. M. S., September 8, 1846, *Religion on the American Frontier, 1783–1840: The Presbyterians*, vol. 2, ed. William Warren Sweet (New York: Cooper Square Publishers, 1964), 695–700; J. S. Utley, "Graves of Eminent Men," in *Publications of the Arkansas Historical Association*, vol. 2, ed. John Hugh Reynolds (Little Rock: Press of Democrat Printing and Lithographing Company, 1908), 259–60; S. Charles Bolton, *Arkansas, 1800–1860: Remote and Restless* (Fayetteville: University of Arkansas Press, 1998), 114–15.

3. For the field-defining syntheses of this slaveholding conservatism, see Eugene D. Genovese and Elizabeth Fox-Genovese, *Fatal Self-Deception: Slaveholding Paternalism in the Old South* (New York: Cambridge University Press, 2011); Elizabeth Fox-Genovese, *Within the Plantation Household: Black and White Women of the Old South* (Chapel Hill: University of North Carolina Press, 1988); and Elizabeth Fox-Genovese and Eugene D. Genovese, *The Mind of the Master Class: History and Faith in the Southern Slaveholders' Worldview* (New York: Cambridge University Press, 2005).

4. Donald G. Mathews, "The Second Great Awakening as an Organizing Process, 1780–1830: An Hypothesis," *American Quarterly* 21 (Spring 1969): 23–44. John Hammond powerfully counters the "Mathews thesis" by insisting that revivals "divided the nation far more than they unified it." See John L. Hammond, "Revivals, Consensus, and American Political Culture," *Journal of the American Academy of Religion* 46 (September 1978): 293–314.

5. Beth Barton Schweiger, "Max Weber in Mount Airy, or Revivals and Social Theory in the Early South," in *Religion in the American South*, eds. Beth Barton Schweiger and Donald G. Mathews (Chapel Hill: University of North Carolina Press, 2004), 31–66; Mathews, "The Second Great Awakening," 23–44; Nathan O. Hatch, *The Democratization of Christianity* (New Haven: Yale University Press, 1989), 3–16; Edwin Scott Gaustad, *A Religious History of America* (New York: Harper Collins, 1990), 139.

6. Barbara J. Fields, "Ideology and Race in American History," in *Region, Race, and Reconstruction: Essays in Honor of C. Vann Woodward*, ed. J. Morgan Kousser and James M. McPherson (New York: Oxford University Press, 1982), 143–77.

7. Anne C. Loveland attributes a "skeptical view of democracy" to southern evangelicals. See Loveland, *Southern Evangelicals and the Social Order, 1800-1860* (Baton Rouge: Louisiana State University Press, 1980), 126-27.

8. For an interpretation that centralizes the "evangelical movement" in the history of the Whig Party of the North, see Daniel Walker Howe, "Religion and Politics in the Antebellum North," *Religion and American Politics: From the Colonial Period to the 1980s*, ed. Mark A. Noll (New York: Oxford University Press, 1990), 121-45. The identity politics of a discordant evangelicalism in the antebellum South, however, precluded the emergence of "interdenominational cooperation" to support evangelical partisanship for the southern wing of the Whig Party. In addition, this essay questions the characterization of southern Whigs as "weak." Whiggish Episcopalians did not need to win elections (or win souls) to maintain their hegemony in southern society.

9. "History of the Real Estate Bank," *Arkansas State Gazette*, March 8, 1843; Charles Grier Sellers, Jr., "Who Were the Southern Whigs?," *American Historical Review* 59 (January 1954), 340; Jeannie M. Whayne, et al., *Arkansas: A Narrative History* (Fayetteville: University of Arkansas Press, 2002), 110-13; Ted R. Worley, "The Control of the Real Estate Bank of the State of Arkansas, 1836-1855," *Mississippi Valley Historical Review* 37 (December 1950), 403-4; *Revised Statutes of the State of Arkansas*, 37-39. For the classical interpretation of planter-controlled banks, see Eugene D. Genovese, *The Political Economy of Slavery: Studies in the Economy and Society of the Slave South* (New York: Vintage Books, 1967), 15-30.

10. "History of the Real Estate Bank," *Arkansas State Gazette*, March 8, 1843; Worley, "The Control of the Real Estate Bank," 408-409; C. Fred Williams, S. Ray Granade, and Kenneth M. Startup, *A System and Plan: Arkansas Baptist State Convention, 1848-1998* (Franklin, TN: Providence House Publishers, 1998), 19, 30, 77-78.

11. Arkansas outlawed the employment of "slaves, or any free negro or mulatto, in any retrial grocery, dram shop, or other place where vinous or ardent spirits are sold in less quantities than one quart." To enhance the Dram Shop Act, Izard and his colleagues threatened to jail Arkansans who "sold to any . . . slave, ardent spirits in any quantity, without the permission of the master." Izard supported an amendment to expand the spirituous-liquors bill to criminalize the sale of "any commodity, of any kind or description" to slaves without the permission of slaveholders. Senators killed that amendment on a motion to table, before passing the Spirituous Liquors Act to complement the Dram Shop Act. In the same session, the senate enacted the Sabbath Breaking Act to curtail the freedom of "free" non-evangelicals in Arkansas who played cards "on the christian sabbath" for either "wager . . . or for amusement." *Journal of the Senate for the Ninth Session of the General Assembly of the State of Arkansas* (Arkadelphia, AR: Pegues State Printer, 1852), 3-4, 78, 89, 93-94, 128, 165, 220, 338, 362, 365, 472, 554, 566; *Acts Passed at the Ninth Session of the General Assembly of the State of Arkansas* (Arkadelphia, AR: Pegues State Printer, 1853), 71-72, 120-21, 205.

12. "To the Public: Protest of the Trustees of the Real Estate Bank," *Arkansas State Gazette*, April 5, 1843; W. B. Worthen, *Early History of Banking in Arkansas*, (Little Rock, AR: Democrat Printing & Litho Company, 1906), 26; Worley, "The Control of the Real Estate Bank," 403-4; Whayne, et al., *Arkansas*, 110-13.

13. William W. Hughes, *Archibald Yell* (Fayetteville: University of Arkansas Press, 1988), 64-68; Michael B. Dougan, "Second Governor: Archibald Yell, 1840-1844," in *The Governors of Arkansas*, eds. Willard B. Gatewood, Jr., Timothy P. Donovan, Jeannie M. Whayne (Fayetteville: University of Arkansas Press, 1995), 8-12; "Public Meeting and the Inauguration," *Arkansas State Gazette*, November 11, 1840; McDonald, *White Already to Harvest*, 12, 26, 59,

66, 78, 475; Ellen Harrell Cantrell, *The Annals of Christ Church Parish of Little Rock, Arkansas, From A.D. 1839 to A.D. 1899* (Little Rock: Arkansas Democrat Company, 1900), 41–42.

14. "Governor's Message," *Arkansas State Gazette*, November 11, 1840; "Governor's Message," *Arkansas State Gazette*, November 9, 1842; James Roger Sharp, *The Jacksonians Versus the Banks: Politics in the States after the Panic of 1837* (New York: Columbia University Press, 1970), 37–38, 45, 117–19; Bolton, *Arkansas*, 55–61, 172–75; Archibald Yell, as quoted in "Ex. Doc. No. 112: Condition of the Banks," *Executive Documents Printed by Order of the House of Representatives during the Second Session of the Thirty-Fifth Congress*, vol. 12 (Washington: James B. Steedman, 1859), 192–94, 206–209; McDonald, *White Already to Harvest*, 25–27; "The West," *The Spirit of Missions* 8 (1843), 97–98.

15. Archibald Yell, Veto Message, *Arkansas State Gazette*, January 25, 1843; "Indignation Meeting," *Arkansas State Gazette*, March 8, 1843; David Orr, "Extract of a Letter from David Orr, Pastor the New Hope Baptist Church, Lawrence County, Arkansas, to the Editor of the *Cross and Journal*, dated Oct. 30, 1835," *Triennial Baptist Register: No. 2.—1836*, ed. I. M. Allen (Philadelphia: Baptist General Tract Society, 1836), 217–18; Williams, Granade, and Startup, *A System and Plan*, 16–19, 24, 30; "The Reverend David Orr," *Arkansas Gazette*, May 15, 1833.

16. "Indignation Meeting," *Arkansas State Gazette*, March 8, 1843.

17. Cantrell, *The Annals of Christ Church*, 57; McDonald, *White Already to Harvest*, 9–10, 15, 43, 376; ". . . County Clay Club," *Arkansas State Gazette*, December 27, 1843; "Dr. Walker," *Arkansas State Gazette*, May 22, 1844; *Arkansas State Gazette*, May 15, 1844; Hughes, *Archibald Yell*, 75–76; "To the People of Arkansas," *Arkansas State Gazette*, September 18, 1844; An inviting camp-meeting hymn riddled with the raw emotionalism of the plain folk is deserving of more consideration. For example, the fourth verse: "Jesus all the day long / Was my joy and my song / O that all his salvation might see! / He hath loved me, I cried / He hath suffered and died / To redeem such a rebel as me." See Joshua Leavitt, *The Christian Lyre; A Collection of Hymans and Tunes Adapted for Social Worship, Prayer Meetings, and Revivals of Religion* (New York: Robinson & Franklin, 1839), 97. Some sources spell "Trapnall" as "Trapnell."

18. "The West," *The Spirit of Missions*, 97–98; McDonald, *White Already to Harvest*, 25, 28, 42; "To the People of Arkansas," *Arkansas State Gazette*, September 18, 1844.

19. "The Election" and "Pulaski County," *Arkansas State Gazette*, October 16, 1844; Hughes, *Archibald Yell*, 76; Michael J. Dubin, *United States Congressional Election, 1788–1997: The Official Results of the Elections of the 1st through the 105th Congress* (Jefferson, NC: McFarland & Company, 1998), 139. Gene Wells Boyett, "The Whigs of Arkansas, 1836–1856," (PhD diss., Louisiana State University, 1972), 252; E. H. English, *A Digest of the Statutes of Arkansas: Embracing All Laws of a General and Permanent Character in Force at the Close of the Session of the General Assembly of 1846; Together with Notes of the Decisions of the Supreme Court upon the Statues* (Little Rock: Reardon & Garritt, 1848), 71. Boyett presents election returns that slightly differ from Dubin by suggesting that Yell earned 58.9 percent of the vote. Thomas W. Newton secured a seat in the Arkansas senate. Newton won 458 votes (53 percent), while his Democratic challenger finished with 403 (47 percent) votes. Voters in Pulaski County awarded Frederick W. Trapnall with a seat in Arkansas's House of Representatives.

20. Henry C. Lay, *Pastoral Letter to the Clergy and Members of the Protestant Episcopal Church in the State of Arkansas* (Memphis: Southern Publishing House, 1861), 13–16.

21. McDonald, *White Already to Harvest*, 41–60; John N. Norton, *Life of Bishop Freeman of Arkansas* (New York: Gen. Prot. Episc. S.S. Union and Church Book Society, 1867), 93–94, 104–106, 114–20; Seventh Census of the United States, 1850, Pulaski County, Arkansas,

Slave Population, National Archives Microfilm Series M-432, reel 32; Seventh Census of the United States, 1850, Pulaski County, Arkansas, Free Population, National Archives Microfilm Series M-432, reel 29; Eugene D. Genovese, *Roll, Jordan, Roll: The World the Slaves Made* (New York: Vintage Books, 1976), 3–7, 138–93, 280–84. Colossians 4:1 (TNIV): "Masters, provide your slaves with what is right and fair, because you know that you also have a Master in heaven."

22. "Extract from the proceedings of the Arkansas Annual Conference of the Methodist Episcopal Church, South," *Arkansas State Gazette*, December 15, 1845; "Camp-Meeting in Dallas," *Arkansas State Gazette*, October 21, 1847; Williams, Granade, and Startup, *A System and Plan*, 44–60.

23. John Rogers, *The Biography of Elder J. T. Johnson* (Cincinnati: John Rogers, 1861), 19–20; Leroy Garrett, *The Stone-Campbell Movement: The Story of the American Restoration Movement* (Joplin, MO: College Press Publishing Company, 2002), 173–96; Robert Richardson, *Memoirs of Alexander Campbell: Embracing a View of the Origin, Progress and Principles of the Religious Reformation Which He Advocated* (Philadelphia: J. B. Lippincott & Company, 1870), 379–81; Hatch, *The Democratization of American Christianity*, 163–68; "Religious Discussion," *Arkansas State Gazette*, January 30, 1847; "We Mentioned," *Arkansas State Gazette*, February 17, 1845; J. T. Johnson and R. C. Ricketts, "Foreign News: Georgetown, Kentucky, May 1st, 1845," *Christian Messenger and Family Magazine; Devoted to the Dissemination of Primitive Christianity*, vol. 1 (London: Simpkin, Marshall, and Company, 1845), 243; "A Christian to Mr. Borden," *Arkansas State Gazette*, February 13, 1847; Alexander Campbell, "Slavery and the Fugitive Slave Law," *The Millennial Harbinger*, vol. 1 (Bethany, VA: A. Campbell, 1851), 171–72; Thomas A. DeBlack, "Johnson, Benjamin," *Arkansas Biography: A Collection of Notable Lives*, eds. Nancy A. Williams and Jeannie M. Whayne (Fayetteville: University of Arkansas Press, 2000), 150–51; James M. Woods, "Johnson, Robert Ward," *Arkansas Biography: A Collection of Notable Lives*, eds. Nancy A. Williams and Jeannie M. Whayne (Fayetteville: University of Arkansas Press, 2000), 152–53.

24. Hughes, *Archibald Yell*, 87–91; Worley, "The Control of the Real Estate Bank," 410–11; Cantrell, *The Annals of Christ Church*, 13–14, 110; "Election Returns," *Arkansas State Gazette*, August 10, 1846; "To the People of Arkansas," *Arkansas State Gazette*, November 23, 1846; Dubin, *United States Congressional Election, 1788–1997*, 143–44; "Election for Representative in Congress," *Arkansas State Gazette*, December 26, 1846; "Election for Member in Congress," *Arkansas State Gazette*, January 16, 1847; Boyett, "The Whigs of Arkansas," 295. Newton entered the congressional race after his constituency of Pulaski County had just re-elected him as a state senator with over 67 percent of the county's vote. Although Pulaski County leaned toward the Whig Party, a congressional campaign required Newton to secure the support of less-receptive statewide voters. In terms of actual votes, Newton prevailed statewide by twenty-three votes. The three candidates who ran against Newton under the Democratic Party's banner collectively earned over 57 percent of Arkansas's popular vote. Once again, Boyett presents election returns that slightly differ from Dubin's tabulation. Boyett lists Newton's margin of victory as thirty votes.

25. Newton's support for the WAB padded the 89-72 vote in the US House of Representatives. Over 30 percent of the WAB's expenditures improved western rivers either in, near, or connected to Arkansas. The Episcopalian senator Ashley safeguarded the Arkansas spending in the WAB when the legislation arrived his chamber. Ashley opposed an amendment introduced by an Alabama senator to delete the improvements for the "Mississippi Missouri, and Arkansas rivers" from the WAB. Only six senators voted for the amendment, while thirty-eight senators voted against the rescission—including the Episcopalian from

Arkansas. The unamended bill passed the senate. President James K. Polk, however, vetoed the WAB because he shuttered at a congressional exorbitance that "sweeps into the vortex of national power . . . not only harbors and inlets, rivers and little streams, but canals, turnpikes, and railroads." Polk detected "no middle ground" as he confronted "the immensity and danger of the power which the principle of this bill involves." Thomas W. Newton, "Additional General Officers," *Appendix to the Congressional Globe . . . of the Second Session of the Twenty-Ninth Congress* (Washington: Blair and Rives, 1847), 429; "Col. R. W. Johnson," *Arkansas State Gazette*, July 27, 1848; "Col. Newton is opposed," *Arkansas State Gazette*, July 20, 1848; "H.R. 84 . . . An Act to Provide for Continuing a Certain Public Work in the Territory of Wisconsin, and for Other Purposes," Bills and Resolutions, House of Representatives, Twenty-ninth Congress, Second Session, https://memory.loc.gov/ammem/amlaw/lawhome.html; *Journal of the House of Representatives of the United States: Being the Second Session of the Twenty-Ninth Congress* (Washington: Ritchie & Heiss, 1847), 394–96; *Journal of the Senate of the United States: Being the Second Session of the Twenty-Ninth Congress* (Washington: Ritchie & Heiss, 1847), 269–70; James K. Polk, "Veto of the River and Harbor Bill," *The Congressional Globe of the First Session of the Thirtieth Congress* (Washington: Blair and Rives, 1848), 30–33.

26. John Davis, "For the Arkansas State Gazette," "John Davis to the Editor," and "To the Associated Mechanics of Little Rock," *Arkansas State Gazette*, November 23, 1846.

27. "Little Rock Bible Society," *Arkansas State Gazette*, May 4, 1848; Dubin, *United States Congressional Election, 1788–1997*, 151; "Election Returns," *Arkansas State Gazette*, September 7, 1848; Boyett, "The Whigs of Arkansas," 321; "Legislative Proceedings," *Arkansas State Gazette*, November 23, 1848. Newton retained his strong base of support in the five river counties along the Mississippi. For instance, the bank cashier won over 52 percent of the vote in the Delta county of Chicot. Frederick W. Trapnall, vestryman emeritus of Christ Church and longtime associate of Newton, attempted to resuscitate Newton's career with a fanciful nomination in 1848 for a seat in the United States Senate. Newton finished third on the general assembly's first two ballots and then his senatorial candidacy ended.

28. "C. W. Wilson," *Arkansas State Gazette*, June 29, 1848; "Elections," *Arkansas State Gazette*, August 17, 1848; "Official Returns of the Votes Given in Pulaski County," *Arkansas State Gazette*, August 10, 1848.

29. "The Whig Candidate for Governor," "G. B. Hayden, etc. to Cyrus W. Wilson," and "Cyrus W. Wilson to Gentlemen," *Arkansas State Gazette*, January 25, 1849; "Fellow Whigs," "Extracts," and "One More Word about the Election," *Arkansas State Gazette*, March 8, 1849; "C. W. Wilson," *Arkansas State Gazette*, June 29, 1848.

30. "It Becomes Our Painful Duty" and "Died" *Arkansas State Gazette*, September 27, 1849. Ben M. Barrus, Milton L. Baughn, and Thomas H. Campbell, *A People Called Cumberland Presbyterians* (Memphis, TN: Frontier Press, 1972), 285–88; B. W. McDonnold, *History of the Cumberland Presbyterian Church* (Nashville: Board of Publication of the Cumberland Presbyterian Church, 1893), 100; C[ephas] Washburn to A.H.M.S., September 8, 1846, in *Religion on the American Frontier*, 695–700.

31. Barrus, Baughn, and Campbell, *A People Called Cumberland Presbyterians*, 146–51; Thomas H. Campbell, et al., *Arkansas Cumberland Presbyterians, 1812–1984: A People of Faith* (Memphis: Arkansas Synod of the Cumberland Presbyterian Church, 1985), 108.

32. "E. to the Editor," *Arkansas State Gazette*, February 15, 1849; "The Election for Governor" and "To the Voters of the State of Arkansas," *Arkansas State Gazette*, February 1, 1849.

33. "The Whig Candidate for Governor," *Arkansas State Gazette*, January 25, 1849; "To the Voters of the State of Arkansas," *Arkansas State Gazette*, February 1, 1849.

34. Barrus, Baughn, and Campbell, *A People Called Cumberland Presbyterians*, 221–22; Boyett, "The Whigs of Arkansas," 347–53, 387–90, 399–400; Michael J. Dubin, *United States Gubernatorial Elections, 1776–1860: The Official Results by State and County* (Jefferson, NC: McFarland & Company, 2003), 9–12; Michael J. Dubin, *United States Gubernatorial Elections, 1861–1911: The Official Results by State and County* (Jefferson, NC: McFarland & Company, 2010), 48–59; "Ex. Doc. 107: Condition of the Banks throughout the United States," *Executive Documents Printed by Order of the House of Representatives during the First Session of the Thirty-Fifth Congress*, vol. 12 (Washington: James B. Steedman, 1858), 219–20; "Ex. Doc. No. 112: Condition of the Banks," *Executive Documents Printed by Order of the House of Representatives during the Second Session of the Thirty-Fifth Congress*, vol. 12 (Washington: James B. Steedman, 1859), 237–40; Carl H. Moneyhon, *The Impact of the Civil War and Reconstruction on Arkansas: Persistence in the Midst of Ruin* (Baton Rouge: Louisiana State University, 1994), 81–91. Dubin omits two minor candidates included in the returns provided by Boyett. Dubin, therefore, awards Roane 50.5 percent of the vote and Wilson 49.5 percent. For a discussion of Governor Roane's support for internal improvements, see Carl H. Moneyhon, *The Impact of the Civil War and Reconstruction on Arkansas: Persistence in the Midst of Ruin* (Baton Rouge: Louisiana State University, 1994), 81–91.

35. *Journal of the Proceedings of the Bishops, Clergy, and Laity of the Protestant Episcopal Church in the United States of America, Assembled in a General Convention . . . 1850*, (Philadelphia: King & Baird, 1851), 200–204; Orville W. Taylor, "Arkansas," in *Religion in the Southern States*, ed. Samuel S. Hill (Macon: Mercer University Press, 1983), 30–31; *Journal of the Proceedings of the Bishops, Clergy, and Laity of the Protestant Episcopal Church in the United States of America, Assembled in a General Convention, Held in the City of New York, from Oct. 7th to Oct. 29th, Inclusive, in the Year of Our Lord 1868* (Hartford, CT: Church Press Company, 1869), 353; *Journal of the Executive Proceedings of the Senate of the United States of America: From December 4, 1848, to August 31, 1852, Inclusive* 8 (Washington: Government Printing Office, 1887), 98, 233, 321–22; George W. Freeman, "Report of the Rt. Rev. G. W. Freeman, D. D., Missionary Bishop of the South-West," *The Spirit of Missions* 16 (August 1851), 373; William G. McLoughlin, *After the Trail of Tears: The Cherokees' Struggle for Sovereignty, 1839–1880* (Chapel Hill: University of North Carolina Press, 1993), 98–100.

36. L. Scott Stafford, "Daniel Ringo," in *United States District Courts and Judges of Arkansas, 1836–1960*, ed. Frances Mitchell Ross (Fayetteville: University of Arkansas Press, 2016), 57–64; Cantrell, *The Annals of Christ Church*, 41–43, 113–14, 376–77; *Biographical and Historical Memoirs of Pulaski, Jefferson, Lonoke, Faulkner, Grant, Saline, Perry, Garland and Hot Spring Counties, Arkansas* (Chicago: Goodspeed Publishing Company, 1889), 377; Norton, *Life of Bishop Freeman of Arkansas*, 182–84; Seventh Census of the United States, 1850, Chicot County, Arkansas, Slave Population, National Archives Microfilm Series M-432, reel 32. Only death extinguished Frederick W. Trapnall's faith in the Whig Party. Trapnall followed in Newton's footsteps by running for Congress in Arkansas as a Whig. Trapnall gained his party's nomination in 1853, but died during the campaign. See, Margaret Smith Ross, "Sandford C. Faulkner," *Arkansas Historical Quarterly* 14 (Winter 1955), 307–311; Boyett, "The Whigs of Arkansas," 384–85; James M. Woods, *Rebellion and Realignment: Arkansas's Road to Secession* (Fayetteville: University of Arkansas Press, 1987), 22–23. Planters who remained in the Delta suffered minimal impairment from camp meetings or the bank war. Slaves accounted for 77.9 percent of Chicot County's total population in 1850, and that percentage jumped to 81.4 percent by 1860. Slaves comprised a mammoth 85.7 percent of Chicot County's total population growth between 1850 and 1860. The most revealing evidence of permanence arises from the plantations in Chicot County with attachments to the

Episcopal Church. Those plantations surpassed countywide trends. The slave population on John Lwelleyn's plantation climbed from twenty-two slaves in 1850 to forty-seven slaves in 1860. Likewise, a war against the REB may have rattled the institution's former president, but the melee did not attenuate Davies's standing in the planter class. The number of enslaved people on Davies's plantation in Chicot County soared by 50 percent between 1850 and 1860. The demographic evolution of Newton's county of matrimony in the Delta corroborated the shallowness of the wounds inflicted upon planter-class Episcopalians by either camp meetings or a bank war. For that data, see J. D. B. DeBow, *The Seventh Census of the United States: 1850* (Washington: Robert Armstrong, 1853), 535–37; Joseph C. B. Kennedy, *Population of the United States in 1860; Compiled from the Original Returns of the Eighth Census, under the Direction of the Secretary of the Interior* (Washington: Government Printing Office, 1864), 12–19; Seventh Census of the United States, Chicot County, Arkansas, Slave Population, National Archives Microfilm Series M-432, reel 32; Seventh Census of the United States, Chicot County, Arkansas, Free Population, National Archives Microfilm Series M-432, reel 25; Eighth Census of the United States, Chicot County, Arkansas, Free Population, National Archives Microfilm Series M-653, reel 38; Eighth Census of the United States, Chicot County, Arkansas, Slave Population, National Archives Microfilm Series M-653, reel 53. For some astute examinations of the ritualism, paternalism, and reciprocity that defined Christmas gifts on southern plantations, see Kathleen M. Hilliard, *Masters, Slaves, and Exchange: Power's Purchase in the Old South* (New York: Cambridge University Press, 2014), 132–53; Ted Ownby, *American Dreams in Mississippi: Consumers, Poverty, and Culture, 1830–1998* (Chapel Hill: University of North Carolina Press, 1999), 33–60, 79–81; and Stephen Nissenbaum, *The Battle for Christmas: A Social and Cultural History of Our Most Cherished Holiday* (New York: Vintage Books, 1997), 258–300.

37. George W. Freeman, "Report of the Rt. Rev. G. W. Freeman, D.D., Missionary Bishop of the South-West," *The Spirit of Missions* 15 (1850), 273–74; McDonald, *White Already to Harvest*, 47; J. S. Utley, "Graves of Eminent Men," in *Publications of the Arkansas Historical Association*, vol. 2, ed. John Hugh Reynolds (Little Rock: Press of Democrat Printing and Lithographing Company, 1908), 259–60; Ross, "Sandford C. Faulkner," 301–314; "The Methodist Church," *Arkansas State Gazette and Democrat*, September 15, 1854; "From the Arkansas Traveler," *Arkansas State Gazette and Democrat*, June 26, 1858.

38. "Diocesan School of Arkansas," *Arkansas State Gazette and Democrat*, August 24, 1855; Otis Hackett, "Excerpts from the Diary and Letters of Reverend Otis Hackett from the Files of St. John's Episcopal Church, Helena, Arkansas," ed. G. H. Hackett, *Phillips County Historical Quarterly* 1 (Summer 1962), 24–30; Otis Hackett, "Helena—Rev. Otis Hacket [sic]," *The Spirit of Missions* 23 (1858), 276–77; James H. Otey, "Report of the Rt. Rev. James Henry [sic] Otey, D.D., Acting Missionary Bishop of Arkansas," *The Spirit of Missions* 23 (1858), 612–13; Otis Hackett, *Romish and Presbyterian Aspersions against the Protestant Episcopal Church Repelled: A Discourse Preached at Planters, Ark., June 20, 1858; with a Reply to an Attack Made upon It by the Rev. Thos. R. Welch, Minister of the Old School Presbyterian Church* (Memphis: Hutton & Clark, 1858), 5; Eighth Census of the United States, Phillips County, Arkansas, Slave Population, National Archives Microfilm Series M-653, reel 54; Eighth Census of the United States, Phillips County, Arkansas, Free Population, National Archives Microfilm Series M-653, reel 47.

39. Hackett, *Romish and Presbyterian Aspersions*, 5–8, 36–37.

40. "Bishop Lay Detained on the Arkansas River," and "Letter from Bishop Lay," *The Spirit of Missions* 25 (New York: Daniel Dana, Jr., 1860), 236–39, 350–52; McDonald, *White Already to Harvest*, 48–57; *Journal of a Tour in the "Indian Territory" Performed*, 10–11, 37–38.

41. Lay, *Pastoral Letter*, 12–16.

42. "At a Meeting of the Mechanics' Institute," *True Democrat*, September 22, 1858; John Ashworth, *Slavery, Capitalism, and Politics in the Antebellum Republic: Volume 1: Commerce and Compromise, 1820–1850* (Cambridge: Cambridge University Press, 1995), 104–105.

43. "City Election," *True Democrat*, January 19, 1858; "To 'A Mechanic,'" *True Democrat*, October 8, 1858; Cantrell, *The Annals of Christ Church*, 4, 13, 91–94, 122–26; Eighth Census of the United States, Pulaski County, Arkansas, Slave Population, National Archives Microfilm Series M-653, reel 54; Eighth Census of the United States, Pulaski County, Arkansas, Free Population, National Archives Microfilm Series M-653, reel 49; *Journal of the Executive Proceedings of the Senate of the United States of America From December 3, 1855, to June 16, 1858, Inclusive*, vol. X (Washington: Government Printing Office, 1887), 382.

44. To complement that propaganda, Arkansas's planters maneuvered to protect slavery by drafting a new law designed to simultaneously enrich slaveholders while feeding the white supremacy of the movement of mechanics (MM). Legislators in Arkansas introduced a bill to "exclude from residing in the State of Arkansas, all free colored persons" by outlawing "emancipation" and declaring any previously legal action "giving freedom to any slave" "a nullity, and void from its making." "The Movement of the Mechanics," *True Democrat*, September 29, 1858; "An Important Bill," *True Democrat*, January 5, 1859.

45. "Socialism," *True Democrat*, October 6, 1858; "The Movement of the Mechanics," *True Democrat*, September 29, 1858; Christine Leigh Heyrman, *Southern Cross: The Beginnings of the Bible Belt* (Chapel Hill: University of North Carolina Press, 1997), 154–60.

46. "Appointments of the Arkansas Conference," *Arkansas State Gazette and Democrat*, November 27, 1858; "Died," *Arkansas State Gazette and Democrat*, September 25, 1858; "The General Assembly," *Arkansas State Gazette and Democrat*, November 6, 1858; "The Protracted Meetings in the Baptist and Methodist Churches," *Arkansas State Gazette and Democrat*, August 14, 1858.

47. "The City Election," *True Democrat*, January 5, 1859; Cantrell, *The Annals of Christ Church*, 4, 24–25, 188, 238, 290, 304, 335, 354, 377–78; Eighth Census of the United States, Pulaski County, Arkansas, Slave Population, National Archives Microfilm Series M-653, reel 54; Eighth Census of the United States, Pulaski County, Arkansas, Free Population, National Archives Microfilm Series M-653, reel 49.

48. Seven of the eight aldermen elected in 1859 following the MM dwelled in slaveholding households inside of the city limits. An inspection of the MM's leadership accounts for the susceptibility of the association to coopting by slaveholders. In a plebiscite, the MM anointed a humble carpenter as the combination's secretary, but that same ballot crowned carriage-maker A. J. Ward as the association's president. Mechanics had embraced a false prophet of bourgeois modernization as their president, because promoters considered Ward's establishment comparable to "anything . . . from the north." Ward managed a "carriage warehouse" and multiple "workshops." The alleged mechanic employed "twenty workmen" in his "large carriage factory." That workforce, however, consisted of one slave owned by Ward. Beneath the northern veneer of the factory, Ward eagerly solicited "Plantation Work." Ward embodied in a single individual, therefore, how slaveholders and modernizers united around an interregional objective: the artificial division of laboring people in antebellum America. See "At a meeting of the Mechanics' Institute," *True Democrat*, September 22, 1858; "Little Rock Carriage Manufactory," *True Democrat*, September 29, 1858; "New Carriage and Buggy Manufactory," *Arkansas State Gazette and Democrat*, January 9, 1858; Eighth Census of the United States, Pulaski County, Arkansas, Slave Population, National Archives Microfilm Series M-653, reel 54; Eighth Census of the United States, Pulaski County, Arkansas, Free Population, National Archives Microfilm Series M-653, reel 49.

49. George W. Freeman, "Report of the Rt. Rev. G. W. Freeman, D.D. Missionary Bishop of the South-West," *The Spirit of Missions* 17 (New York: Daniel Dana, Jr., 1852), 420; George W. Freeman, "Report of Bishop Freeman," in *Journal of the Proceedings of the Bishops, Clergy, and Laity of the Protestant Episcopal Church in the United States of America Assembled in a General Convention, 1853* (Philadelphia: King & Baird, 1854), 298–99.

Race and the Visions of John Lafayette Girardeau

Otis W. Pickett

The name John Lafayette Girardeau carries conflicting meanings depending on the context. Among southern Presbyterians, he is known as a great orator, preacher, seminary professor, missionary to enslaved African Americans, and the first southern Presbyterian to ordain African Americans to the office of ruling elder. Among African Americans in Charleston, South Carolina, Girardeau is known as a minister to the antebellum enslaved community, as well as an advocate for education and racial reform via ecclesiastical equality in the years after the Civil War. In stark contrast, historians and Lost Cause advocates are mostly familiar with the name Girardeau for his role in perpetuating a civil religion that served to undergird the tenets of the Lost Cause during Reconstruction.[1]

Yet Girardeau's life and world presents a much more complex picture than his missionary activity, representative Calvinism, efforts toward ecclesiastical reform, or Lost Cause ideology reveal. In *Race and Reunion: The Civil War in American Memory*, David Blight cast three disparate visions of the legacy of the Civil War in American memory, and Girardeau can be found in all three (reconciliationist, white supremacist, and emancipationist), each during the same epoch.[2] This complicates our understanding of the roles of Christian clergy in the Civil War era and displays that they could often possess different personas and competing ideologies. The rival visions of Girardeau during

Reconstruction further cloud the already murky waters through which historians have thought about the role of clergy in the Civil War-era South.

Indeed, applying Blight's visions to three separate phases of Girardeau's career perhaps paints a more representative picture of a conflicted southern clergy whose theology and ecclesiology often challenged their views on race and slavery while fully embracing and supporting the social, economic, political, and racial status quo. Girardeau's postbellum ecclesiastical reform in ordaining African Americans and pushing for their ecclesiastical equality places him among emancipationists. However, his work on the battlefield as a Confederate chaplain, his aid to the public in coping with death and destruction after the Civil War, and his service as pastor of an integrated church places him in the reconciliationist camp. His work as a defender of the Lost Cause, which helped justify the racial violence perpetuated by Lost Cause adherents, places him within the emerging norms of a white supremacist vision.[3]

In *Baptized in Blood: The Religion of the Lost Cause, 1865–1920*, Charles Reagan Wilson uses Girardeau to display the "traditional Calvinist explanation" for an interpretation of the Civil War and also as an example of their "hope of future vindication."[4] Indeed, as Girardeau penned in 1866, Confederate ideals would one day, "in some golden age, sung by poets, sages, and prophets, come forth in the resurrection of buried principles and live to bless mankind, when the bones of its confessors and martyrs shall have moldered into dust."[5] Further, W. Scott Poole shows in his *Never Surrender: Confederate Memory and Conservatism in the South Carolina Upcountry* that the religion of the Lost Cause was rooted in a deep pessimism about "the possibilities of society that issued in both sad praise for a conquered past and a critique of the materialistic and utilitarian present."[6] We see this on display in Girardeau's Lost Cause apologetics during Reconstruction. At the same time that Girardeau was speaking at Confederate Memorial Day ceremonies and disseminating a Lost Cause ideology, he was also challenging the racial status quo in one of, if not the most, racially conservative denominations in the country: the Presbyterian Church in the United States (the southern branch of the Presbyterian Church). This denomination, known for James Henley Thornwell's writings in defense of the institution of slavery and later Robert Lewis Dabney's work *A Defense of Virginia and the South*, a book lauding the institution of slavery on theological and cultural grounds, was the same space where Girardeau found himself becoming an advocate of for the equality of African Americans in the church courts, in membership, and in leadership roles.

Prior to the Civil War, Girardeau was pastor of one of the largest congregations of African Americans in the entire South, and he continued to serve as pastor to an interracial Presbyterian church from 1865 to 1874. He became the first member of the Presbyterian Church in the United States (PCUS) to ordain African American elders (which is the highest form of leadership in the local Presbyterian Church) and was the lone dissenting vote in the 1874 General Assembly of the PCUS against what was called "organic separation" or racial segregation. He would also later serve alongside African American freedmen as coequal members and as elders on the session (the governing body in the local Presbyterian Church) at Zion Presbyterian Church (Glebe Street). Girardeau did all of this while simultaneously speaking at Confederate Memorial Day services and embracing a Lost Cause ideology that sought to prevent African Americans from taking their rightful place as first-class citizens through newly granted and hard-won civic equalities.[7]

Girardeau seemed to be a man torn between two worlds, yet these worlds collided during Reconstruction in familiar ways, reflecting similar tensions in southern culture in the antebellum context. In one context, Girardeau was a Civil War veteran who fought with and served the Confederacy as a chaplain in the Twenty-third Regiment of South Carolina Volunteers. In another, he was a missionary to Charleston's enslaved African American population, many of whom saw him as a spiritual father, as a racial moderate, and as a man who advocated for their ecclesiastical rights.[8]

After the war, a strange marriage occurred between these competing visions. Girardeau was called upon by leading lights of the Lost Cause in Charleston to speak on the justness and holiness of the Confederate cause, one that included the defense of the perpetual enslavement of African Americans as one of its main tenets.[9] Girardeau spoke partly because he was attempting to cope with, and help his listeners grasp, the changing nature of their racial and political surroundings. He was also providing the men and women in the audience a vision to deal with defeat by displaying a postbellum version of southern honor, built on both gentility and violence through continued sectionalism and white superiority.[10] There is a staunchly unreconstructed tone throughout this speech, and, even in defeat, Girardeau remained defiant arguing that there "are two senses in which it must be admitted that they [Confederate soldiers] lost their cause—they failed to establish a Confederacy as an independent country, and they failed to preserve the relation of slavery," which led southerners to forms of government considered the "evils which now oppress us."[11]

Serving as a minister of civil religion in the Lost Cause provided Girardeau with a powerful postwar public platform. He found himself in the process of redefining what it meant to be a "southerner" and a "Presbyterian" minister in the latter half of the nineteenth century, helping the landscape heal after a crippling military defeat while also helping shape, define, and put into practice what would later become Jim Crow segregation. Girardeau had never before had such broad audiences, and he found himself not only preaching to his biracial church but also to the broader citizenry about the justness, rightness, and holiness of the Confederate war effort and how it should be honored. He went from being a local missionary to enslaved Africans to a Confederate chaplain to becoming a statewide and regional defender of the memory of the Confederate dead and advocate for the Lost Cause, which helped forge a postwar identity of white South Carolinians bent on redemption and wresting political, economic, and social control away from African Americans and Republicans.

While serving as a minister of the Lost Cause, Girardeau also became the leading southern Presbyterian advocate for ecclesiastical integration. He experienced an enormous degree of pushback from Robert Lewis Dabney and other leading theologians of southern Presbyterianism during Reconstruction. It seems as if Girardeau was comfortable with this contradictory clash between African American ecclesiastical equality and civic inequality, was completely unaware of the distinctions between the two, or was adapting and redefining his religious and racial identity by publicly serving as a minister-patriot of the Lost Cause while also helping to expand some rights for African Americans in a local-church context.

To be sure, his unquestioned loyalty to the Lost Cause and his embodiment of it as a living testament to Confederate memory in Charleston, South Carolina, would make it difficult for detractors to question Girardeau when it came to his moderate stance on race in the church. Girardeau seemed to use those powers of influence in complex ways in ecclesiastical circles, which oftentimes ran counter to accepted broader cultural standards of racial hierarchy and sometimes even contradicted certain emerging tenets of Lost Cause dogma.

To understand Girardeau's later negotiations within the ecclesiastical and social context of postwar South Carolina, we must know something of his career prior to the Civil War. Before the war, Girardeau introduced measured reforms of the ecclesiastical roles of African Americans within the interracial Zion Presbyterian Church. Zion was a largely enslaved, independent (not under care of Second Presbyterian, but instead an autonomous "particular" church) congregation whose members were allowed to hold lay leadership positions called "watchmen." Girardeau often used these watchmen as catechists or teachers to other members. They were "given responsibility for assisting the ministers in visiting the people, gathering the congregation for worship, and leading public worship when ministers were not present. They also served as superintendents over the Sabbath schools."[12] While seating was separated along racial lines, the African American congregants occupied the best seats, or "the places of honor,"[13] in the pews directly in front of the pulpit, not in the balconies above the pews where white visitors sat. Also, Girardeau recorded both the first and surnames of members (recognizing their family lineage and humanity) in the roll books, affirmed names chosen by enslaved members rather than names given by owners, performed baptisms and weddings (thereby affirming the basic humanity of members), and taught Sunday school as well as catechism classes.[14]

This type of mission work, however, was short-lived. After the Civil War, in conjunction with taking up their old ministries in churches and pulpits throughout the South, many Confederate chaplains also assumed prominent roles in southern society disseminating the rhetoric of the Lost Cause. Their moral authority, status as Confederate officers, formal education, and oratory skill made ex-Confederate chaplains perfect trumpets for the Lost Cause. Girardeau was the full embodiment of this phenomenon since he had a war record to back up his status as a walking testament to Confederate ideals. He also possessed a great reputation among southern Presbyterians for this theological acumen, sharp mind, orthodoxy, and his tremendous preaching ability, which earned him the moniker "Spurgeon of the South."[15]

Confederate Memorial Day speeches became prime spaces for proliferating Lost Cause ideology, and Girardeau fit the mold as a brilliant orator, chaplain, and spiritual spokesman for the defeated Confederacy. Girardeau's military service provided him the necessary credentials to speak with legitimacy, offering the crowd an image of a fighting clergyman who was able to preach with a bible in one hand and fight Yankees with the other. Nothing was more acceptable or more valid to a white southerner during Reconstruction than the image of a fighting Confederate clergyman.

After the war, around five hundred African American members, now freedmen, remained at Zion and expressed interest in Girardeau continuing to serve as pastor. Members of the old antebellum Zion, who had been enslaved during Girardeau's pastorate, formally requested that Girardeau return and minister to them as freedmen during Reconstruction. There is some evidence for this continued relationship between Girardeau and his African American congregants in a letter dated July 27, 1865, from Paul Trescot, now a freedman, who was previously one of the enslaved membership from the antebellum Zion church:

Revd Sir & Pastor

> We the undersign members of Zion Presbyterian Church embrace this opportunity, as one among the many good ones we have engaged in the past and in doing so you have our best wish for your health & that of your loveing family. The past relations we have engaged together for many years as pastor and people are still in its bud in our every heart. Therefore we would well come you still as our pastor. To inform you that you past congregation will be the same in future and til death provide past relations with you are and considered the same.[16]

Despite the earnest affections of his congregants, Girardeau "had great difficulties to contend with." "The attendants upon our services," he wrote, "were ridiculed and twitted with [by other freedmen for] being still under the control of rebels. But the work went steadily on" and the membership continued to rise.[17] This experience helped push Girardeau to become an advocate for expanded ecclesiastical rights among African Americans in Charleston and in southern Presbyterianism. He would even become known in PCUS circles for his article in the *Southern Presbyterian Review* entitled "Ecclesiastical Relations to Freedmen," in which he laid out his beliefs regarding the equality, at least in church courts, of African Americans.

Now that the Civil War was over and slaves were free, Girardeau felt that the church had to offer ecclesiastical emancipation to free African Americans from their minority status in the church. Indeed, "he was convinced that blacks and whites ought to remain together"[18] and his desire was "to maintain the unity of the black and white congregations."[19] Immediately following the Civil War, factions within the Presbyterian Church in the United States began to debate the ecclesiastical status of emancipated African Americans and whether or not they could become full members with voting rights or even teaching or ruling elders or deacons. To resolve the matter, the general assembly of the PCUS called Girardeau to serve as chair on a committee in order "to consider the relations of the church to the freedmen and report on the whole subject."[20] As a result, he drafted a report to the general assembly in 1866 called "Ecclesiastical Relations to Freedmen." Many at the assembly commended the report, and "the assembly adopted the committee's resolution and ordered that Girardeau's paper be published in the *Southern Presbyterian Review*."[21]

In the report, Girardeau explained his fundamental beliefs on the equality of freedmen in the church, citing several biblical texts supporting his views. First, he pointed to the scriptural doctrine of the specific unity of the human race, citing several biblical passages to prove that "all mankind sprang from one original pair, are involved in the consequences of Adam's fall, and depend for their recovery solely upon the mediation of the Lord Jesus Christ. Therefore God hath made of one blood all nations of men to dwell on the face of the earth."[22] This was not fully accepted by many in southern Presbyterian circles, many of which mistakenly used biblical texts regarding Noah's curse on his son Ham to argue that African people descended from Ham and, therefore, Noah's curse forever condemned Ham's descendants to be servants and slaves.

Second, Girardeau claimed in his report that all believers in Christ were united in goodwill, which is not affected by distinctions of race, nationality, sex, culture, or civil status. He cited Galatians 3:28, in which Paul the Apostle affirms that there is neither Jew nor Gentile in Christ, dispelling any notion of a racial priority in salvation. Girardeau's position struck a chord with many of his contemporaries, most notably Robert Lewis Dabney, whose *A Defense of Virginia* (1867) and *Ecclesiastical Equality of Negroes* (1868) referred to African Americans as a "subservient race; made to follow, and not to lead; that his temperament, idiosyncrasy, and social relation make him untrustworthy."[23]

To support further his position, Girardeau suggested in his report that the new civil climate of Reconstruction demanded a renewed consideration of the status of African Americans in the church. In accordance with the emancipation of the slaves, Christians were now under a civil obligation to grant ecclesiastical equality to former enslaved Africans. As Girardeau wrote, "The ecclesiastical disabilities which attached to them, growing out of the state of slavery, are no longer in existence. It must be admitted that, technically speaking, their minority in the church must be removed."[24] According to Girardeau, it was time for exploring new forms and notions of civil, social, and ecclesiastical freedom.

In April of 1866, the presbytery ordered the consolidation of the Glebe Street Church with Zion Presbyterian Church. A formal installation service took place on December 29, 1867. The consolidation included both African American as well as white members. Zion retained "the offices of both congregations in the united church, including the pastor, and holding the name Zion Church, the regular worship being conducted on the building on Glebe Street."[25] On March 25, 1867, the white session of the church nominated seven African Americans to be superintendents over the new congregation. Many were the same men who had served as class leaders or "watchmen" in the old Zion Mission church before the Civil War. Between Zion Presbyterian and the Glebe Street Presbyterian Church there were 440 African American members, not including sixty new members added in 1868. By March of 1869, the black congregation numbered 561. African American membership "constituted more than one-half the total membership of Girardeau's flock in 1869."[26] Later that year, Girardeau's work towards ecclesiastical equality of freedman came to fulfillment: "Upon recommendation of the Session, the following African American men were nominated to serve in the office of Ruling Elder—Paul Trescot, William Price, Jacky Morrison, Samuel Robinson, William Spencer, and John Warren."[27] As a result, Girardeau became the first white member of the Southern Presbyterian Church to ordain African Americans to the position of elder.

At nearly the same time, he also took on the mantle of a fervent defender of the Lost Cause.[28] Increasing hostility throughout the South towards freedmen from 1871 to 1873 led to complete racial segregation in southern Presbyterian churches in 1874. In 1871, Girardeau began speaking at Confederate Memorial Day ceremonies, openly advocating a racially charged Lost Cause ideology by prompting his audience to never forget the cause for which Confederate veterans died. In the late nineteenth century, Confederate Memorial Day ceremonies often included ex-Confederate chaplains who not only reaffirmed the holiness of Confederate troops but also preached about the sanctity and verity of the Confederate cause. Such clergy were central to the development of a collective Confederate identity and memory. The combination of their education, oratorical skill, and their firsthand account of the Civil War gave Confederate chaplains powerful positions in postbellum southern society. Furthermore, their education, spirituality, and ability to comfort and inspire their audiences made them effective speakers for Memorial Day events, such as the one that the Ladies' Memorial Association of Charleston hosted at Magnolia Cemetery on May 10, 1871.

Four ministers participated in the event: the Rev. John Bachman, the Rev. Ellison Capers, the Rev. Edward R. Miles, and the Rev. John Lafayette Girardeau. Of these four ministers, two served as Confederate chaplains (Capers and Girardeau). Girardeau delivered the main address.[29] The purpose of the event was the reinternment of South Carolinian Confederate troops who died at Gettysburg. As Girardeau wrote, "the circumstances which assemble us in the streets of this City of the Dead are" that "the bones of our brethren have for nearly eight years been sleeping in the bloody battlefield of Gettysburg" and are now returned to "the State that they had loved so well." In some strange combination of afterlife mysticism (not common among Calvinist Presbyterians of the nineteenth century) and sectionalism, he awkwardly proposed the theory that the soldiers, "as dying children to a mother, yielded up their gallant spirits" and "breathed the fervent entreaty: 'Send our bodies to South Carolina to be buried there!'"[30] (This is a strange statement from a southern Presbyterian who, according to theological principles laid out in the Westminster Confession of Faith, to which Girardeau ascribed, the "bodies of men, after death, return to dust, and see corruption: but their souls, which neither die nor sleep, having an immortal subsistence, immediately return to God ... where they behold the face of God.")[31].

Girardeau was insulted at the thought of South Carolina's sons lying in a grave for "rebels and traitors." If Girardeau believed these men to be "beholding the face of God" and had immediately "returned to God" along the lines of an orthodox view of the Westminster Confession, then why would the souls in question be worried about whether their bodies of dust were in Pennsylvania? Worse, Girardeau presumed that the corpses were deeply offended. He asked his audience, "Was it in their latest moments of consciousness" that "they recoiled from the thought that they would be interred in an enemy's soil?"[32] This important question from an authority on the subject of religion, death, and the Civil War suggested to listeners the verity of memorializing their fallen fathers, brothers, and sons. What was also implied in this statement was that, to honor these men properly, the listener and preserver of their memory could not consider the soil of Pennsylvania as in union with the soil of South Carolina. To Girardeau and his audience, Pennsylvania in 1871, six years after the surrender at Appomattox, was still enemy ground.

For Girardeau, to honor the dead, his listeners must remember that Confederate soldiers gave their lives in defense of a state, a cause, and a way of life. "There are living issues which emerge from these graves," Girardeau claimed, "gigantic problems affecting our future, which starting up in the midst of these solemnities demand our earnest attention. The question which thrills every heart is, 'Did these men die in vain?'"[33] In response to his own question, Girardeau first declared that Confederate soldiers "had, as a peculiar people, occupied graces by themselves—in death as in life adhering to a noble and sacred, though despised and execrated, Cause." The cause to which Girardeau was referring was the right to preserve the southern way of life in its cultural, social, political, and economic dimensions. The most important aspect of this way of life was the preservation of the institution of slavery and the perpetuation of an antebellum racial hierarchy well into the late nineteenth and twentieth centuries. In admitting failure on behalf of the Confederate dead, he noted, that "they failed to preserve the relation of slavery," which "underlay and pervaded that complex whole which we denominated our Cause."[34]

Girardeau asserted that it was the duty of the living to remember the Confederate cause in noble and sacred ways rather than to accept current political, social, or economic conditions as a possibility for an acceptable future. Rather than admit that the South's soldiers had died in vain, Girardeau implored for southern civic duty among his listeners: "Shoulder to shoulder they stood; now let them lie side by side. Confederates in life, confederates let them be in death." This duty was to honor and possess an "unspeakable love," a "boundless admiration," and an "undying gratitude" for the "heroes of a defeated but glorious Cause."[35]

In clear terms, Girardeau asserted what the white South's cause was about: "'There are two ways in which it must be admitted that [the soldiers] lost their cause—they failed to establish a Confederacy as an independent country, and they failed to preserve the relation of slavery."[36] Underneath these two main tenets Girardeau placed other fundamental principles, such as preserving an antebellum social order as well as civil and religious liberty. According to Girardeau's statements, it may be properly assumed that the intent of the Confederate cause was to establish a government under which slavery might continue to grow, flourish, and perpetuate. The question posed to the audience forced them to consider how antebellum social relationships could be perpetuated in a country that had outlawed slavery and the Confederacy had been defeated and no longer existed.

Girardeau then connected listeners to his or her role in this cause: "And the question whether those who fell in its support died in vain . . . must depend for its answer upon the course which will be pursued by the people of the South." In a not so subtle shift, Girardeau transferred the burden of supporting the principles of the "cause" from the fallen Confederate soldiers to the remaining civilian population of the South. He claimed that "our brethren will not have died in vain, if we cherish in our hearts ... the principles for which they gave their lives."[37]

For Girardeau and his audience, it was the duty of every southern man and woman to remember the Confederate cause, to continue to preserve state sovereignty in practical ways, and to keep freedmen in a separate and unequal social order. Girardeau was prodding his listeners toward a sense of transferred guilt and unfinished duty, thus perpetuating the cause of the Confederacy into the next generation. Not honoring and remembering the dead—and the "cause" for which they died—was akin to desecration. Girardeau therefore contributed to the development of an explicit southern white memory of the Civil War. However, this memory was not just philosophical and ethereal. It had real, tangible, and palpable application for his listeners and for African Americans living in Charleston. "Honoring" soldiers and their memory required a buttressing of racial divides, a perpetuating of racial hierarchy, and violence, if necessary, to preserve the "southern way of life." To the men in the audience who did not fight in the Civil War, Girardeau was communicating that they could still prove their masculinity by upholding the racial and social culture of the white South via the memory of their slain forefathers. They could even act violently to preserve this way of life. The spilling of blood adequately honored the memory of Confederate veterans.

Girardeau did not mince words. "Let us cling to our identity as a people! The danger is upon us of losing it—of its being absorbed and swallowed up in that of a people which having despoiled us of the rights of freemen assumes to do our thinking, our legislating and our ruling for us" which would remove and "wipe out every distinctive characteristic which has hitherto marked us."[38] This firmly unreconstructed statement displayed continued defiance to federal authority and disdain for South Carolina's largely integrated state government during Reconstruction. The identity, not so subtly referred to, was that of white superiority solidified in a "states' rights" ideology promoting African inferiority and thus forcing African Americans to live and work in a state of subservience. For Girardeau, the characteristic that marked southern people was their commitment to white control, white virtue, and resistance to interracial familiarities. He mentioned "there is a race, which, coming down through the centuries enveloped with antagonistic influences and hostile nationalities, has stood out in perpetual protest against amalgamation with other peoples."[39] With this statement, Girardeau connected the listener's identity with an uncomplicated, "white" European ancestry, which had supposedly remained unmixed and even "today preserves its characteristics, as the current of the great Wester River flows into, without blending with, the multitudinous waters of the Gulf."[40] To win daily the Lost Cause, his listeners would need to maintain white solidarity and supremacy, and would be responsible for teaching the next generation of the virtues of race-based social and political ordering.

Connecting racism to public culture, Girardeau insisted that "appointing anniversaries" for the commemoration of "the deeds of men who died for our fundamental liberties and constitutional rights" would be necessary in order to maintain the cause. Further, a dogmatic adherence to perpetuating "the phraseology of the past—making it a vehicle for transmitting our posterity ideas which once true are true forever, all opposition to them by brute force to the contrary notwithstanding."[41] It was clear that the education of new generations of white southerners would be necessary in order to maintain antebellum political, economic, and social relations. It would be necessary to make "nurseries, schools, and colleges channels for conveying from generation to generation our type of thought, sentiment and opinion; by stamping on the minds of our children principles hallowed by the blood of patriots."[42] In a seemingly eerie glimpse of the modern era, Girardeau predicted the prevalence of segregated southern public and private universities replete with Confederate markers and flags, the development of segregationist academies after *Brown v. Board of Education*, and the pervasiveness of history textbooks that perpetuated myths of Reconstruction and, in some cases, used Lost Cause rhetoric and historical interpretations well into the late twentieth century.

Finally, Girardeau closed with the image of a dying Thomas J. "Stonewall" Jackson, who "faint from the loss of blood, and suffering from excruciating pain, he partly raised himself from his prostrate posture and in a tone of authority said: 'Hold your ground, Sir!'" One can only speculate as to the heightened volume and theatrics offered by Girardeau in this moment, but given his use of pronounced language and facial expressions to drive home a point in the pulpit, it is likely that he embellished the scene for his audience. Turning the hearts and minds of his listeners to the revered Confederate general was calling the crowd to hold their own cultural, economic, political, and social ground. "We must," Girardeau concluded, "by God's help, hold our ground, or consent to be traitors to our ancestry, our dead, our trusts for posterity, to our fire-sides, our social order, and our civil and religious liberties."[43]

With this statement, Girardeau was essentially offering what can only be called a military-style order to a civilian population to continue the Confederate fight. Invoking the memory of Jackson and recreating his call for them to "hold their ground" was a clear clarion call to maintaining the antebellum order at all costs. This kind of rhetoric proved incredibly successful as South Carolina would help lead the nation over the next century in preventing integration, perpetuating racial violence, and "holding the ground" on states' rights. Whites in the state refused to implement anti-lynching laws and regained full control of politics while successfully limiting educational and economic opportunities for African Americans well into the twentieth century.

Just a year and a half prior to his Lost Cause speech, Girardeau became the first white Presbyterian to ordain African American freedmen to leadership positions in an interracial church. And, while giving the speech, Girardeau was simultaneously pastor of a church with African American members, many of whom he helped gain expanded ecclesiastical rights. How was Girardeau able to reconcile these two seemingly contradictory stances? Girardeau did so by suggesting that white men and women of the South ought to choose a public and political course supported by the Lost Cause's racial and political implications while blatantly rejecting the same order in their own local church and more private ecclesiastical contexts. Girardeau also saw the church as a vehicle for promoting the kind of education and instruction that undergirded the religion of the Lost Cause. At the same time, Girardeau saw the church as an institution that could, over time, bring African Americans beyond ecclesiastical equality to full civic equality, and he needed to play a contrasting public role to give him space to maneuver in the ecclesiastical sphere. Whatever his designs, broader denominational forces were also at work to prevent fuller endorsement by Girardeau and other Presbyterians of broader racial equality.

In 1874, Benjamin Morgan Palmer, as moderator of the Columbus, Mississippi, general assembly, among other southern presbyters, called for the organic separation of African Americans from white Presbyterian churches. Girardeau cast the only vote of the general assembly to remain integrated. His effort to retain an integrated church ultimately failed and "with the establishment of the African Presbyterian Church, Girardeau's cause for an integrated church was lost."[44] On July 5, 1874, "after much discussion, the members unanimously voted their agreement 'to the severance, in good feeling, of our organic relations to said church, with a view to the formation of a separate Coloured Presbyterian Church with its Presbyteries, Synods, etc.'"[45] Later, Girardeau penned, "Your affectionate and generous conduct towards me has increased my obligations to you, and bound my heart to you more closely than ever. I am profoundly grateful to you for all of your kindness; I love you tenderly and deeply; and only a conviction of duty impels me to take this painful step."[46] He later reflected on the separation with a close friend, writing "Dear Brother Joe . . . Last night the mystic tie which has so long bound me to the coloured people in this city was formally severed. The Calhoun St. Congregation adopted the Assembly's recommendation for organic separation."[47] Girardeau's long pastorate among the African American population in Charleston dating back to 1853 had reached its end.

Girardeau's postwar ministerial career in Charleston, South Carolina, was multifaceted. He was a slave missionary before the Civil War who became an advocate for the ecclesiastical equality of freedmen during Reconstruction while simultaneously arguing that white Charlestonians should defend a cause undoing any potential civic or social equality. Charlestonians, Presbyterians, Lost Cause advocates, educators, and scholars have all used his life and memory to display different aspects of the role of religion in the South. Presbyterians remember Girardeau as the great missionary to the slaves who devoted his life to their spiritual growth, theological education, and leadership development. The administration of the College of Charleston erected a marble plaque in Randolph Hall in 1937 commemorating the college's "first honor graduate" and "distinguished theologian" who was a "pioneer" in interracial work in the city. Meanwhile, scholars of the Lost Cause have viewed Girardeau as a staunch advocate of the Confederacy and representative of an unreconstructed mentality in the South. African Americans at Zion-Olivet Church, which is the remnant church of Girardeau's Zion Mission, but who left the PCUS and joined with the northern and later national Presbyterians (PCUSA), remember Girardeau as a benevolent missionary who was "familiar with the Gullah dialect; hence his sermons appealed to his listeners."[48]

In 1948, in the midst of a segregated South Carolina, Zion-Olivet members recalled the work of the antebellum slave missionary and postbellum pastor on the nineteenth anniversary of the church. The Rev. Sandy David Thom produced a souvenir booklet noting in the forward that "we now come to this nineteenth anniversary with grateful hearts and souls overflowing with thanksgiving. This booklet is dedicated to the Honorable Past, the Prosperous Present, and the Promising future." He went on to remark: "Here we view the road long and dismal; the white friends that shepherded the slaves in the Second Presbyterian Church and later organized them into a separate Church. We can never know the great multitudes of lives that have been awakened . . . and must never forget or be ashamed to 'Look unto the rock whence ye are hewn and to the hole of the pit whence ye are digged.'"[49] Throughout the booklet, produced by this congregation of African Americans in the very midst of a segregated Jim Crow South, there persisted a sense of remembrance for the "white friends" who had "shepherded" the enslaved Africans of the 1850s.[50]

Indeed, the memory and legacy of Girardeau is mixed based on who is speaking, a fact indicative of the complex nature of southern interracial worship as it flowered and wilted in the midst of denominational conflicts and the rise of Lost Cause religion. John Lafayette Girardeau's legacy as a rare interracialist on matters of race and church runs parallel with his career as an orator of the Lost Cause. Girardeau therefore complicates our understanding of southern white clergy and competing notions of masculinity, identity, and morality in the postwar South. It also helps us understand further the positions that whites elected to stake out regarding racial ecclesiastical integration in a burgeoning Lost Cause state.

Despite Girardeau's efforts toward ecclesiastical reform, it was the Lost Cause that ultimately left the most lasting legacy in the post-Reconstruction South. The southern population had the authorization and even orders from a Confederate chaplain to maintain an antebellum order at all cost. More broadly, the leading lights of southern Presbyterianism not only helped defend an antebellum southern way of life in the postbellum South, but also helped mobilize an embittered and resentful population toward reclaiming political, economic, and social control through violence. The church, an organization that was to be a place for all people, would become a steadfast bastion in the effort to "hold your ground" on issues of racial inclusion. To be sure, at different points in his career, Girardeau embodied all three of Blight's visions. Ultimately, however, Girardeau could not detach himself from the white supremacist vision so common among Lost Cause advocates in the postwar South and today.

Girardeau continued to honor, make sacred, and memorialize a Lost Cause movement during the course of Reconstruction. At times, his work in the church undermined several of the tenets of the Lost Cause. However, capitulation to culture on issues of race was his life's legacy. Like his predecessors and many contemporaries, whether Presbyterian or not, Girardeau would increasingly reflect the broader cultural mores of fellow southerners bent on maintaining segregation, white control, and the political and economic exploitation of African Americans.

Notes

1. Charles Reagan Wilson, *Baptized by Blood: The Religion of the Lost Cause, 1865–1920* (Athens: University of Georgia Press, 1980), 73.

2. David Blight, *Race and Reunion: The Civil War in American Memory* (Cambridge, MA: Harvard University Press, 2001), 2.

3. Several texts have shaped this understanding of Christianity, slavery, and the southern response, including John B. Boles, *Black Southerners, 1619–1869* (Lexington: University Press of Kentucky, 1983); Robert M. Calhoon, *Evangelicals and Conservatives in the Early South, 1740–1861* (Columbia: University of South Carolina Press, 1988); David B. Chesebrough, *Clergy Dissent in the Old South, 1830–1865* (Carbondale: Southern Illinois University Press, 1996); Edward R. Crowther, *Southern Evangelicals and the Coming of the Civil War* (Lewiston, NY: E. Mellen Press, 2000); James D. Essig. *The Bonds of Wickedness: American Evangelicals against Slavery, 1770–1808* (Philadelphia: Temple University Press, 1982); Paul Harvey, *Freedom's Coming: Religious Culture and the Shaping of the South from the Civil War through the Civil Rights Era* (Chapel Hill: University of North Carolina Press, 2005); Samuel S. Hill, *Southern Churches in Crisis Revisited* (Tuscaloosa: University of Alabama Press, 1999); Samuel S. Hill, *One Name but Several Faces: Variety in Popular Christian Denominations in Southern History* (Athens: University of Georgia Press, 1996); Samuel S. Hill, ed., *Varieties of Southern Religious Experience* (Baton Rouge: LSU Press, 1988); E. Brooks Holifield, *The Gentlemen Theologians: American Theology in Southern Culture, 1795–1860* (Durham, NC: Duke

University Press, 1978); Victor B. Howard, *Conscience and Slavery: The Evangelistic Calvinist Domestic Missions, 1837–1861* (Kent, OH: The Kent State University Press, 1990); Donald G. Mathews, *Religion in the Old South* (Chicago: University of Chicago Press, 1977); John R. McKivigan and Mitchell Snay, *Religion and the Antebellum Debate over Slavery* (Athens: University of Georgia Press, 1998); William G. McLoughlin, ed., *The American Evangelicals, 1800–1900* (New York: Harper and Row, 1968); W. Scott Poole, *Never Surrender: Confederate Memory and Conservatism in the South Carolina Upcountry* (Athens: University of Georgia Press, 2004); Mitchell Snay, *Gospel of Disunion: Religion and Separatism in the Antebellum South* (New York: Cambridge University Press, 1993); Kenneth Moore Startup, *The Root of All Evil: The Protestant Clergy and the Economic Mind of the Old South* (Athens: University of Georgia Press, 1997); and Charles Reagan Wilson, *Baptized in Blood: The Religion of the Lost Cause, 1865–1920* (Athens: University of Georgia Press, 1980); Charles Reagan Wilson; *Religion in the South* (Jackson: University Press of Mississippi, 1985). I am forever indebted to Charles as an incredible advisor, mentor, historian, writer, and friend. Thank you, Charles.

4. Wilson, *Baptized in Blood*, 66, 73–74.

5. Ibid., 74.

6. Poole, *Never Surrender*, 56.

7. Otis W. Pickett, "We Are Marching to Zion: Zion Church and the Distinctive Work of Presbyterian Slave Missionaries in Charleston, South Carolina, 1849–1874," *Journal of the South Carolina Historical Association*, May 2010, 91–101; C. N. Willborn, "John L. Girardeau: Pastor to Slaves and Theologian of Causes" (PhD diss., Westminster Theological Seminary, 2003).

8. Pickett, "We are Marching to Zion," 91–101.

9. John L. Girardeau, College of Charleston Special Collections Pamphlets, "Confederate Memorial Day at Charleston, SC: Reinternment of the Carolina Dead from Gettysburg" (Charleston, SC: W. G. Mazyck, 1871).

10. Bertram Wyatt-Brown, *Southern Honor: Ethics and Behavior in the Old South* (New York,: Oxford University Press, 1982).

11. Girardeau, "Reinternment of the Carolina Dead," 6–7.

12. Erskine Clarke, *Our Southern Zion: A History of Calvinism in the South Carolina Low Country, 1690–1990* (Tuscaloosa: University of Alabama Press, 1996), 241.

13. Lois A Simms, *A History of Zion, Olivet, and Zion-Olivet Churches, 1850–1985, Charleston, South Carolina* (Mercury Micro Computer Products, 1987), 2.

14. Pickett, "We Are Marching to Zion, 92–97.

15. The Rev. J. M. Buckley, editor of the *New York Christian Advocate*, quoted by Dr. John B. Mack in George A. Blackburn, ed., *The Life Work of John L. Girardeau, D.D., LL.D.*, 52. This is interesting given the hatred of Charles Spurgeon among many southerners due to his disdain for slavery and slaveholding.

16. Paul Trescoat to John Girardeau, July 27, 1865, Microfilm Roll #160, Blackburn Family Papers, South Caroliniana Library, University of South Carolina.

17. Prefatory notes, Thomas Smyth Papers: Second Presbyterian Church Papers: Records of Anson Street and Zion church kept by Dr. Girardeau, collection 24, box 5, folder 6. South Carolina Historical Society.

18. Erskine Clarke, *Wrestlin' Jacob: A Portrait of Religion in the Old South, 1830–1865* (Carbondale: Southern Illinois University Press, 1996), 178.

19. Willborn, "John L. Girardeau," 194.

20. Ibid., 192.

21. Ibid., 193.

22. John Lafayette Girardeau, "Ecclesiastical Relations to Freedmen," *Southern Presbyterian Review* 18 (1866): 2.

23. Robert L. Dabney, *Discussions of Robert Lewis Dabney*, vol. 2 (London, England: Banner of Truth Trust, 1891), 204.

24. Girardeau, "Ecclesiastical Relations to Freedmen," 4.

25. Blackburn, *Life Work and Sermons of John L. Girardeau*, 137.

26. Willborn, "John L. Girardeau," 203.

27. Ibid., 203. Indeed, as Thomas Law recalled, "All these Brethren, I venture to say, drew their inspiration and encouragement for the higher work from their consecrated and ever zealous pastor." See Blackburn, *Life Work of John L. Girardeau*, 147.

28. Pickett, "We Are Marching to Zion," 91–101; Willborn, "John L. Girardeau," 203.

29. Girardeau, "Reinternment of the Carolina Dead," 3.

30. Ibid., 6.

31. *The Westminster Confession of Faith* (Lawrenceville, GA: Committee for Christian Education & Publications), 96–97.

32. Girardeau, "Reinternment of the Carolina Dead," 6.

33. Ibid., 8.

34. Ibid., 7–8.

35. Ibid., 8.

36. Ibid.

37. Ibid., 8–9.

38. Ibid., 17.

39. Ibid., 19.

40. Ibid.

41. Ibid., 18.

42. Ibid.

43. Girardeau, "Reinternment of the Carolina Dead," 20.

44. Willborn, "Girardeau," 205.

45. Ibid., 205.

46. Blackburn, *Life Work and Sermons of John L. Girardeau*, 160.

47. William Banks Papers (1814–1875), letter from John L. Girardeau to the Rev. J. B. Mack, July 29, 1874, South Caroliniana Library, 2–4.

48. Simms, *A History of Zion*, 2.

49. Souvenir Booklet, *Anniversary of Zion Presbyterian Church, 1858–1948*. Vertical File, Churches-Presbyterian-Zion-Olivet, Avery Research Center for African American History and Culture.

50. Within this booklet is an article entitled "Dr. Girardeau Devoted to Negro Work," which is filled with stories of his kindness and warmth towards African Americans, both slave and free.

Having Our Own

The Colored Methodist Episcopal Church and the Struggle for Black Autonomy in Education

ALICIA JACKSON

Knowledge did'nt agree with slavery— /
'Twould make us all too wise
—FRANCES HARPER, "Learning to Read," 1872

In January of 1906, Catherine Cottrell Hall, the women's dormitory of Mississippi Industrial College (MI), opened its doors to scores of students lined up in Holly Springs, Mississippi, to register for the school's first class. Their enthusiasm resulted from the dedication of the men and women of the Colored Methodist Episcopal Church's (CME Church) third district who had met their goal of raising over $50,000 to build the dormitory and Washington Hall. The establishment of MI, as it became known, reflected the ability of rural African Americans to raise large amounts of money and build their own educational institutions without the assistance of whites.

Education was a common pursuit of black leaders, especially in black churches. Many felt that they would obtain the tools to demand their civil rights if they could educate members of their own communities. In a 1903 editorial in the *Christian Index*, R. T. Brown described the importance of education to the CME Church: "Education increases the aspirations of individuals, and if that be true, it will increase those of a race."[1]

Education was a key component of freedom to many blacks, and African American churches worked tirelessly to establish their own educational institutions. For the CME Church, determination to make their own schools mirrored their determination to make their own all-black denomination. Established in 1870 in Jackson, Tennessee, the CME Church arose from the soils of the Deep South, drawing the bulk of its membership from Alabama, Georgia, Texas, Arkansas, Louisiana, and Mississippi. The story of MI exemplifies southern blacks' collective efforts to educate their communities; it represents their continual struggle to maintain funding for their education, to govern the direction of their institutions, and to escape their dependence on paternal white supporters.

MI's success is connected to its birthplace: Holly Springs. As late as 1874, the town was a safe haven for blacks in and around north Mississippi. The community, located roughly thirty miles southeast of Memphis, is most famous for being the hometown of Ida B. Wells. But Holly Springs and surrounding Marshall County were more than that; both were the home of hundreds of blacks who lived between the emerging realities of the Jim Crow South and the secure familiarity of black community during and after Reconstruction.[2] From 1860 to 1880, the county's black population grew from 17,447 to 18,338, while the number of whites living there decreased from 11,376 to 10,992.[3] During Reconstruction, Union generals stationed nearly two hundred troops in the town, and the establishment of a Freedman's Bureau office in 1868 further heightened a sense of security for black residents.

Holly Springs was also a center for political power: Secretary of State James Hill lived in Marshall County, and from 1873 to 1880, he was one of its eight black representatives and senators in the Mississippi legislature. Holly Springs provided another key magnet for black migration: education. Established in 1866 by the Freedman's Aid Society and funded by the Methodist Episcopal Church in the North (MEC), Rust College educated the black population both in and around Holly Springs. In addition, Holly Springs State Normal School was one of just two public colleges for African Americans in the state; the other was Alcorn, located nearly three hundred miles south and focused on agricultural and industrial training.[4] The Normal School, with its teacher training and preparatory track, was an indispensable pipeline for black education. In 1890, 162 students were enrolled in the school's normal and preparatory programs. By 1900, enrollment had increased to an average of 250 students.[5]

Unfortunately, its annual state funding of $3,000 dropped to $2,500 from 1877 to 1890; by 1903, the Holly Springs School was on the verge of losing state funding completely.[6] During his 1903 gubernatorial campaign, Democrat James K. Vardaman openly characterized black education as foolish, believing that "blacks belonged to an inferior race that was incapable of acquiring meaningful education—and dangerous because even a rudimentary education might rekindle the Negro's ambitions to vote and hold office." In his campaign, he promised to repeal the Fifteenth Amendment, modify the Fourteenth Amendment, and completely defund "Negro education."[7] Vardaman kept his campaign promise: On March 15, 1904, he vetoed the legislature's funding for the State Normal School in Holly Springs, permanently closing the only publicly funded teacher training school for blacks in north Mississippi.

Blacks in Holly Springs and the surrounding area did not relent. By 1908, two new African Americans schools were launched: the short-lived Baptist Normal and the CME Church's Mississippi Industrial College, formed under the leadership of Bishop Elias Cottrell.[8] Having lived in Holly Springs, Cottrell was quite familiar with the Normal School and preached at the graduating class' commencement in May of 1890.[9] Earlier, Cottrell had characterized Vardaman as "Bigoted" and a "Political demigogue [sic]."[10]

Robust, forceful, and argumentative, Bishop Cottrell embodied the struggle for southern black autonomy in education.[11] He was born on January 31, 1853, and grew up a few miles outside of Holly Springs in Old Hudsonville, Mississippi.[12] Cottrell joined the CME Church in January of 1877 and was soon after ordained. In December of 1878, he left Mississippi and began religion classes at Central Tennessee College in Nashville, Tennessee, while serving as pastor of Capers Chapel.

Cottrell's fight to see African Americans building, supporting, and leading their own educational institutions led to his appointment in 1892 as commissioner of education in the CME Church. He was called to solicit funds for the denomination's educational pursuits, and he helped to established four colleges, including Miles Memorial College in Alabama, Homer Seminary (later renamed Homer College) in Louisiana, and Haygood Seminary in Arkansas.[13] In 1900, he established a board of trustees and spent the next three years raising money to build a school in Holly Springs. Three years later, he purchased land, and Mississippi Theological and Industrial Seminary opened in January 1906 with two impressive buildings: Catherine Cottrell Hall and Washington Hall. Later that year, the school was renamed Mississippi Industrial College; Hammond Hall was added to the campus in 1907. By 1908, 450 students were enrolled in the elementary, secondary, agricultural, and industrial departments, and teacher training remained the focus of MI's curriculum.[14] By 1910, the college had the highest number of students of all the CME Church's schools.[15]

Cottrell's worked to develop community-run schools modeled after Booker T. Washington's Tuskegee Institute. Just a few years after the school's opening, he received acclaim from Washington and other black leaders throughout the South for his service as treasurer in the Mississippi chapter of the National Negro Business League—its most respected chapter. On October 8, 1908, during his tour of Mississippi, Washington stopped in Holly Springs to visit leading African Americans of the town. Reporting on Washington's tour, the *AME Church Review* described Cottrell as a champion of his race for establishing MI in particular and for the "splendid buildings all paid for by colored people themselves." Washington noted in his diary that "[the new school], considerably larger in every way, is in part the result of [Gov. James K. Vardaman's] attitude."[16] In an address during the visit, Washington focused on the great progress of African Americans in Mississippi—and especially in Holly Springs, emphasizing the role of education in that progress.[17] For Cottrell, the visit was monumental in that he shared the stage with the man then known as the leader of the black race.[18] Support from Washington was essential for any black leader hoping to secure funding from the General Education Board (GEB), where Washington influenced white philanthropic leaders.

John D. Rockefeller, Sr., established the GEB in 1902 with a $1 million endowment that was later supplemented by other endowments, which totaled $129 million by 1921. Cottrell and other black educators knew that a large portion of the GEB's funding was given to black institutions that focused on industrial education.[19] The GEB supported the establishment of black schools that modeled themselves after the Hampton-Tuskegee model with its emphasis on industrial and agricultural training.

Witnessing the success of Booker T. Washington's fundraising from northern sources and the ever-growing challenges facing black farmers, Cottrell repeatedly sought additional funding for MI through the GEB; however, his black nationalistic rhetoric, his outspoken criticism of James Vardaman, and his promotion of MI as an institutional challenge to the governor's racist policies placed him and his vision for his school in direct opposition to Wallace Buttrick, a GEB trustee. Buttrick espoused the view of many southern white reformers, stating, "I recognize the fact that the Negro is an inferior race and that the Anglo-Saxon is the superior race."[20]

Cottrell's criticism of Vardaman ebbed, and his requests to the GEB yielded a meager amount of funding.[21] In fact, less than 20 percent of the funds given by the GEB reached black institutions despite its mandate.[22] Regarding MI, the GEB did not see a large enough emphasis on industrial training; by Cottrell's design, MI was an industrial school in name only for the purpose of getting funding from organizations like the GEB. Cottrell disguised his educational ambitions in his correspondence to the GEB by stressing that Mississippi needed an industrial school similar to Booker T. Washington's. Imitating Washington's brickmaking tutelage, Cottrell solicited funding from the GEB for the purchase of a brickmaking machine. In its curriculum, however, MI placed industrial education second to more academically oriented studies.[23] Instructors taught chemistry, physics, and mathematics; they organized literary societies and taught Latin and Greek, focusing on MI's original goal of teacher training.[24] For Cottrell, local ministers, and their community, MI continued the vision set forth by the CME Church, which in 1873 mandated that "an education is second only to true Religion and Piety" and that bishops should establish schools in their respective districts.[25]

White leaders often held a paternalistic view of blacks, and black-controlled educational institutions tacitly challenged their control. Black-controlled schools were prominent among Methodists in black denominations like African Methodist Episcopal Church (AME), AME-Zion, and CME churches.[26] Cottrell believed that a school in Holly Springs owned, controlled, and staffed by African Americans themselves, unlike Rust College, would provide greater benefit for black students. Yet, with Rust directly across the street from MI, he knew that GEB trustee Wallace Buttrick would see little need to fund another African American school. Buttrick believed that for black students, courses in Latin, Greek, and fine arts should be abandoned for industrial and agricultural training.

Rust College complicated MI's ability to receive funding. Its alumni were well-known: M. W. Dogan, president of Wiley College; J. B. F. Shaw, president of Central Alabama Institute; Perry W. Howard, an assistant attorney general of the United States; former US senator Hiram Revels, who also taught at the institution for several years. Rust's glowing reputation also perpetuated the perception that its students were better off financially. Although both schools provided financial aid to students whose parents exchanged crops and livestock for a portion of their children's education, many considered MI a poorer school for children of sharecropping and tenant farming families.[27]

For leaders at MI, the fact that its school buildings were primarily paid for by black sharecropping and tenant farming families was a source of dignity, and the value of its school buildings and property differentiated it from Rust. By 1923, MI had 110 acres of land, worth $6,000, and the net worth of its buildings totaled $206,500. Each structure cost between $60,000 and $75,000, and all were paid for primarily by African Americans.[28] Rust's campus farm of sixty acres was worth $4,500, and the net worth of all buildings on its campus totaled $107,000, according to a 1919 statistical report.[29] For Cottrell and others, the value of property and the quality of structures spoke to the unity and strength found within the black church and surrounding black community. The school "fostered by struggling farmers with very little assistance from white people from the North or South" highlighted African American resolve, and Cottrell characterized blacks as "simply bearing our burdens manfully."[30]

Raised in the all-black rural community of Wall Hill, Mississippi, Pearlie Phillips grew up in a sharecropping family. Her mother had attended the Holly Springs Normal School before its closure in 1904. According to Phillips, "MI students were on the left-hand side, and Rust people were on the right hand side. They would hardly speak to you if you met them face to face. I think it came from their teaching. Rust was run by whites, and MI was run by blacks. I believe that was the reason [that Rust students] felt like they were more important than we were."[31]

The board of trustees at Rust College was made up of both whites and blacks, with most of the school controlled by members from outside of the area. In contrast, MI's board had regional ties. Twenty members were from the denomination's north Mississippi Conference, and the majority of trustees were preachers and farmers representing small communities throughout the area.[32] Several trustees were from Holly Springs, and their service on the board allowed them to have input into the school, especially since they led efforts to raise money.[33]

Like all bishops in the CME Church, Elias Cottrell used the annual conferences of his district to solicit funds for building CME Church institutions like MI. The majority of funding for education was raised during local and state conference meetings, and many ministers felt the pressure to give to institutions within their conference while maintaining scant church budgets.

Many rural supporters gave, in spite of their meager incomes and great hardship. In 1910, Marshall County and neighboring counties, which were heavily dependent upon black sharecroppers and tenant farmers, saw cotton crops devastated by drought and an infestation of boll weevils. With few options available, Cottrell looked for funding outside of his constituents. In a letter to the GEB dated January 25, 1910, he wrote: "We have raised $13,715.87 from colored people alone in the state of Mississippi, not one dollar out of state. This too comes from the black belt from the struggling farmers who have had short crops, less than 50 percent also infested by boll weevils"[34]

While black leaders promoted CME Church schools to challenge the Jim Crow South, white Methodist Episcopal Church South (MECS) leaders supported CME Church schools as a way to control future black leaders. Some of the first CME Church schools were influenced by the paternalistic tendencies of the MECS, but in Holly Springs, MI marked a transition as its founders pursued black autonomy and independence from the MECS.

Originally, CME Church bishops, such as Lucius Holsey, Henry Miles, and Isaac Lane, were drawn to Methodism because of their familiarity with the MECS. The CME Church relationship with the MECS initially helped establish many of its congregations. This relationship, however, conveyed the sense that the CME Church was not simply supported but rather controlled by the MECS. Many in rival Methodist denominations believed former slaveholders directed CME Church affairs toward the goal "to lead colored people back to slavery."[35] Some denounced and ridiculed the CME Church as "the little slave church" or the "bootlick Church."[36]

The relationship between the two denominations was shaped by CME Church leaders' need for financial support and by MECS leaders' desire to maintain the paternalistic nature of their relationship. CME Churches often lacked financial support from their laity, many of whom were still trying to get their footing in the post-Civil War South. The MECS offered significant help. In 1907, J. D. Hammond, a secretary of education for the MECS, procured funding for Hammond Hall, the boys' dormitory on MI's campus. Other funding efforts by white MECS leaders yielded roughly $20,000 from 1913 to 1923 for the completion of other building projects.[37]

MECS support was often contingent upon CME Church leaders adhering to policies set forth by the MECS as shown in the establishment of Paine College in Georgia. The white denomination supported the educational efforts of the CME Church because white leaders were concerned that Methodists from the North would influence southern blacks and that whites would lose influence in rural black communities. White Methodist leaders prohibited any political speeches in CME churches as a condition to transferring property to the smaller black denomination. In an editorial, J. D. Barbee wrote what many in the MECS most feared—that establishing schools for blacks in the South would provoke black leaders to be more politically active: "The Colored Methodist Episcopal Church in America professes to teach pure and simple Christianity without any mixture of politics. Let them be encouraged and let their spiritual mother especially give them her sympathies and sustain them in the above enterprise."[38]

The philanthropy of the MECS grew out of a philosophy known as the "Paine Principle."[39] The acceptance of this principle arose from the failed efforts of Bishop W. H. Miles, who in 1873 tried to established schools in Sardis, Mississippi, and Louisville, Kentucky. Both eventually closed because Miles was unable to secure enough funding from emancipated African Americans to maintain the schools. White leaders were unwilling to support his efforts because Miles pushed for black staff and leadership in the schools. Following the closing of the two schools, leaders like Lucius Holsey pragmatically adopted the Paine Principle. To him, CME Churches needed the MECS to remain solvent.

Lucius Holsey established Paine College and tied the college closely with the MECS, receiving a substantial percentage of funding from the older denomination. In fact, various Methodist publications have listed Paine College as a MECS, school, not recognizing its tie to the CME Church. The college had a white president until 1971, and the institution is listed as both a CME Church and United Methodist College to this day. While receiving funding from the MECS, Paine College purposely avoided funding from organizations in the North, unlike other CME Church institutions.[40]

As CME Church leaders worked toward greater autonomy in their institutions, funding by the MECS dropped. Suffering with crop failures and heightened fears of black lawlessness, economic support among less progressive MECS members wavered. From 1914 to 1934, the MECS gave a little over $600,000 to CME Church educational institutions, and funding went primarily to Paine and Lane Colleges. Some CME Church leaders began to question whether strong ties with the MECS were truly beneficial as they became increasingly frustrated with the lack of equality experienced by blacks in the South. Lucius Holsey, a one-time proponent of the Paine Principle, was angered by this inequality. After 1910, he distanced himself from Paine College and became increasingly critical of the institution.[41]

At Lane College the push for equality and recognition was apparent by 1902. In 1882, Bishop Isaac Lane established Lane Institute in Jackson, Tennessee (it was later named Lane College). Initially, the school was established as a training institution and received a great deal of funding from the MECS. But views on the extent of white control over black institutions fluctuated. According to Othal Lakey, bishop and historian of the denomination, a substantial number of letters to the *Christian Index* submitted around 1902 called for a black president at Lane, suggesting that the college should become the central institution of the CME Church. The following year, the Rev. T. F. Saunders, a white Methodist leader whose salary was paid by the MECS, resigned as president. The next year, Lane College installed its first black president, James Bray, a graduate of Paine College.

By 1910, African Americans headed all CME Church schools except for Paine College. Many in CME Churches saw black leadership as vital to African Americans' opportunities for education and employment. A 1908 editorial in the *Christian Index* praised the separate school systems in Philadelphia, Mississippi, because they gave black students "an opportunity to develop teaching qualities in our own young people."[42] Many whites did not want black schoolteachers and, in his 1916 autobiography, Bishop Lane discussed his belief that the CME Church's former slaves should have schools run by African American faculty and staff: "I saw that we could not maintain our Church as a separate organization with our intelligent representatives who were able to defend its doctrines and support its polity. So it became necessary and urgent for us to establish and operate a school of high grade for our Church."[43]

Unlike leaders at Paine College who refused to solicit funds from northern philanthropic organizations, Lane and Cottrell openly sought whatever funding they could for education. MI encouraged black leadership and autonomy, but the college received significant funding from white leaders. In addition to J. D. Hammond's financial support, Andrew Carnegie donated $25,000 in matching funds to construct an auditorium. On the condition that the school raised the first $25,000, a two thousand-seat auditorium was built, making it the largest auditorium space for blacks in Mississippi.[44] Raising additional funds was extremely difficult for a newly founded school, yet despite its white sources of funding, MI proudly advocated black autonomy by having an African American faculty and staff.

Church involvement was integral to black lives in the South, and the minister often served as a race leader. Consequently, many believed that heeding the bishop's call for funds to build a school was equivalent to doing God's will. Not regarding their own needs, many ministers saw their contributions to education as essential to African Americans. Efforts to raise funds for education gave a sense of unity and solidarity among the laity, who saw the establishment of their own institutions as a continuation of the fellowship and refuge they felt while worshipping in black churches and living in rural communities. CME Church members also saw education as a way out of poverty and the only means for advancing their social standing and interests, and many parents from small rural communities in northern Mississippi, east Arkansas, and southwest Tennessee registered their children to attend MI.

The cost of tuition, board, and other living expenses was overwhelming for many families in the late 1890s through the 1940s. Sending children to school also meant the loss of an extra hand to work the field and bring in a crop. Many parents demanded that students do their best while in college, and students knew that school was a chance to leave farming and gain a skill that would provide an opportunity for the social and economic advancement of their entire family and community. Bishop Cottrell recognized the sacrifices that families in rural communities made to support and attend black-controlled institutions: "Some [black men and women] . . . don't own their own homes, some of them are very poor, living in one, two and three rooms—in log cabins, without an education themselves, yet so wrapped up in the idea of encouraging the rising generation, and paving the way for the education of their children—that they are willing to give five, ten, and fifteen dollars out of their own pockets for the support of a school."[45]

The expense often caused parents to choose a single child, often a girl, to attend school. Black parents saw professional teaching as a noble and respectable job for black women, and MI supported a teacher training school located in the rear of Catherine Hall. Many parents sent their daughters to this school, believing that their sons could find manual occupations and would not have to risk working in white homes where there was greater potential for mistreatment.

As CME Church leaders empowered black students from their congregations through education, laity in turn supported integrationist efforts. Miles College graduate Autherine Lucy's enrollment in a master's program at the then-segregated University of Alabama in February of 1956 confirmed the hopes of CME Church leaders and their challenge of the Jim Crow system that crippled educational opportunities for people of color in the South.

Lucy's challenge was an important precursor to student activism in the South; in fact, it was a challenge to Governor George Wallace's segregationist policies and it mirrored Elias Cottrell's previous challenge to James K. Vardaman, who was governor of Mississippi at the turn of the twentieth century. Fifty years after Cottrell's stand and the establishment of Mississippi Industrial, Lucy believed that it was "time to move forward"; her actions served as "a stepping-stone in the civil rights movement."[46] Two weeks after her enrollment, she endured expulsion but remained hopeful of returning to the university. "I have no fear of going back. God will take care of me," she affirmed in the *Christian Index*, the CME Church's journalistic instrument, which concluded that "Miles College and the [CME Church] have just reason to be proud of this young woman and Sunday School teacher ... Miss Lucy is right on her faith that God will take care of her. She is not alone in her struggle. Her battle is our battle."[47]

By the 1960s, the legacy of Cottrell's vision for black autonomy in education found voice in a new generation as MI students worked together with Rust students to integrate local stores and support chapters of the Student Nonviolent Coordinating Committee and the NAACP.

Unfortunately, the boll weevil infestation, the falling price of cotton, and the onset of the Great Depression led to the closing of cotton mills and rail lines in Mississippi. With the rise of Memphis as an industrial center in the 1940s and '50s, many blacks left farming in Mississippi for opportunity elsewhere.[48] Today, the once vibrant MI campus lies in ruins. Closed in 1982, virtually all of its remaining buildings are either sagging or leaning. In 2008, Rust College bought the property. Soon after, discussions of revitalizing the campus emerged but never materialized. Catherine Cottrell Hall, the girls' dormitory and one of the first buildings on MI's campus, was razed in 2012 and now is gone.

Notes

1. R. T. Brown, editorial, *Christian Index*, February 7, 1903; James Anderson, *The Education of Blacks in the South, 1860–1935* (Chapel Hill: University of North Carolina Press, 1988); Adam Fairclough, *A Class of Their Own: Black Teachers in the Segregated South* (Cambridge, MA: Belknap Press of Harvard University Press, 2006).

2. See Patricia A. Schechter, *Ida B. Wells-Barnett & American Reform, 1880–1930* (Chapel Hill: University of North Carolina Press) and Mia Bay, *To Tell the Truth Freely: The Life of Ida B. Wells* (New York: Hill and Wang, 2010).

3. United States Census Bureau, "Population, by Race, Sex, and Nativity," Population, by Race and by Counties: 1880, 1870, 1860, table V, http://www2.census.gov/prod2/decennial/documents/1880a_v1-13.pdf (accessed April 1, 2016). See also Ruth Watkins, "Reconstruction

in Marshall County," *Reconstruction in Northern Counties of Mississippi*, Mississippi Historical Society, vol. 12.

4. Stuart Grayson Noble, *Forty Years of the Public Schools in Mississippi, with Special Reference to the Education of the Negro* (New York: Teachers College, Columbia University, 1918), 89. Because Alcorn was created as a land-grant institution, the school received federal funding. See Robert L. Jenkins, "Development of Black Higher Education in Mississippi (1865–1920)," *Journal of Mississippi History* 45, no. 4 (November 1983): 278.

5. Noble, *Forty Years of the Public Schools in Mississippi*, 84, 87.

6. Ibid., 89. On opposition to funding for African American education, see also Anderson, *Education of Blacks in the South*; Neil McMillen, *Dark Journey: Black Mississippians in the Age of Jim Crow* (Champaign: University of Illinois Press, 1989); Fairclough, *Class of Their Own*, 142–47.

7. William F. Holmes, *The White Chief: James Kimble Vardaman* (Baton Rouge: Louisiana State University Press, 1970), 103.

8. Booker T. Washington, *The Booker T. Washington Papers*, vol. 10: 1909–11, eds. Louis R. Harlan and Raymond W. Smock (Urbana: University of Illinois Press, 1981) 63.

9. *Christian Index*, May 30, 1891.

10. Cottrell to Robert C. Ogden, March 29, 1906, General Education Board. General Education Board Records, Series 1 Appropriations, Subseries 1, Early Southern Program, Box 96 Folder 859, Miss 39, Rockefeller Archive Center for the Study of Labor and Industrial Relations, Sleepy Hollow, NY (hereafter cited as Rockefeller Archives).

11. *Autobiography of Bishop Isaac Lane, LL.D., with a Short History of the C.M.E. Church in America and of Methodism* (Nashville, TN: M. E. Church, South, 1916), 164.

12. Olga Pruitt, *It Happened Here: True Stories of Holly Springs* (Holly Springs, MS: South Reporter Printing, 1950), 25.

13. Charles Wesley, "Personal Notes," *Journal of Negro History* 23 (1938): 261–63.

14. Larry G. Murphy, ed., *Encyclopedia of African American Religions* (New York: Garland Publishing 1993), 502.

15. *Christian Index*, January 9, 1908.

16. Booker T. Washington, *The Booker T. Washington Papers*, vol. 9: 1906–1908, eds. Louis R. Harlan and Raymond W. Smock (Urbana: University of Illinois Press, 1980), 676.

17. Washington, *The Booker T. Washington Papers*, vol. 10, 60

18. Washington, *The Booker T. Washington Papers*, vol. 9, 674. See Charles C. Bolton, *The Hardest Deal: The Battle Over School Integration in Mississippi, 1870–1980* (Jackson: University Press of Mississippi, 2005).

19. Tera Hunter, "The Correct Thing: Charlotte Hawkins Brown and the Palmer Institute," *Southern Exposure* 11 (September–October 1983), 37–43. The article discusses the defunding of Brown's school once she moved away from agricultural education.

20. James D. Anderson. *The Education of Blacks in the South, 1860–1935*, 92.

21. By 1914, Cottrell's criticism of Vardaman in General Education Board correspondence ended once his tenure as governor ended.

22. Eric Anderson and Alfred A. Moss, Jr., *Dangerous Donations: Northern Philanthropy and Southern Black Education, 1902–1930* (Columbia: University of Missouri Press, 1999), 9. See also Fairclough, *Class of Their Own*, 147–54, 182–90; David Sansing, *Making Haste Slowly: The Troubled History of Higher Education in Mississippi* (Jackson: University Press of Mississippi, 1990), 67–69.

23. It was a common practice for African American educators to identify their schools as industrial training schools to secure funding. Cottrell to General Education board, June 1, 1909, Rockefeller Archives. See Anderson, *The Education of Blacks in the South*, 135.

24. "Report on Mississippi Industrial College by Jackson Davis, 11 April 1918," Cottrell to General Education Board, June 28, 1907, Rockefeller Archives; Robert Jenkins, "Development of Black Education," 277.

25. *General Conference Minutes, 1873*, "Report of Committee of Education," 61, Christian Methodist Episcopal Church Archives, Memphis Tennessee.

26. Both Bishop Lucius Holsey of the CME Church and Bishop Henry McNeal Turner of the AME Church advocated black nationalism. Holsey suggested the creation of a black state and Turner suggested emigration of blacks back to Africa.

27. Pearlie Phillips, Holly Springs, March 17, 2003. Letter from Dr. L. M. McCoy, November 23, 1928, Rust College Archives, Holly Springs, Mississippi. The letter recounts one student's parents giving the school two mules in order to pay for a son's education. In another case, three daughters worked all summer long harvesting crops and working on father's farm to pay for schooling. In another case, a family gave a calf and some hogs as payment.

28. Washington, *The Booker T. Washington Papers*, vol. 10, 63.

29. Statistical Report of Rust College, Holly Springs School year ending May 31, 1919, Rust College Archives, Holly Springs, Mississippi.

30. "Letter to General Education Board from Elias Cottrell," in GEB Box 96, Folder 859, Miss 39, Rockefeller Archives.

31. Pearlie Phillips, interview by author, August 2, 2002. The tensions between the schools was noted in "Excerpt from Fred McCuiston's Report on Colleges for Negroes—Colored M E Church 1932," which suggested MI and Rust merge, but "they have been rivals for so long that it is difficult for them to cross the road in the most obvious types of collaboration," General Education Board, 8 September 1944, Rockefeller Archives.

32. "Report on Mississippi Industrial College by Jackson Davis sent to General Education Board, 11 April 1918," Rockefeller Archives.

33. Ibid.

34. "Letter to General Education Board, 25 January 1910," Rockefeller Archives.

35. Fayette Montgomery Hamilton, *A Plain Account of the Colored Methodist Episcopal Church in America: Being an Outline of Her History and Polity; Also Her Prospective Work* (Nashville, TN: M. E. Church, South, 1887), 18.

36. Lucius Holsey, "The Colored Methodist Episcopal Church," in *African American Religious History: A Documentary Witness*, ed. Milton C. Sernett (Durham, NC: Duke University Press, 1999), 251.

37. "Letter to General Education Board from Jackson Davis, 7 April 1924," Rockefeller Archives.

38. J. D. Barbee, "Bishop Beebe and the Colored Methodist Episcopal Church in America," *Christian Advocate*, June 18, 1881.

39. Othal Hawthorne Lakey, *The History of the CME Church (Revised)* (Memphis, TN: CME Publishing House, 1996), 443.

40. Early on, CME Church leaders made a distinction between institutions supported solely by the CME Church and those institutions supported by both the CME Church and MECS, like Paine College. In advertisements for both schools, the advertisement for Lane states in big, bold letters that it is a CME Church-supported school. See *Christian Index*, October 8, 1887.

41. Glenn T. Eskew, "Black Elitism and the Failure of Paternalism in Postbellum Georgia: The Case of Bishop Lucius Henry Holsey," *Journal of Southern History* 58, no. 4 (November 1992): 663.

42. *Christian Index*, December 3, 1908.

43. *Autobiography of Bishop Isaac Lane*, 98.

44. United States Department of the Interior, National Park Service, *National Register of Historic Places Inventory—Nomination Form* (October 1979), http://focus.nps.gov/pdfhost/docs/NRHP/Text/80002290.pdf (accessed April 1, 2016).

45. National Negro Business League, "Tenth Annual Convention" (conference proceedings, Louisville, KY, August, 18–20, 1909).

46. Brian Lanker, *I Dream a World: Portraits of Black Women Who Changed America* (New York: Stewart, Tabori & Chang, 1989), 126; Raymond Somerville, *An Ex-Colored Church: Social Activism in the CME Church, 1870–1970* (Macon, GA: Mercer University Press, 2004), 150.

47. Somerville, *An Ex-Colored Church: Social Activism in the CME Church, 1870–1970*, 150.

48. David M. Callejo-Pérez, *Southern Hospitality: Identity, Schools, and the Civil Rights Movement in Mississippi, 1964–1972* (New York: P. Lang, 2001), 20–23.

Religious History beyond Institutions

Spirit in the Air

Pentecostal and Holiness Media Innovation in the Twentieth-Century South

RANDALL STEPHENS

Charles Reagan Wilson has fittingly observed that one of the most significant religious phenomena of the 1980s was the emergence, or at least widespread public awareness, of the electronic church. When combined with the conservative political activities of key white televangelists, it proved to be a development that not even the editorial team of the *New York Times* could ignore. Writing in the wake of TV preacher scandals, journalist Peter Applebome remarked: "Religious broadcasting is stronger and more diverse now than it was when the scandals erupted."[1] Of the thriving and public visibility of televangelism Wilson noted: "This was not exclusively a southern phenomenon. But many of the leading televangelists easily emerged from the southern religious culture— Pat Robertson and Jerry Falwell in Virginia, Jimmy Lee Swaggart in Louisiana, Oral Roberts in Oklahoma, James Robertson in Texas. Even non-southerners like Jim and Tammy Faye Bakker had to come south, to North Carolina, to make their evangelical empire of the air."[2] Indeed, in 1987, according to Nielson ratings, four of the most-watched religious programs on television were hosted by southern Pentecostals. Jimmy Swaggart's *Gospel Hour* vied for the top spot with Robert Schuller's *Hour of Power*.[3] In 1985, the *Directory of Religious Broadcasters* counted 1,043 radio stations and ninety-six TV stations. Just four years later, in the Reagan era of deregulation, that number had jumped to 1,485 radio stations and 336 television stations.[4] The 1980s was a boom time for the electronic church, and southern Pentecostals led the way. In coming years, African American Word of Faith and Pentecostal ministers like T. D. Jakes and Creflo Dollar would join the ranks of these highly visible religious stars.

The link between Holiness and Pentecostal faith and tech savviness was not accidental. Accordingly, the religious studies scholar Birgit Meyer takes note of the "technological mastery and up-to-dateness" of Pentecostals. This is a feature that largely defines the movement around the globe. Writes Meyer: "Many researchers have been struck by Pentecostalism's skillful and efficient appropriation of modern mass media, such as radio, television, film, and audio-cassettes." Pentecostals have used these resources, says Meyer, to spread the movement. She points out how "traveling crusades, the circulation of books, tapes, and DVDs, and the beaming of televangelists' radio and television programs have been central to capturing broad audiences."[5] Yet some questions about the American and southern context deserve further exploration. Why did so many celebrity TV preachers hail from the South, and why were so many of them Holiness people or Pentecostals? What were the links between this ecstatic faith, pop culture, and media innovation?

Some of the most high-profile TV preachers of the 1970s and '80s, like fundamentalist Baptist Jerry Falwell, who first began his TV broadcasts in 1956, proclaimed that their growing audience and wide appeal was a sure sign of God's hand. There were certainly more mundane factors involved. Historian Daniel Williams comments that the development "reflected a national trend in which young, dynamic pastors create colossal church empires in metropolitan areas by reaching out to recent Southern migrants who had come to the city in search of industrial jobs."[6]

The message went well beyond US borders, too.[7] And while media-driven Pentecostalism made enormous headway in the Global South, it also gained ground in other unlikely places as well. A well-known Pentecostal megachurch televangelist from San Antonio, John Hagee, appears on Christian TV in Norway's Bible Belt, stretching across the country's southern regions. To the east, in Sweden, Livets Ord Theological Seminary in Uppsala operated for twenty years as a branch of Oral Roberts University, training charismatic ministers in Scandinavia.[8] It may be that the prosperity gospel and the linking of new media and ecstatic faith are among America's largest, most successful religious exports. Religious studies scholar Kate Bowler notes that "the prosperity gospel proved readily exportable. ... [W]e can see clearly that preachers and ideas bounced back and forth in the global spiritual market."[9] The gospel of wealth, health, and happiness, preached with such vigor on the Trinity Broadcasting Network and Daystar Television, gained ground in European nations as well as Brazil, the Philippines, South Korea, and Nigeria. Pentecostal ministers outside the states proved just as adept at using radio, TV, and, later, social media to champion the cause.

In the postwar American boom years "pastorpreneurs" in Dixie and across the Sunbelt took advantage of new technological developments and coordinated sophisticated ministries with paid professionals. Their typical message as well—promising success, riches from heaven, control over life's problems, and strong families—was well-suited for postwar consumers, who had been marinated in positive thinking and had come to expect great things from technological innovation. Yet this was true of much of America. So why were radio and television ministries so disproportionately dominated by Holiness and Pentecostal groups? Were observers wrong to class believers with the anti-modern forces of resistance to change?

For much of the twentieth and even twenty-first centuries, critics in the secular media and the academy have described traditional conservative Protestantism as regressive, out of step with modernity, and lacking innovative qualities. Birgit Meyer and Annelies Moor note such false associations in their work on media and religion: "If religion assumes a marked public role, this is taken to be a sign of the society's backwardness or at least the backward orientation of the religious movement in question. This perspective on the public sphere as a secular space is intrinsic to a modernist attitude toward society. Such a view was mobilized in the colonial era to legitimize the alleged necessity of the colonial state to control and contain religion, above all Islam."[10] In recent years, popular and influential new atheists such as Richard Dawkins, Sam Harris, and Christopher Hitchens have argued that traditional conservative religion is necessarily reactionary, atavistic, and bad for society as a whole. Media and religious studies scholar Heidi Campbell remarks that "there's been a tendency throughout history to see science, technology, and modernity as essentially in conflict with religion and religious communities. . . . This continues to be a popular and often overarching characterization in contemporary times that religious groups and institutions are innately suspicious of technology and thus typically reject or strongly resist new forms, especially media technologies."[11]

This standard perspective neither recognizes nor explains the importance of innovation and creativity within American evangelicalism, Pentecostalism, and fundamentalism, the key religious pillars (along with traditionalist Catholicism) of the modern conservative movement. Stalwarts in the South and across the US grappled with the challenges of the modern world in theological and culturally innovative ways. Missionary outreach, evangelistic techniques, and the shock of the new all challenged believers to reimagine the faith in the modern era. The call to evangelize frequently drove the innovative impulse.

"Innovation" in itself is a slippery term. But for the sake of some working definition, it might be defined in the following ways: doctrinal (new beliefs and ideas), technical (participation in or support of scientific developments and/or new modes of dissemination of ideas/beliefs/values), and social/public (conversion of doctrinal/technical innovation into new social/political/economic policies, programs, and activism). Certainly believers innovated in any number of ways: the early use of radio and television by religious communities and individuals, media and Billy Graham's world crusades, evangelical internationalism and American foreign policy, Pentecostal healing ministries, megachurches and media, and evangelical involvement in space exploration and engineering. For the sake of a more fine-tuned study, the focus here will be on Pentecostals and Holiness people in the South and will show how they used and made sense of technological developments.

A look back to the beginning of the twentieth century helps contextualize Pentecostal innovation. After that, a focus on two significant southern media pioneers, one black and one white, within the Holiness-Pentecostal tradition will shed further light on how and why spirit-filled believers adopted the latest means to promote their old-time message. It was not just in the realm of new media that southern Pentecostals, Holiness people, and charismatics set themselves apart. From the outset, enthusiasts from Dixie proved to be pioneers in other ways as well. Since the beginning of the century, they had been eager to promote their message in almost any fashion that would yield maximum success.

Since Pentecostalism's inception in a gaudy, castle-like Victorian mansion in turn-of-the-century Topeka, Kansas, and its growth and spread after a more forceful, wide-reaching revival in Los Angeles in 1906, initiates used technologies and novelties to evangelize with gusto. Indeed, even their forebears in the Holiness and Higher Life movements employed singing evangelists and gospel wagons bedecked with banners that read "Jesus Is Coming Soon!" It is likely that Holiness folk and Pentecostals' furious denunciation of the theater and moving pictures had something to do with the threat such entertainment posed. Could the stage antics of the most athletic and exuberant revivalist compete with the magic of the silver screen? How would the acrobatic, masculine preaching of even a Billy Sunday stand up against the swashbuckling heroism of Douglas Fairbanks or the comic capers of Charlie Chaplin?

In the 1950s, a similar fear fanned out over churches across the Bible Belt. Did the old-time religion have to compete now with newfangled celebrities and sideburned rock and rollers? In 1957, a Wichita radio station threatened to drop a local pastor's show because the station hoped to update its formatting with new music. Incensed, the Nazarene preacher wondered how society had sunk so low as to drive religion off the dial. "I just can't believe that thousands of people in care homes, hospitals, and religious people who are unable to attend the church of their choice," said the Holiness pastor, "would rather listen all day Sunday to Elvis Presley and 'Hound Dog,' the Coasters and 'The Idol with the Golden Head,' or Little Richard and 'Rock around the Clock.'" Of course, the latter was not a Little Richard song. Yet despite his confusion, the radio pastor's message was clear enough. Outraged listeners swamped the station with phone calls, telegrams, and protest letters. The minister's show was reinstated.[12]

Long before the advent of celebrity pop culture, Holiness and Pentecostal mavericks put much of their energy into print media, competing for attention with novels, secular newspapers, and more. It may be true that their tongues-speaking faith thrived as an oral culture, but its spread across the globe in the era before the radio also had much to do with the flurry of newspapers, tracts, books, and pamphlets that believers rolled off their presses.[13]

One of these enterprising Holiness printers was L. L. Pickett, born in Mississippi two years before the outbreak of the Civil War. He later lived in Texas, Arkansas, and South Carolina. Pickett became an influential evangelist, temperance reformer, and a writer of weepy, heartstring-tugging hymns. The printing press, he assured whoever would listen in the 1890s, would play a central role in spreading the message of Holiness around the world in these last days before the return of Christ. The Holiness movement, he wrote with a sense of Victorian hyperbole, was "harnessing the press to the car of a more spiritual and unctuous religious experience than has prevailed for many years." He was sure that "books, papers, and tracts are opening many eyes to the beauties of holiness, and feeding the many hungry souls with this 'hidden manna' of the Lord."[14]

The Kentucky revivalist and so-called tramp evangelist W. B. Godbey certainly agreed. He produced more printed material than perhaps anyone else in the movement, anxious to spread the perfectionist message throughout the land. By the time of his death in 1920, Godbey had written 230 books and booklets and penned hundreds, if not thousands, of editorials in Holiness journals. Godbey was one of many Holiness diehards who were quick to denounce Pentecostalism. He described the new offshoot faith in one of his many pamphlets as just another one of "Satan's Sidetracks for Holiness People."[15] He even made the trek to the Azusa Street revival of April 1906. Unlike countless other pilgrims who flocked to the rundown former barn and tombstone shop, Godbey was not impressed. The preacher, who styled himself an expert in languages ancient and modern, reported of his visit: "I had a language, but they did not, as the demons who imparted the counterfeit . . . cannot give a language."[16]

During the interwar years, most Pentecostals had shed some of their more peculiar features. Many who had once championed pacifism had decided, with the onset of World War II, that military participation did not conflict with gospel truth. There were fewer women in the ministry now, too, with the exception of high-profile evangelists like Sister Aimee Semple McPherson and later Kathryn Kuhlman. The biracial revival had fanned out from Azusa Street in Los Angeles and made its way across the country to the inner coastal plains town of Dunn, North Carolina. But the racial interchange that drew so much outrage from critics could not last. In 1912 the *Atlanta Constitution* ran a typically scandalous headline about one such meeting: "'Rollers' Have No Color Line. West End Citizens Object to Whites and Blacks Mingling." In court, the reporter remarked, "Several witnesses stated that many white women joined the negroes in their wild demonstrations of 'religious intoxication,' as one termed it, and that the sight of a white woman in the embrace of a negress, dancing and shouting in the center of the congregation was a common spectacle."[17] The dictates of Jim Crow, along with the ubiquitous fear that Holiness and Pentecostals services were just one "embrace" shy of a mixed race orgy, disrupted the movements' interracialism. Black and white mixing did remain present among some groups. Oneness Pentecostals were one example. As the historian Paul Harvey puts it, "White Pentecostals gradually dissociated themselves from the racial interchange of their earlier origins. The early biracial Pentecostal services produced some genuine sentiments of Christian interracialism, but by the 1920s black and white believers had settled into racially distinct separate organizations."[18] In subsequent years, and until the influx of Mexican immigrants, the congregations of the Church of God in Christ, the Assemblies of God, the Pentecostal Holiness Church, and the Church of God (Cleveland, Tennessee) took on a monochromatic hue.

First-generation Pentecostals also had to learn the hard way that they were not as ready as they had thought to preach the gospel in every land before the second coming of Jesus. What seemed to them like the gift of xenoglossia was, in fact, anything but. Missionaries who entered the field equipped with what they believed were native languages quickly discovered that they were mistaken.[19] With all the harsh lessons and the discontinuity there were certain features of the faith in both black and white communities that remained constant. From the outside, journalists and academics pinpointed the unrestrained worship they witnessed in Holiness and Pentecostal churches. They also found that the music, the range of musical instruments, and the clapping or syncopated beats set such churches apart from other Christian communities. For their part, insiders were quick to confirm that Holy Ghost religion was lively, powerful, and unique. In the mid-1960s, an Ohio anthropologist heard as much in interviews he conducted with the saints of inner-city black storefront churches. One interviewee for the study wanted to set things right: "A lot of folks talk about getting too emotional," he confided. "I wouldn't give two cents for a religion that wouldn't make me move. My God is a living God." Energetic services and spirited music in this telling proved the truth and godliness of the movement.[20]

In the middle years of the century, other sociologists and scholars of religion found much the same when it came to the churches they researched. Some asked just how did Pentecostalism and Holiness churches differ from their religious competitors. In the late 1950s, Cloyd V. Gustafson, a University of Chicago sociologist of religion, completed his dissertation on fundamentalist churches in Portland, Oregon. Here he spent some time observing Assemblies of God services and interviewing ministers and laypeople. He hoped to learn more about the social, economic, and belief systems of his subjects. One white Assemblies church included in his study was situated in an industrial section of town, surrounded by auto-supply shops and wholesale agencies. Though far removed from the denomination's stronghold of the South and border South, the congregation worshipped, sang, and prayed in ways quite similar to fellow believers across the country. The Portland church, made up of sixty or sixty-five persons, thought Gustafson, was composed primarily of lower-class believers. Regardless of the plight of the people and the church's shabby decor, he noted, it "was brightened by a grand piano, an electric organ, and there was a microphone on the pulpit and a loud speaker for the benefit of the hard-of-hearing."[21] Gustafson then delved into the music and the order of the service. The music was powerful and played to lift the spirits and heighten emotions:

> Usually the piano was played by a middle-aged woman, and the electric organ by her sixteen-year-old daughter, but Rev. T, the pastor, played one or the other on occasion and sometimes played his accordion in the service besides. Mrs. T., wife of the pastor, usually led the singing. On one occasion she accompanied her husband's accordion number on the double bass. All of this music seemed designed to keep up the courage and enthusiasm of the group, and this was clearly an effort at times. In one of these services the writer first heard "speaking in tongues" by an elderly man, apparently an aged relative of the pianist. Mrs. T. had led in a hymn, then came the call for prayer. All prayed aloud at once, eyes closed and arms uplifted. The glossolalia began without marked emotion, a jumble of syllables uttered smoothly and without hesitation as though it were routinized by frequent repetition. There was frequent repetition of hard consonants like K, G, also T, B, and R, and the vowels seemed broad, so that the effect vaguely resembled Japanese. The voice rose and fell in normal melody and inflection meanwhile. At subsequent services this performance was repeated several times. Each instance would last for three or four minutes.[22]

Gustafson found that the Assemblies of God churches he visited conformed with fundamentalists along certain doctrinal and organizational lines. Their speaking in tongues, of course, set them apart, as did their much more demonstrative worship. Related to that, claimed Gustafson, their "use of orchestral instruments such as the accordion, clarinet, trombone, and bass violin in formal worship is divergent from conventional Protestantism." Then, with a note of condescension, Gustafson ventured: "The use of these instruments probably represents an adjustment to the prevailing tastes which popular radio programs have inculcated in an uncritical constituency."[23]

These innovations in worship, music, and style appeared among black Pentecostal or sanctified churches as well. Researchers, who sat for hours in tumble-down tabernacles, glory barns, or storefront churches encountered worshipers who played the drums, electric guitars, and trumpets, shouted at the top of their lungs, stomped their feet in unison, all the while carving out a new and exciting religious identity for themselves.

Another sociologist, Vattel Elbert Daniel of Wiley College in Texas, surveyed the black religious landscape of Chicago in the late 1930s and early 1940s, populated as it was by recent arrivals from the South. Along with looking at liturgical and mainstream Protestant congregations, he and his research assistants also observed the workings of a group of what he termed "Ecstatic Cults." Instruments in such churches included piano, "percussion, such as drums, tamborines [sic], triangles and sometimes a wind instrument, usually a trumpet." The services, with a charismatic leader at the helm, were "highly theatrical and it is recognized by rapid and rhythmic movement; at times, in some of the cults, the ecstasy becomes so great that pandemonium reigns." Daniel took in what he thought amounted to chaos with some sense of wonder:

> In most cases, the frenzy includes yelling, tapping, stamping, shouting, and, in some instances, running and jumping, including the type which resembles the movements of a jumping jack. Loud praying while standing with hands uplifted, and speaking in tongues while in a similar position constitute the climax of the ecstatic behavior, although this was not so prevalent as were the rhythmic hand-clapping and foot-patting.[24]

Such worship contrasted markedly, he thought, with the worship that took place in more traditional churches—Congregational, Presbyterian, and Episcopal. Referring to his "Ecstatic Cults" with the derogatory term "holy rollers," Daniel figured that they set themselves apart from so many other churches by

> speaking in tongues, in which the believers repeat rapidly and loudly unintelligible symbols; . . . healing ritual, in which the sick are anointed with oil and surrounded by a praying, singing, and dancing group; saint-making ritual, in which believers are supposed to receive the Holy Ghost, after white-robed saints kneel with them and pray loudly, accompanied by rapidly repeated rhythmical assent, while the pianist plays a revival hymn. . . .[25]

Roughly twenty years after Daniel's study, journalists were still trying to figure out what attracted people to these strange "cults." But some had a more sympathetic eye than others. Louis Cassels, a prominent, prolific religious reporter who was employed by United Press International, began taking stock of Pentecostalism's growth and influence in the early 1960s, not long after *Life* magazine included a lengthy feature story and photo essay on the movement.[26] "At their worship services," wrote Cassels in August of 1960, "Pentecostals display their feelings in an uninhibited and often exuberant way. They shout, clap hands, sing, and march." Even more unusual, he reported, was that "some may speak in tongues or fall to the floor in a trance." The latter gave birth to the notorious "holy roller" epithet.[27] Other pejorative labels included "tonguers" and "bible thumpers." Unlike twentieth-century Methodists, Baptists, or Presbyterians, Holiness folk, and Pentecostals faced heavy criticism and the outright condemnation of outsiders.

Outsider and mainline Protestant disdain for Holiness or Pentecostal practices can be traced to any number of sources. Methodists and Baptists found the worship, tongues-speaking, and demonstrative gestures as scandalous as they were ludicrous.[28] Non-Pentecostals also recoiled at what they sensed was a kind of sanctified pride or boastfulness within these communities. One Louisiana Methodist had that in mind when he penned a letter to *Christianity Today* in 1963 to chastise Pentecostals: "I have found Pentecostalists choosing to dissociate themselves from the major orthodox denominations," he vented, "because they claim to offer the Holy Ghost (pronounced HO-lyghost) as a bonus to people already 'saved.'" He wondered, in jest, if this amounted to a "Christian aristocracy."[29] Others may have been stung by the excitement and success the new movement generated. Indeed, Holiness and Pentecostal groups grew at an extraordinary rate in the twentieth century.

In addition, Pentecostals proved even more enthusiastic about publishing and new media than their grumbling, anti-tongues Holiness brethren. Not surprisingly in the 1920s, on the eve of the radio era, stalwarts eagerly embraced the new technology to serve their purposes. In California, Sister Aimee Semple McPherson made much of radio's wonder-working powers. It may be that believers' tendency to infuse technology with religious meaning made them more willing to use it than non-Holiness or non-Pentecostal groups and individuals. Like other Pentecostals of her generation, McPherson rhapsodized about the staggering, evangelistic potential of technology. For her, radio was

> like some fantastic dream! Like a visionary tale from the Arabian Nights! Like an imaginary fairy tale is the Story of Radio.... These are the days of invention! The days when the impossible has become possible! Days more favorable than any that ever have been known for the preaching of the blessed Gospel of our Lord

and Saviour, Jesus Christ! Now, the crowning blessing, the most golden opportunity, the most miraculous conveyance for the Message has come—The Radio!³⁰

An equally exuberant contemporary of Sister Aimee's used recordings, radio, television, and Hollywood showmanship as few other ministers did. In 1934, a reporter at the *Washington Post* called the African American Holiness preacher Elder Lightfoot Solomon Michaux "the best known colored man in the United States today." The savvy, popular preacher, said the journalist, "is a combination of all the qualities of Billy Sunday, Ben Franklin, Aimee Semple McPherson . . . and Father Coughlin, rolled into one."³¹

Michaux's early history is shrouded in some mystery. But he was likely born in 1884 in Newport News, Virginia, one of thirteen children in a strict Baptist household. He followed his father and became a fishmonger, developing a profitable business particularly during World War I. Still, as a youth he was attracted to the Church of Christ (Holiness) and its lively style of worship. Ordained in the relatively new denomination, he rose quickly within its ranks. About fifty years later, one critic recalled that Michaux preached "on street corners and small southern Virginia towns—with a whoop-it-up religion that attracted hundreds."³² When the denomination's leader and founder Charles Jones called on Michaux to take a pulpit that was not to his liking, Michaux, now in his late thirties, bolted from the Church of Christ (Holiness) and would go on to form a new denomination, the Gospel Spreading Church of God. He set himself apart early on as a powerful preacher, with an unusual presence in the pulpit. His vocal range and animated gestures stood out. One researcher, who conducted numerous interviews with Michaux's flock, recounted his "inflection, making his voice subdued and clear, loud and raspy." The well-known minister also "moved from an ordinary speaking rhythm to a sing-song cadence, holding certain words longer for emphasis."³³

At the end of the 1920s, this energetic, high-spirited minister made a name for himself and launched a local radio show on WJSV in Alexandria, Virginia. The show was soon featured on fifty stations. Called the *Radio Church of God*, the program was reaching an astonishing twenty-five million listeners on Saturdays in 1934. In addition, two million listeners tuned into it on a daily basis. In 1933, Michaux had begun publishing a twelve-page monthly newspaper called *Happy News* to run alongside his radio work. It was little wonder that the celebrity preacher received roughly one thousand pieces of mail each day. But that was just part of what this entrepreneurial and innovative evangelist set his hands to in these years. Michaux set up an employment agency, established a low-cost housing complex, and launched what he called the Happy News Café, which fed his Washington, DC, congregants in exchange for their work.

Michaux also held massive outdoor revivals at Griffith Stadium in Washington, DC, with crowds ranging over thirty thousand.[34]

So widespread was Michaux's fame in the Depression years that *Time* magazine took note. One of its reporters recounted the razzle-dazzle of the minister's radio sermons, peppered as they were with positive thinking and rousing songs, like his enormous record and radio hit "Happy Am I." Written by two whites from Georgia, the song became such a standard for the preacher that he bought its copyright in 1932.[35] For Michaux's massive meetings, noted a writer in *Time* magazine,

> he needs large auditoriums or stadiums. Announcing all his programs as coming from "the banks of the Potomac," Elder Michaux sometimes conducts mammoth baptismal services, with white-clad participants splashing in the river or Chesapeake Bay and spectators on gaily decorated barges and excursion boats. Last summer he scandalized District of Columbia officials by asking leave to baptize a flock in the reflecting pool in front of the Lincoln Memorial.[36]

The writer thought such gimmicks linked Michaux with another celebrated, if highly controversial, Pentecostal minister, Father Divine, though the former made no claims to divinity. It is little wonder that Michaux and the equally famous African American Pentecostal leader Daddy Grace, who, not to be outdone, conducted his mass outdoor baptisms with a fire hose, would become archrivals.[37] Such creative spectacles awed other observers. The Pulitzer Prize–winning novelist William Styron witnessed the mass baptisms of Michaux and Daddy Grace many times in his youth, as he recalled to a friend in the late summer of 1980. These events, reminisced Styron, "were held in the shallow water near the Little Boat Harbour, where the ferry to Norfolk docked.... Thousands of Negroes showed up from all over Va. & N.C. Tidewaters," he said, "and I remember the Fox Movietone newsreel people also covered it. Quite a sight, all those black people (mostly women) in their white turbans and robes, hollering Hallelujah."[38]

Michaux lived in style, much like Grace and other African American celebrity preachers of the era. In the late 1930s, Michaux oversaw his works from an extravagant house and presided over seven churches. He gave a reporter a tour of his home in 1938. Walking across an expensive Kodiak bear rug to his living room, he bragged, "I could be a millionaire if I wanted to, but I don't care about money." Nonetheless, when the well-known minister and song evangelist died in 1969, he left a multimillion-dollar estate and ranked as one of the wealthiest African American figures of the postwar era. Michaux seemed to care deeply and have a level of pride about his influence and his multiethnic ministry.[39] For instance, he counted Franklin Delano Roosevelt as a fan. The president enjoyed his high-energy programs and his sunny, cheery message for Depression-era America.[40] Michaux, in fact, was instrumental in ushering tens of thousands of African Americans into the Democratic Party. As one headline aptly put it in this era: "Elder Michaux, Evangelist, Battles Devil, Republicans."[41]

Certainly much of the celebrity Holiness preacher's appeal came from his skillful packaging of the gospel message. In his willingness to use gimmicks, stunts, and headline-grabbing showmanship, he followed in the footsteps of Sister Aimee and Billy Sunday. For instance, Michaux conducted spectacular dramatic tableaus in Griffith Stadium. His 150-member "Cross Choir" dazzled those who attended his church services and others who listened on the radio. The church advertised enormous outdoor baptisms and other campaigns in newspapers and through area businesses. Busses and cars were bedecked with announcements. On one occasion in 1950, Micahux had twelve barrels of water shipped from the Jordan River, supposedly verified by a missionary in Israel. Michaux not only appears to have had a knack for whimsical religious spectacles, he and his church also fostered some of the best musical talent of the age. One of the most prominent figures associated with Michaux's radio show and church services was Mahalia Jackson, the gospel legend and a soloist in the minister's impressive choir. Jackson began performing in the church while still in her late teens. From radio stardom, she recorded her trademark blend of gospel and blues with Decca and Apollo Records. In the coming decades, she would launch her own radio program, sing at the Eisenhower White House, and perform at John F. Kennedy's 1961 inauguration.[42] Joining Jackson on stage and over the airwaves under Michaux's direction was the lauded "first lady of gospel music," Clara Mae Ward. On the WJSB Radio Church of God the two were the most conspicuous, and later to become world-renowned, singers from the church.[43]

The choir, though, was just one of many of Michaux's selling points. His thundering message and flair for the theatrical drew in white and black crowds. On one occasion, he even held extravagant "funeral services" for the Devil, splayed out in a glass coffin. In the chilly international climate of the Cold War, Elder Michaux held a series of revivals in Alaska. While there, he charted an airplane, costing $100 an hour, which piloted him over the Bering Sea near Siberia. Here he had a Bible dropped into the churning waters, proclaiming that the current would wash it to the Soviet shore. He confidently told reporters, "what the Russians need is an atomic Bible, not an atomic bomb."[44]

Michaux's gospel of happiness and Holiness purity drew the ire of plenty of detractors. Just as ministers, critics, and journalists had aimed their sites at Father Divine and Sweet Daddy Grace, they turned their angry attention to the "Happy Am I" preacher. Black as well as white high-profile evangelists faced similar scorn. In 1956, the southern Pentecostal television healing revivalist Oral Roberts confronted an array of doubters. The Oklahoman's nationwide evangelism was little more than tawdry big business, observed the *Hartford Courant*.[45] Michaux's flashy, religion-as-entertainment style and Holiness music did not sit well with numerous black critics either. In 1934, a writer in the *Baltimore Afro American* newspaper extolled and criticized Michaux in the same breath. The "jazz pastor" had amassed "the largest and most widely distributed radio audience that any member of our group has developed in this country. He has a larger interracial congregation of regular listeners than any preacher." What accounted for all the success, journalists wanted to know. Michaux was little more than "a showman." He appealed to the base emotions of his congregants and his avid, if misguided, radio listeners. Said the critic, he did not "encourage active thinking."[46] That kind of naysaying did little to dent the minister's popularity or appeal, which remained strong into the 1950s. From 1949 to 1951, Michaux even branched out into the new world of television ministry.

Never as well known, or as influential, as Michaux, the white southern Pentecostal minister James Hamill also experimented with media and new music. Hamill spent most of his career pastoring an Assemblies of God church in Memphis. Born in 1913 in Pugh's Mill, Mississippi, Hamill began preaching in country churches in his late teens after feeling called to the ministry. As an evangelist, he traveled widely and served as a pastor in Columbia, Tennessee; Hattiesburg, Mississippi; Hope, Arkansas; and Okmulgee, Oklahoma. In 1944, Hamill took up the pastorate of Memphis First Assembly, where he remained for thirty-seven years.[47] The congregation itself actually predated the denomination and was originally a radical Holiness church. Two early figures who were attached to the church, M. M. Pinson and H. G. Rodgers, became leading first-generation Pentecostals in the South. In these first years, the church even published its own newspaper, *Grace and Truth*. Before Hamill entered the First Assembly pulpit, the congregation had had a rocky history, filled as it was with break-off factions and numerous moves from buildings, tents, and tabernacles. It finally secured a more permanent building at 1084 East McLemore in 1948.[48]

In the same year the church settled into its new home, a family of three, hailing from Tupelo, Mississippi, made the move to the bustling city. Soon after their arrival, Vernon and Gladys Presley, along with their teenage son Elvis, began attending Hamill's growing, thriving First Assembly. Hamill described the young Elvis as a shy country boy whose clothes did not quite fit and whose hair was too long. The youngster, remembered Hamill, was always polite and became a fixture in the church.

In this same period, Pastor Hamill, now becoming a popular denominational leader, reported on the successes of the church.[49] "Scores have been saved and baptized in the Holy Spirit," he enthused in the denomination's magazine.

"Seldom a Sunday has passed but that from one to a dozen have professed Christ as Savior. The membership of the church has more than doubled." There were other signs of growth and achievement in these prosperous postwar years. The Sunday school that young Elvis was attending had grown from 130 in 1944, to 371 in 1946, and then 1,361 in 1952.[50] In 1947, the church reported $1,500 in foreign mission offerings. A decade later that had risen to $25,000.[51]

Hamill was certainly a rising star in the denomination and a highly sought-after speaker and revivalist. The Assemblies of God proudly described Hamill as "one of the outstanding Pentecostal preachers in the South." Hamill's educational programs claimed the second-largest attendance in the General Council, only outpaced by an Assemblies of God church in Dallas.[52] He sent regular updates of his growing church's work to the denomination's chief publication. "We recently concluded a successful revival," he announced in November 1950. "Many times the crowd overflowed the auditorium and balcony," rhapsodized Hamill. He also reported that some were baptized with the Holy Spirit, often accompanied with speaking in tongues, and many testified that they had been healed.[53]

Hamill found ways to broaden his constituency and build on his growing reputation. The Memphis pastor did not have the same reach and appeal attained by Michaux, but Hamill nonetheless was experimenting with peppy music and new media in similarly inventive ways. He launched a weekly newspaper for the congregation called the *Memphis Mirror*. First Assembly also developed a new radio program, *Words of Life*, not long afterward.[54] By 1957, the church was even sponsoring a weekly television program, *Christ Is the Answer*, which became one of the most popular, wide-reaching religious telecasts in the American South. In the mid-South, it was second only to Billy Graham's TV program.[55]

The Assemblies of God had already been putting a great deal of effort into radio broadcasting with its popular *Revivaltime* program, launched in 1950 out of Springfield, Missouri. Soon, ABC Radio was broadcasting the show to three hundred stations across the country. Listeners sent in between 12,000 and 15,000 letters each month. Host C. M. Ward spoke directly to his audience, personalizing the message for the masses.[56] Ward embodied the kind of astute Pentecostal pragmatism that historian Grant Wacker has detailed. In a kind of spirit-filled celebration of technology, Ward proclaimed that pastors "must not apologize for jet, television, penicillin, kidney transplant, travel to the moon. He must be quick to detect motions of the Spirit of God in the movements of society. He must have gifts operative of discernment and interpretation."[57]

Hamill tapped into his denomination's existing eagerness to proclaim the gospel over the air and with vibrant music. When asked about the nature of his church's growth and success, Hamill told a denominational official: "The secret in my opinion is spirituality, good organization, consecrated personnel, the consistent improvement of facilities, sound and sensible promotion of the program, and hard work!"[58] It most certainly also owed something to the lively, stirring music the church sponsored and the willingness to use the latest technologies. Hamill, like Michaux, was more than willing to bring in flashy, new gospel quartets.

At Memphis First Assembly, a young and impressionable Elvis sat at the feet of gospel greats like the Blackwood Brothers and the Stamps Quartet. These two major vocal groups proved to be critical innovators of white southern gospel. Members from both attended First Assembly. Elvis regularly attended the Blackwood Brothers' live radio broadcasts at WMPS. One of the group's songs of this era—their 1953 cover version of Thomas Dorsey's "Everyday Will Be Sunday By and By" (1950)—includes an upbeat tempo and bouncy piano, vocal harmonies soaring from bass to high tenor. The influence on Elvis's style and delivery is unmistakable. It is little wonder that the future star also went to the popular gospel concerts held at Memphis's Ellis Auditorium.[59] An eager fan, he even hoped to join a local group called the Songfellows Quartet. The teenage Elvis auditioned for them at the time that he was still working as a truck driver. The group's leader told the enthusiastic Elvis that he could not hear harmony and the quartet turned him down. The rejection did nothing to diminish his love of gospel music, made stronger during these crucial years at First Assembly.[60]

In 1972, Elvis, in something of a pill-induced haze, recalled the influence such groups had on him: "We grew up with it. From the time I was ... like two years old ... because my folks took me there. When I got old enough, I started to sing in church." The interviewer pressed further. Was that why he became a singer? It was among the reasons, replied Elvis. "The gospel is ... what we grew up with, more than anything else."[61] Not long after Elvis hit it big in 1956, he occasionally reflected on his religious and musical education in Hamill's church and other Pentecostal tabernacles he and his family frequented. In September, he opened up to a Canadian reporter who was asking the twenty-one-year-old star about his musical roots. "'Ah never sang anywhere before except in church,' said Elvis. 'Ah sang for 12 years in the choir of the First Assembly of God, a Pentecostal church in my hometown of Osceola. Where's that? About forty miles from Memphis, Tennessee.'" The reporter wanted to know what church people thought about Elvis's novel music. "'Ah don't know,' said Elvis, as though the idea had never occurred to him. 'Of course, truly religious people don't talk about that sort of thing. Ah know Ah gets invited back to church by Reverend James E. Hammill [sic] every time Ah goes home. Ah've also sung at Youth for Christ meetings, and Teen-agers for Christ.'" But was the style of that singing the same, questioned the reporter. "'Well,' said Elvis, 'a hymn is different.'"[62]

More than ten years later, Elvis reflected a little more on the roots of rock during his NBC '68 *Comeback Special*. Sitting next to his original drummer, D. J. Fontana, and guitarist, Scotty Moore, the sweating, leather-clad Elvis observed: "Rock and roll music is basically, uh, Gospel or Rhythm and Blues, and uh, it sprang from that. And people have been adding to it, adding instruments to it, experimenting with it."[63] It surely seemed shocking to Pentecostals to think that their church music had anything to do with rock. But the links were unmistakable. New, vibrant performance styles and the revved up music of Holiness and Pentecostal churches also inspired Little Richard, Johnny Cash, B. B. King, Jerry Lee Lewis, Ray Charles, and a host of lesser-known rockers and R&B performers.

Let us return to the question that we began with—why did southern Holiness and Pentecostal believers prove to be so inventive in their music, styles of worship, use of technology, and the vitality of their message? Richard Flory and Kimon Sargeant suggest that

> Pentecostals have also proven adept at capitalizing on their ability to put different media forms to innovative use in promoting and publicizing their endeavors. While there are certainly examples of Pentecostal groups that are utilizing newer forms of digital media such as email blasts, texting, websites, or Facebook, often the most effective way to reach the masses with their message is through media that is much more pervasive in the areas of the world where Pentecostalism is seeing the most growth: television, radio, or even printing pamphlets to hand out en masse.... Thus in many ways, different forms of mass media, combined with the Pentecostal emphasis on the Spirit and the individual, creates and promotes the democratization of the sacred; it is available to all without the need of it being mediated through a priest, a ritual structure, or a religious hierarchy. This in itself gives Pentecostalism a competitive advantage over the more traditional forms of its Christian (and other) competitors.[64]

In the open marketplace of religion in the US, spirit-filled groups thrived. As English sociologist of religion David Martin observes: "Pentecostalism is a natural denizen of deregulated religious markets; its expansion benefits from, and reinforces, whatever pressure may already exist for deregulation. Thus it arose 'naturally' in the unregulated religious market of the United States but exported the pluralistic and competitive model to a Latin America where the Catholic monopoly subsumed all kinds of inspired religious activity."[65] The same was not true in countries like Britain where radio and television remained largely out of reach for enthusiasts. For instance, in the United States in 1960 the FCC made it easier than ever for religious programs to buy airtime from television and radio stations. In essence, the ruling favored conservative evangelicals, whose entrepreneurial and creative fundraising skills far exceeded their counterparts in the mainline.[66]

How did the mainline fair when compared to evangelicals and Pentecostals? As the evangelical and Pentecostal denominations grew substantially from the 1960s onward, mainline Protestantism declined in strength. Interestingly, this also coincided with the evangelical and Pentecostal embrace of television. That same enthusiasm for new media did not enliven mainline groups. According to Michele Rosenthal, leaders of mainline Protestantism, though passionate about scientific advancement and technological innovation, "remained reticent about television, and reluctant to use this new communications technology to promote their agenda." The Broadcast and Film Commission of the National Council of Churches critiqued television as driven by consumerism and spectacle. Negative appraisals of mass culture cast a critical eye on TV in particular. In a curious twist, writes Rosenthal, evangelicals may have been much more "modernist" in their adoption of new technology and a matching theological framework, whereas mainline liberal Protestants wavered when it came to the use of modern means to promote their message.[67]

Pentecostals' relationship to modernity surely bares some consideration. According to the historian Roger Robbins, the early leader of the movement, A. J. Tomlinson, is perhaps best described as a "plainfolk modernist." Radical Holiness enthusiasts celebrated human progress, believed in a close, personal God, and adopted the ideas and means of modern culture. In a related sense, David Martin suggests that Pentecostalism represents an alternate form of modernity and modernization. "Pentecostalism combines the technical modes of modernity," Martin notes, "with a freedom of the spirit capable of entering into the varied inspirited cultures of the two-thirds world and reassembling them under the Christian aegis of the one Holy Spirit."[68]

Finally, the southern Pentecostal and Holiness use of radio, television, and even newer technologies may also have something to do with their self-proclaimed outsider status. Religious studies scholar Stephen Stein remarks that "it is impossible to understand outsiders without a clear appreciation for the ways they dissented consciously from the mainstream. Any effort to tell the story of religious people at the edges must deal with both the margins and the mainstream, for tensions and dissent are at the heart of the outsider experience."[69] If mainline Protestants shunned media innovation or considered it vulgar or beneath the church, Pentecostals had no such compunctions. Black storefront churches or ramshackle glory barns did not attract members of the local Rotary Club or chamber of commerce. Some Pentecostals clung to their outsider status with pride. "Pentecostals are creating distinctive models for members to follow that will differentiate them from others; they are aware that many outsiders consider their behavior extreme," writes folklore and English scholar Elaine J. Lawless. "By creating standards that seem extreme to the outsider," Lawless writes, "Pentecostals create boundaries between themselves and others. They recognize that in so doing they often create negative images that are difficult to combat. The balance between 'different' and 'freakish' is not an easy one to maintain."[70]

Pentecostals' willingness to use print, radio, film, and television to promote their religion of the spirit may help explain the enormous growth of the movement in the last fifty years. Even further back, journalists were flagging the movement for its tremendous growth rate. Said reporter Louis Cassels in the year that Richard Nixon and John F. Kennedy vied for the presidency: "America's fast-growing Pentecostal movement is composed of more than twenty organized denominations plus uncounted thousands of independent local churches and store-front sects." And with an eye for important trends, Cassels concluded: "Many religious groups are expanding their membership at a faster rate than any other type of church."[71] The Holy Ghost religion that first took root in the US South in the early twentieth century, and which has had such a strong foothold in Dixie ever since, is now one of the largest branches of global Christianity. By the end of the twentieth century, Pentecostalism, and the related charismatic movement, had become one of the fastest-growing segments of world Christianity, numbering some 500 million adherents.[72] That is a very sizable potential TV audience indeed.

Notes

1. Peter Applebome, "Scandals Aside, TV Preachers Thrive: If a Minister Falls, His Viewers Only Need Change the Channel," *New York Times*, October 8, 1989.

2. Charles Reagan Wilson, *Judgment and Grace in Dixie: Southern Faiths from Faulkner to Elvis* (Athens, GA: University of Georgia Press, 1995), 16.

3. Dennis McDougal, "'Jim and Tammy Show' Held 13th Spot among Religious Programs," *Los Angeles Times*, March 28, 1987.

4. Applebome, "Scandals Aside, TV Preachers Thrive." Jonathan L. Walton describes the prevalence of the Pentecostal-style domination of religious broadcasting. He identifies "the neo-Pentecostal, Charismatic mainline, and Word of Faith movements as the three distinctive perspectives that constitute most of African American religious broadcasting.... From these three perspectives the leading producers of African American religious broadcasting, Bishop T. D. Jakes, Bishop Eddie Long, and Pastor Creflo Dollar, have emerged to inform the ministry of others." Jonathan L. Walton, *Watch This! The Ethics and Aesthetics of Black Televangelism* (New York: New York University Press, 2009), 101; Robert Joseph Taylor and Linda M. Chatters, "Religious Media Use Among African Americans, Black Caribbeans, and Non-Hispanic Whites Findings from the National Survey of American Life," *Journal of African American Studies* 15, no. 4 (December 2011): 434–35, 436–37.

5. Birgit Meyer, "Pentecostalism and Globalization," in *Studying Global Pentecostalism: Theories and Methods*, eds. Allan Anderson, Michael Bergunder, Andre F. Droogers, and Cornelis van der Laan (Berkeley: University of California Press, 2010), 123.

6. Daniel Williams, *God's Own Party: The Making of the Christian Right* (New York: Oxford University Press, 2010), 44. See also Jill Terry, "Oral Culture and Southern Fiction," *A Companion to the Literature and Culture of the American South*, eds. Richard Gray and Owen Robinson (Malden, MA: Blackwell Publishing, 2008), 528. For an excellent summary of the development and growth of radio and TV ministries, see R. Laurence Moore, *Selling God: American Religion in the Marketplace of Culture* (New York: Oxford University Press, 1994), 244–65.

7. Writes Helen Taylor: "Over several decades, there has been a large appetite for southern evangelical religion, encompassing gospel music and singers such as Mahalia Jackson as well as high profile preachers from Billy Graham to the founder of moral majority, Jerry Falwell." Helen Taylor, *Circling Dixie: Contemporary Southern Culture Through a Transatlantic Lens* (New Brunswick, NJ: Rutgers University Press, 2001), 12.

8. "Livets Ord: Additional Location," Oral Robert University, www.oru.edu/academics/resources/livets_ord.php.

9. Kate Bowler, *Blessed: A History of the American Prosperity Gospel* (New York: Oxford University Press, 2013), 230–31. See also William K. Kay, "Pentecostalism and Religious Broadcasting," *Journal of Beliefs and Values: Studies in Religion and Education* 30, no. 3 (December 2009): 245–54.

10. Birgit Meyer and Annelies Moor, introduction to *Religion, Media, and the Public Sphere*, eds. Birgit Meyer and Annelies Moor (Bloomington: Indiana University Press, 2006), 5.

11. Heidi Campbell, *When Religion Meets New Media* (New York: Routledge, 2010), 5.

12. "Radio: Wichita Radio Station Abandons Plan to Drop Religious Broadcasts," *Pentecostal Evangel*, November 17, 1957. See also " . . . Rock 'n' Roll Is Worse than Narcotic," *Pentecostal Evangel*, September 22, 1957.

13. On Holiness and Pentecostalism as oral traditions, see J. Lawrence Brasher, *The Sanctified South: John Lakin Brasher and the Holiness Movement* (Urbana: University of Illinois Press, 1994), xii, 69; Deborah Vansau McCauley, *Appalachian Mountain Religion: A History* (Urbana: University of Illinois Press, 1995), 257; Elmer T. Clark, *The Small Sects in America* (Nashville: Abingdon Press, 1965), 85, 98; Cheryl J. Sanders, *Saints in Exile: The Holiness-Pentecostal Experience in African America Religion and Culture* (New York: Oxford University Press, 1996), 49–52, 56; and Robert Mapes Anderson, *Vision of the Disinherited: The Making of American Pentecostalism* (New York: Oxford University Press, 1979), 223–27.

14. L. L. Pickett, prefatory introduction to B. Carradine, *Sanctification* (Nashville: Publishing House of the M.E. Church, South, 1892), 3; William C. Kostlevy, "PICKETT, L(eander) L(ycurgus)," *Historical Dictionary of the Holiness Movement*, ed. William C. Kostlevy (Lanham, MD: Scarecrow Press, 2001), 205.

15. William Baxter Godbey, "Satan's Sidetracks for Holiness People" (Nashville: Pentecostal Mission Publishing Company, n.d.).

16. W. B. Godbey, *Tongue Movement, Satanic* (Zarephath, NJ: Pillar of Fire, 1918), 4–5. W. B. Godbey, *Spiritualism, Devil-Worship and the Tongues Movement* (Cincinnati, OH: God's Revivalist Press, n.d.), 26; Barry W. Hamilton, *William Baxter Godbey: Itinerant Apostle of the Holiness Movement* (Lewiston, NY: Edwin Mellen Press, 2000), 259–64.

17. "'Rollers' Have No Color Line. West End Citizens Object to Whites and Blacks Mingling," *Atlanta Constitution*, June 30, 1912. Randall J. Stephens, *The Fire Spreads: Holiness and Pentecostalism in the American South* (Cambridge, MA: Harvard University Press, 2008), 238–45.

18. Paul Harvey, *Freedom's Coming: Religious Culture and the Shaping of the South from the Civil War to the Civil Rights Era* (Chapel Hill: University of North Carolina Press, 2005), 136. See also Grant Wacker, *Heaven Below: Early Pentecostals and American Culture* (Cambridge, MA: Harvard University Press, 2001), 230–35.

19. Stephens, *The Fire Spreads*, 216.

20. Ira E. Harrison, "The Storefront Church as a Revitalization Movement," *Review of Religious Research* 7, no. 3 (1966): 161.

21. Cloyd V. Gustafson, "The Sociology of Fundamentalism: A Typological Analysis Based on Selected Groups in Portland, Oregon, and Vicinity" (PhD diss., University of Chicago Divinity School, 1956), 85.

22. Ibid., 85–86.

23. Ibid., 89.

24. Vettel Elbert Daniel, "Ritual and Stratification in Chicago Negro Churches," *American Sociological Review* 7, no. 3 (June 1942): 360, quotes on 358 and 359.

25. Daniel, "Ritual and Stratification in Chicago Negro Churches," 355, 358. See California Pentecostal Holiness Church services described in James Bright Wilson, "Religious Leaders, Institutions, and Organizations among Certain Agricultural Workers in the Central Valley of California" (PhD diss., University of Southern California, 1944), 273–88.

26. "The Third Force in Christendom: Gospel-Singing, Doomsday-Preaching Sects Emerge as a Mighty Movement in World Religion," *Life*, June 9, 1958, 113–24.

27. Louis Cassels, "Pentecostal Movement Outgrowth of Religious Revivals of Nineteenth Century," *Lodi (California) News-Sentinel*, August 13, 1960.

28. Grant A. Wacker, "Travail of a Broken Family: Radical Evangelical Responses to the Emergence of Pentecostalism in America, 1906–1916," in *Pentecostal Currents in American Protestantism*, eds. Edith L. Blumhofer, Russell P. Spittler, and Grant A. Wacker (Urbana: University of Illinois Press, 1999), 23–49; Stephens, *The Fire Spreads*, 219–24.

29. Wallace P. Blackwood, "Pentecost," *Christianity Today*, February 15, 1963, 25.

30. *Bridal Call* (July 1923): 15.

31. James Nevin Miller, "Elder Michaux Makes War," *Washington Post*, October 28, 1934.

32. "Minister Who Left Estate Worth $7 Million," *Jet*, April 24, 1969, 20; "Lightfoot Solomon Michaux," in *Prime-Time Religion: An Encyclopedia of Religious Broadcasting*, eds. J. Gordon Melton, Phillip Charles Lucas, and Jon R. Stone (Phoenix, AZ: Oryx Press, 1997), 228–29.

33. Lillian A. Poe, "Elder Lightfoot Solomon Michaux: His Social and Political Interests and Influence" (PhD diss., College of William and Mary, 1975), 41.

34. Jonathan L. Walton, *Watch This! The Ethics and Aesthetics of Black Televangelism* (New York: New York University Press, 2009), 41–42; "WJSV!," *Time*, October 3, 1955, 42; Estrelda Alexander, *Black Fire: 100 Years of African American Pentecostalism* (Downers Grove, IL: InterVarsity Press, 2011), 97–98; "Michaux, Lightfoot Solomon," in Nathan Aaseng, *African-American Religious Leaders* (New York: Facts on File, 2003), 158–59; Poe, "Elder Lightfoot Solomon Michaux" 83, 88–89.

35. Poe, "Elder Lightfoot Solomon Michaux, 82.

36. "Happy Am I," *Time*, June 11, 1934, 37.

37. "Baptizes 200 with Hose and Asks for Cash," *Springfield Republican*, August 20, 1945; "Daddy Grace: Grandiloquent Negro Preacher Has a Half-Million Faithful Followers," *Life*, October 1, 1945, 51.

38. Styron to James L. W. West III, August 18, 1980, in *Selected Letters of William Styron*, eds. Rose Styron with R. Blakeslee Gilpin (New York: Random House, 2012), 546.

39. "Elder Michaux, Evangelist, Battles Devil, Republicans," *Milwaukee Journal*, July 21, 1938; "Minister Who Left Estate Worth $7 Million," *Jet*, April 24, 1969, 20.

40. "Elder Solomon Michaux Dies," October 21, 1968, *New York Times*; J. Gordon Melton, *The Encyclopedia of American Religion*, vol. 1 (Tarrytown, NY: Triumph Books, 1991), 223.

41. "Michaux Talks to Crowd of 5,000 in Roanoke, Va.," *Baltimore Afro-American*, December 22, 1934; "He's Still Fighting the Devil: Baptizes 73 in 20 Minutes at Revival," *Washington Afro-American*, September 28, 1957; Stanley High, "Black Omens," *Saturday Evening Post*, June 4, 1938, 14–15. On Michaux's revival and other campaigns, see Poe, "Elder Lightfoot Solomon Michaux," 61–90.

42. Poe, "Elder Lightfoot Solomon Michaux," 76; "Mahalia Jackson," in *Prime-Time Religion: An Encyclopedia of Religious Broadcasting*, 160–61.

43. "Clara Mae Ward," in *Prime-Time Religion: An Encyclopedia of Religious Broadcasting*, 368–70.

44. "Minister Who Left Estate Worth $7 Million," 20.

45. "His Nationwide Evangelism Is Really Big Business: Oral Roberts Reach His Millions on TV, Radio," *Hartford Courant*, February 12, 1956; "Minister Who Left Estate Worth $7 Million," 20; On Roberts's TV ministry, see David Edwin Harrell, Jr., *All Things Are Possible: The Healing and Charismatic Revivals in Modern America* (Bloomington: Indiana University Press, 1975), 45–46.

46. William N. Jones, "Talking It Over," *Baltimore Afro-American*, June 9, 1934, 12. For more on criticism of Michaux, see Poe, "Elder Lightfoot Solomon Michaux," 57, 70.

47. "Tennessee House Joint Resolution 547," filed April 15, 1996, 1–2.

48. J. Samuel Rasnake, *Stones by the River: A History of the Tennessee District of the Assemblies of God* (Bristol, TN: Westhighlands Church, 1975), 84–88.

49. For more on how Pentecostalism and Memphis First Assembly shaped Elvis, see Peter Guralnick, *Last Train to Memphis: The Rise of Elvis Presley* (Boston: Little, Brown and Company, 1994), 426; Hamill to the Rev. Ralph M. Riggs, August 1, 1956, Flower Pentecostal Heritage Center, Springfield, Missouri; J. D. Sumner quoted in Don Cusic, "Singing with the King: The Groups That Performed with Elvis," *Rejoice! The Gospel Music Magazine* (Summer 1988): 13; Peter Guralnick, *Careless Love: The Unmaking of Elvis Presley* (Boston: Back Bay Books, 2000), 233. See also J. D. Sumner with Bob Terrell, *Elvis: His Love for Gospel Music and J.D. Sumner* (Nashville: W. C. I. Publishing, 1991), 5–19; Don Cusic, "Southern Gospel and Contemporary Christian Music," in *Encyclopedia of Contemporary Christian Music: Pop, Rock, and Worship*, ed. Don Cusic (Santa Barbara, CA: ABC CLIO, 2010), 410; Jennifer Harrison, *Elvis as We Knew Him: Our Shared Life in a Small Town in South Memphis* (Lincoln, NE: iUniverse, 2003), 16–17; Elvis Presley Subject Folder, Center for Popular Music, Middle Tennessee State University; Charles Wolfe, "Elvis Presley and the Gospel Tradition," in *The Elvis Reader: Texts and Sources on the King of Rock 'n' Roll*, ed. Kevin Quan (New York: St. Martin's Press, 1992), 13–27; and Joe Moscheo, *The Gospel Side of Elvis* (New York: Center Street, 2007), 27–36.

50. James Hamill, "Memphis, Tenn.," *Pentecostal Evangel*, February 8, 1947, 14.

51. J. Samuel Rasnake, *Stones by the River: A History of the Tennessee District of the Assemblies of God* (Bristol, TN: Westhighlands Church, 1975), 88.

52. Robert Fierro, "Well-Known Ministers to Speak at General Council," *Pentecostal Evangel*, August 5, 1951, 10. For the typical preaching and youth work Hamill was involved in, see "Southland Briefs," *Los Angeles Times*, April 18, 1946; "Mississippi Couple Conducting Revival at Faith Tabernacle," *Dallas Morning News*, October 8, 1938.

53. James E. Hamill, "Over 800 in Sunday School Each Sunday," *Pentecostal Evangel*, November 20, 1950, 19.

54. "Our History," First Assembly Memphis, http://www.famemphis.net/our-history/. On the music ministry at First Assembly Memphis, see Cameron Wesley Wilson, "We Serve a God of Song," *Pentecostal Evangel*, March 17, 1957, 4–5.

55. "Popular TV Program Sponsored by Memphis Assembly," *Pentecostal Evangel*, October 13, 1957, 10. On youth programming, see "Keen Teen," *C.A. Herald* (June 1958): 24. For a brief description of a revival at First Assembly, see James E. Hamill, "Memphis, Tenn.," *Pentecostal Evangel*, June 10, 1956, 27. Also see the 1980 interview with James Hamill at https://ifphc.wordpress.com/tag/james-e-hamill/.

56. Benjamin A. Wagner, "'Full Gospel' Radio: Revivaltime and the Pentecostal Uses of Mass Media, 1959–1979," *Fides et Historia* 35, no. 1 (Winter/Spring 2003): 108, 121–22. See also Edith Blumhofer, *Restoring the Faith: The Assemblies of God, Pentecostalism, and American Culture* (Urbana: University of Illinois Press, 1993), 192.

57. C. M. Ward, "Old and New," *Revivaltime Radio Sermons*, April 11, 1976.

58. "On the Cover," *Pentecostal Evangel*, January 27, 1952, 4.

59. James R. Goff, Jr., *Close Harmony: A History of Southern Gospel* (Chapel Hill: University of North Carolina Press, 2002), 237.

60. Don Cusic, *The Sound of Light: A History of Gospel and Christian Music* (Milwaukee, WI: Hal Leonard, 2002), 225.

61. Pierre Adidge and Robert Abel, interview with Elvis, March 31, 1972, in *Elvis: Word for Word; What He Said, Exactly as He Said It* (New York: Harmony Books, 2000), 243. See also Rose Clayton and Dick Heard, *Elvis up Close: In the Words of Those Who Knew Him Best* (Atlanta: Turner Publishing, 1994), 13–17; interview with Elvis about religion in Jack Carrell, "I Like Elvis Presley," *Ottawa Citizen*, September 8, 1956; and Elvis's 1966 interview with May Mann, quoted in Guralnick, *Careless Love*, 223.

62. Jack Carrell, "I Like Elvis Presley."

63. Elvis speaking during his *'68 Comeback Special* (December 3, 1968; reissue, New York: Sony BMG Music Entertainment, 2006).

64. Richard Flory and Kimon H. Sargeant, "Conclusion: Pentecostalism in Global Perspective," in *Spirit and Power: The Growth and Global Impact of Pentecostalism*, eds. Donald E. Miller, Kimon H. Sargeant, and Richard Flory (New York: Oxford University Press, 2013), 305–06.

65. David Martin, "Pentecostalism: An Alternative Form of Modernity and Modernization?," in *Global Pentecostalism in the Twenty-First Century*, ed. Peter L. Berger (Bloomington: Indiana University Press, 2013), 42.

66. Walton, *Watch This!*, 23. Pentecostal and Holiness victories against regulated media were long in coming. Evangelicals in general, and Pentecostals or fundamentalists in particular, faced a variety of hurdles in the early days of radio in the 1920s and '30s. The FRC, the precursor to the FCC, favored broad religious programming, intended for a large nonsectarian audience. Officials deemed many conservative Christian radio programs to be propaganda. See Bob Lochte, *Christian Radio: The Growth of a Mainstream Broadcasting Force* (Jefferson, NC: McFarland & Company, 2006), 22–25.

67. Michele Rosenthal, *American Protestants and TV in the 1950s: Responses to a New Medium* (New York: Palgrave Macmillan, 2007), 2, 5, 38, 49, 52, 60–61; Paul Robinson, "Should Canada Allow Christian Radio and Television Stations: Mainline Churchmen Fear Evangelicals Will Dominate," *Christianity Today*, March 5, 1982, 81–84.

68. Roger G. Robins, *A. J. Tomlinson: Plainfolk Modernist* (New York: Oxford University Press, 2004), 5, 19–25; Grant Wacker, "Searching for Norman Rockwell: Popular Evangelicalism in Contemporary America," in *The Evangelical Tradition in America*, ed. Leonard I. Sweet (Macon, GA: Mercer University Press, 1984), 294, 301, 307–309. See also Thomas A. Tweed, *Crossing and Dwelling: A Theory of Religion* (Cambridge, MA: Harvard University

Press, 2006), 125–27; Martin, "Pentecostalism: An Alternative Form of Modernity and Modernization?," 43.

69. Stephen J. Stein, "Religious Innovation at the Edges," in *Perspectives on American Religion and Culture*, ed. Peter W. Williams (Malden, MA: Blackwell Publishers, 1999), 23.

70. Elaine J. Lawless, *God's Peculiar People: Women's Voices and Folk Tradition in a Pentecostal Church* (1988, repr., Lexington: University of Kentucky Press, 2005), 38.

71. Louis Cassels, "Pentecostal Movement Outgrowth of Religious Revivals of Nineteenth Century," *Lodi (California) News-Sentinel*, August 13, 1960.

72. "Spirit and Power: A Ten-Country Survey of Pentecostals," Pew Forum on Religion and Public Life, October 5, 2006.

"The Pure of Body Are Pure of Soul"

Religion and the Emerging Sports Culture of the New South

Arthur Remillard

In week five of the 2014 college football season, the Alabama Crimson Tide traveled to Vaught-Hemingway Stadium in Oxford to face the University of Mississippi. Ole Miss entered the game ranked eleventh in the nation, while Alabama stood at number three. The proximity of these two teams in the polls, however, obscures Mississippi's historic lack of success in this match and in college football more generally. The last time Mississippi defeated the Tide had been in 2003. So Ole Miss came into this game with a potent mix of momentum and high hopes. From the opening kickoff onward, drama, tension, and controversy marked nearly every second of the contest. And when the final ticks of the clock passed, the scoreboard confirmed an Ole Miss victory: 23-17.[1]

Then, in an instant, as security guards blithely shifted their gaze, fans stormed the field and tore down the goalposts. To be sure, this brand of mass hysteria is a time-honored tradition in college football. But the Mississippi fans quickly put a unique stamp on this ritual, making the goalposts a featured object in a victory procession. As members of the crowd hoisted the metal poles, they departed from the stadium and marched onward to the Grove, a ten-acre grassy plot at the center of campus.[2]

This collective decision was entirely intentional. In the early 1980s, then-coach Billy Brewer began taking his team through the Grove before games, hoping to develop a visceral bond between the players and the fans. Coach Brewer's vision would quickly materialize. In a relatively short period of time, the Grove evolved into what the *Sporting News* once called "the Holy Grail of tailgating sites." Here Ole Miss fans gather by the thousands to eat, drink, and socialize. Winning is nice, but not necessary. "We may not win every game," goes one Ole Miss saying, "but we've never lost a party."[3] So, in the aftermath of their landmark victory over Alabama, a sacred place with an established tradition met a sacred object that had just been christened.

After a brief stay in the Grove, the journey of the goalposts continued on to the various postgame celebrations of the evening. One group of students carried a portion to their apartments. The next morning, they began slicing the goalposts into chunks intending to distribute the relics to worthy followers of the team. As they labored, the young men documented their activities on social media. The university's athletic director soon took notice and decided to enter this digital discussion—not to chasten the students but to politely request a piece for himself and the head football coach. The students obliged, hand-delivering sections to the athletic department.[4]

The university was able to gather more full sections of the goalposts, which they would soon put to use for an entirely practical purpose—fundraising. In addition to needing two new goalposts for the stadium, Ole Miss was fined $50,000 for allowing fans to storm the field. Accordingly, to anyone willing to separate with $500 or $1,000, the university sent three-and six-inch portions of the goalposts respectively. Within hours of starting their campaign, the university exceeded its goal of $75,000. Remarked one enthusiastic owner of a metal relic, "I just knew this was going to be the coolest piece of Ole Miss I could ever have."[5]

Football fever was not limited to Oxford on that weekend. In-state rival Mississippi State had secured a win over Texas A&M. With Mississippi and Mississippi State both undefeated and hovering near the top of the polls, the governor of the state proclaimed that October 4 would thereafter be known as Football Celebration Saturday.[6]

For Mississippi football fans, these victories marked a break in time, a moment when the state set aside its assorted issues, and instead, celebrated gridiron glory. To the cynic, all of this reeks of triviality—an obscene story of drunken revelry, sprouting from a violent game played for majority white audiences by eighteen-to-twenty-two-year-olds, many if not most African American men, who will likely be suffering the physical aftereffects of their careers for decades to come. Even those who follow the game might detect a hint of unhinged extremism. But the "fan" in this sport, or any sport, rarely makes clear-headed decisions, especially when the thrill of a victory seizes them. After all, the word "fan" derives from the Latin *fanaticus*, which translates to "possessed by a deity."[7]

To see college football as Charles Reagan Wilson would, we might say that in the minds of fans, "the spirit" of an athletic contest is otherworldly.[8] It controls the devoted viewer in a unique way, compelling them to do strange things, such as revering an inanimate metal object. In thinking through this story, it also helps to recall Brent Plate's book, *A History of Religion in 5 ½ Objects*. Here, Plate explains how stones, incense, drums, crosses, and bread have come to assume a variety of sacred meanings, dependent on the setting, topic, time, and population. All the while, Plate emphasizes that religion is not simply a matter of belief in gods or creeds. Rather, this human activity holds a central place in our senses, in how we see, touch, hear, smell, and taste the sacred.[9]

For Plate, the religious life unfolds through bodily contact with material things, or tangible experiences of what people perceive as transcendence. To apply this to the goalposts, we need not say that this story of metal things becoming sacred objects proves that Ole Miss football is a religion. Instead, to invoke David Chidester, it is more productive to frame this account as an example of people behaving in "characteristically religious ways."[10] On the field, in the Grove, and at their apartments, a victory became a place for people to experiment with their collective identity, to elevate a single object to a privileged position so as to capture a moment of ecstasy. To do this, they needed something to literally hold on to.

Objects are significant in college football, as they are for other sports. Baseball fans, for example, might experience something "wholly other" at the "Sacred Ground" exhibit at the Baseball Hall of Fame. This site houses over two hundred artifacts from the storied past of baseball. Here, the sights, sounds, and even smells of baseball's history literally assault the senses, seeking to bring visitors into a deep connection with the game. As Gary Laderman observes, this exhibit "is just one of many examples that demonstrate how the world of sports is infused with religious frames of reference and meaning." He elaborates: "God or no God, play can animate religious energies that bind communities of fans, athletes, and teams together around idols that are worshipped in ways that, for some, create shared experiences and memories as impressive and meaningful as any other sacred encounters in this life."[11]

Beyond the language of God and belief, then, the insights of Laderman and others issue a challenge to scholars to identify and contextualize the "sacred encounters" associated with athletics. What if we applied this challenge to the sports culture of the New South? It might help us to think differently about how religion worked through sports in the years between the Civil War and the 1920s. The standard narrative starts by noting that in the North at this time, progressive reformers embraced the "muscular Christian" movement, as they promoted sports as means of "toning" both body and spirit. In the South, however, evangelicals were wary. As William Baker explains in *Playing with*

God, "The liberal social gospel that attached gyms and recreational programs to churches scarcely made a dent in the conservative South."[12]

Baker goes on to document examples where the drama of southern resistance to sports unfolded. For example, in 1887, John Franklin Cronwell, a Pennsylvania native, began his tenure as the president of Trinity College (now Duke University). A Yale alumnus, Cronwell channeled his muscular Christian convictions to argue that football would improve the moral character of young men. As the Trinity team began playing, they found a measure of success on the field as well as a loyal fan base among the student body. Disapproving evangelicals who were affiliated with the school, however, criticized the violent game, recoiling at rumors of its culture of cheating, drinking, gambling, and foul language. Under pressure, Cronwell resigned in 1894. The new president, John Klingo, a southerner and Methodist minister, promptly abolished the program, deeming football "an evil that the best tastes of the public have rebelled against." Emory and Henry College and Wake Forest soon followed Trinity's lead.[13]

Baker points to the 1920s as a transitional decade, when a rising generation of evangelicals developed a more accommodating view of athletics. By 1947, Billy Graham invited world-class runner Gil Dodds—aka "the Flying Parson"—to a crusade in Charlotte, North Carolina. Dodds dazzled the crowd as he ran an exhibition race and gave his testimony. A high-profile Christian athlete, Dodds's presence at the event no doubt drew spectators. At a symbolic level, he also solidified a marriage between sports and evangelical Christianity in the South.[14] The following decades have seen a proliferation of "born-again" athletes in the region, epitomized by Tim Tebow. While playing quarterback at the University of Florida, Tebow gained a reputation both for his spectacular play and his Christian pronouncements and gestures.[15] Baker's story arc, therefore, holds water insofar as it traces a transition from resistance to embrace among white evangelicals. But it does not offer a context for the Ole Miss goalposts. In other words, we find scarce mention of those legions of devoted followers in the New South who generated a stout defense of sports and heralded its unique ascetic, physical, moral, social, and spiritual benefits. These voices weren't always self-identifying as evangelicals or as members of any formal religious body. Still, amid this burgeoning discourse, we witness the traces of religious activity and of creative encounters with the sacred on the field of play.

Additionally, even the story of New South evangelicals is not as exceptional as we might expect. In the North and throughout the world, pockets of evangelicals actively resisted their respective sports cultures, just as in the South. Consider the moral history of the prizefighter Jack Johnson. In 1908, Johnson faced Tommy Burns for the heavyweight title in Australia. As the fight approached, the Sydney Anglican Synod formally denounced the "inherent brutality and dangerous nature" of prizefighting and worried that it would "corrupt the moral tone of the community." When Johnson won, ministers of all Protestant stripes took to the newspapers and pulpits to continue denouncing the "carnival of savagery."[16]

Similar moral pronouncements echoed in the United States, gaining strength in 1910, when Johnson defeated the "great white hope" Jim Jeffries in Reno, Nevada. In response, Bostonian William M. Shaw, general secretary of the United Society of Christian Endeavor, contacted governors, mayors, and other elected officials in the South, beseeching them to outlaw films of the fight. Shaw and his society were part of a nationwide Christian purity crusade to eliminate the "distinctly beastly art."[17] State and local leaders in the South acted promptly on Shaw's dire warnings that the films would incite race warfare. Interestingly, though, the *Richmond Times-Dispatch* was flummoxed when city officials passed legal measures to prohibit the fight film. "It looks to us as if a very big mountain is being made out of a very little mole hill," the author of the newspaper article wrote. He puzzled over why governors and municipalities were giving so much credit to Shaw, a northerner who, the newspaper assured, could never fully understand how "friendly" race relations were in the city.[18]

The story of southern white evangelicals denouncing sports connects to broader national and international discourses over questions of athletics, race, and public morality. Put another way, southern white evangelicals were not entirely distinct in their mobilized opposition to sports like prizefighting. This complicates an understanding of religion and sports in the New South as being a time when, as William Baker phrased it, "Dixie took a different stand." Certainly, the "muscular Christian" movement had few advocates in the South even as it flourished in the North. But when considering the response to prizefighting, we see that Dixie's white evangelicals were not taking a "different stand" so much as they were finding common cause with likeminded members of the faithful throughout the nation and abroad.[19]

Beyond this specific conversation about traditional religious identity and sports, though, is a broader question of where we look for "religion" in sports culture of the New South. A close examination of those who advocated on behalf of sports brings a new dimension to this story. On the fields, among the fans, and in the print culture, athletes and athletics continued to develop a mythic stature. They too deployed not only evangelical language in the elevation of physical activity, but also a generalized discourse of the sacred. For sports enthusiasts in the South, prizefighting was set apart, special, and deeply meaningful. For an example, we might return to Jack Johnson.

On the eve of the aforementioned Johnson-Jeffries match, one New Orleans sportswriter theorized that the fight had become an "absorbing topic of interest" in the city and nation. To the "moralists" who preached against it, the author responded that this fight was between two great athletes, one black and the other white. Unconcerned with the racial optics, the author lauded both for their routine of "constant exercise and careful self-denial," adding, "the fact remains that the English-speaking race dearly loves a brutal fight, especially where there is every guarantee of fair play and an exhibition of nerve, skill, and physical endurance."[20]

The editorialist's words tactically carved a moral discourse for the prize ring, celebrating toned bodies in motion and regulated combat. In addition to being a vigorous defense of boxing, it was also an exultation of the aesthetics of the sport.[21] This moral discourse was neither unique to the 1910s nor to prizefighting. In 1869, a Wilmington, North Carolina, newspaperman articulated a vision for what he called a new age of "Brain and Muscle." He opened by noting the city's growing number of baseball teams, a testament to a sprouting awareness that "neglect of physical culture" is the enemy of "the healthy round limbed boy or girl." The author castigated fathers and mothers for neglecting their children's physical development, labeling this parental habit "the wretched insulter of deity." In contrast, those helping to build a robust "physical culture" were assuring a prosperous future not simply for individuals but also for the South more generally. "Health in body," the author concluded, "superinduces health in mind, and the pure of body are pure of soul."[22]

Among sports enthusiasts, the toned-body-toned-soul motif became a common refrain. So too was an emphasis on the social benefit of sports. In 1871, Henry Chadwick offered a firsthand account of baseball's popularity in the region. Known as the "Father of Baseball" in America, Chadwick's wife was originally from Richmond, where he was briefly a correspondent during the Civil War.[23] Chadwick recounted visiting the city right after the war, only to see "a great change in the young Southerners in regard to sports." Baseball in particular, Chadwick delighted, had "proved to be contagious." And it was the "inherent attributes of manliness" embodied by the southern youth that made the game appropriate for the population. "The late war proved conclusively their powers of physical endurance, as it did the courage, pluck and nerve." Now, these attributes had been transferred to baseball, an urbane expression of southern male identity.[24]

Chadwick's sanguine appraisal of baseball was certainly not shared by all in his time or after. Gambling, cursing, and Sabbath desecration were among the catalog of sins cited by "moralists" who sought legal restrictions on the game. Professionalism was also a source of concern, both by ardent opponents of baseball as well as by the game's purists. An 1876 editorial in Memphis nostalgically recounted the early days of baseball in the city, when players understood the game as a "muscle-developer and brain-strengthener." As its popularity grew, the author continued, baseball-language found its way into the broader culture, as businessmen and laborers began using the game's rhetoric in their respective professional conversations. Even preachers would illustrate sermons with "some peculiar phrases of the great national game." But, the author lamented, the "absorbing" game of baseball had professionalized, thereby draining its vitality and leaving the "old admirers" thoroughly disillusioned.[25]

The ideological contours of baseball had become a work in progress, as fans, players, journalists, and critics erected moral boundaries to separate the game from an assortment of perceived pollutants. Football, as previously noted, produced similar conflicts, although the game was played mostly on college campuses. While Trinity and other denominationally affiliated schools abandoned the sport, public schools enthusiastically adopted it. Many justified the game using the language of "school spirit," mirroring the sentiments of an 1893 editorial in the University of North Carolina's student newspaper. Students attending the games, the author exclaimed, could witness the "grit" and "manliness" of the players, while also developing a profound attachment to the university.[26]

While the game changed in the coming decades, the rhetoric of "school spirit" remained. "Is the Carolina spirit dead?" an editorial asked in 1918. "To the new men or to a stranger it might seem so. But those of us who have been here know that such spirit as the Carolina spirit can never die. That the glorious spirit is not dead is evidenced at the football games in the hearty cheering given the team."[27] Spirit-language of this sort became part of college football's developing appeal, helping to make it "more than a game." In the eyes of enthusiasts, it was a collective and poetic expression of regional distinction and institutional affiliation. The evangelical establishment would eventually warm to this perspective. In 1920, a Baptist minister in Florida extolled the "educational force" of team sports, proclaiming: "A good foot-ball and base-ball team, if properly conducted and controlled, is a school of character."[28] And in 1921, the Praying Colonels of Centre College in Kentucky traveled north to take on the mighty Harvard Crimson. The relatively unknown Presbyterian school from the bluegrass state won 6-0, behind the leadership of quarterback Bo McMillin. While teams like Vanderbilt and Auburn had experienced some success in interregional contests, Harvard was a football powerhouse that no southern team could defeat. So with pride and pleasure, the *Atlanta Constitution* announced: "Centre Saves South," as they dubbed McMillin a "New Immortal."[29]

Centre's chaplain would capitalize on this celebrity by telling the story of these "pious" southern athletes on the revival trail. And when Trinity reconstituted its football program, they intentionally adopted the combination of playing and praying modeled by the Centre stars.[30] Not everyone was impressed with Centre, though. The Praying Colonels lost their final game of the 1921 season to Texas A&M in the Dixie Classic by a score of 14-22. Fuzzy Woodruff, a noted sportswriter of the era, was an unabashed booster for the southern football cause. While he fawned over Auburn and Georgia Tech, though, Centre drew only his scorn. He dismissed the victory against Harvard as insignificant and cheered when the Praying Colonels "were utterly annihilated" by A&M. Woodruff listed two principal objections to Centre. First, he suspected that they used "ringers," or paid players. And second, Centre was not a member of the Southern Intercollegiate Athletic Association, a regulatory body championed by Woodruff for their commitment to the "purification of college athletics."[31]

Woodruff and his ilk, then, happily allowed Centre's victory to become a distant memory once Alabama defeated the Washington Huskies in the 1926 Rose Bowl. The victory certainly caused a stir in Tuscaloosa, and it has since become known as "the game that changed the South."[32] For decades prior, though, any number of interregional contests garnered similar accolades. Some contests were more surprising than others, but not necessarily because of the final score. In 1906, Vanderbilt hosted the Carlisle Indians on Thanksgiving Day. The Carlisle team had become a formidable squad in the northeast due in large part to the efforts of their legendary coach, Pop Warner. Warner left in 1903, but the team clung to their aura of dominance. So, for a southern football population that sought national recognition, the contest promised to serve this end.[33] In pregame commentaries, the racial component of the game was a secondary concern to beating Carlisle. Attendance exceeded all expectations, as 8,000 people crowded the field to watch Vanderbilt win 4-0. Among the viewers that day was Georgia Tech's coach, John Heisman, who reported on the game for Atlanta's newspapers. "Magnificent is the fitting word to stamp their play," he exclaimed. "That is a great deal for Vanderbilt, and for the entire South."[34]

Other teams would take on Indian colleges during these years, using wins as a platform to announce the arrival of southern football. Another curious contest happened on Christmas Day in 1907, as LSU became the first team to play football on foreign soil, facing a local team in Havana, Cuba. Called the Bacardi Bowl, a reference to the Cuban-based alcohol producer that sponsored the game, the Tigers won 56-0. Approximately 10,000 fans attended, most of them from the US military or traveling from Louisiana. In the buildup to the game, the LSU team and coach were confident in their abilities, even though they were unsure of the team that they would face. According to one report, "They say they are willing to meet all comers, excepting negroes."[35]

While white teams gleefully played Native Americans and "native" Cubans, sharing a field with African Americans simply was not an option. By the 1920s, black colleges and universities had fielded teams in hopes of replicating the "school spirit" demonstrated by their white counterparts. They had an additional aspiration. "Athletics is the universal language," announced a Howard editorialist. "By and through it we hope to foster a better and more fraternal spirit between the races in America and so to destroy prejudices; to learn and to be taught; to facilitate a universal brotherhood."[36]

Alas, interracial football was a long way off in the South. Other sports also used the color line to establish boundaries around who could, and could not, participate. Jack Johnson briefly occupied the most visible crown in prizefighting, but he dared not defend this title in the southland, even though New Orleans was a hub of boxing at the time. And black jockeys—a mainstay on the turf until the early 1900s—had all but disappeared from the sport as Jim Crow strengthened its grip.[37] In the New South era, then, white fans and journalists produced heroes, mythic moments, and communities of supporters. But they also produced racial distinctions and applied their unbending and ever-strengthening racial structures to the fields of play. This racial legacy continues today, as is readily evident on college football fields and basketball courts.

The relative "sanctity" or "religiousness" of sports is the product of human intentions, of decisions about what is sacred and why it merits such a distinction. Exhibitions of unity on the field of play create a collective sense of "us," which at the same time directly and indirectly generates a troublesome "them." This essay's effort to revise an existing understanding of religion and sports in the New South accounts for the most noteworthy sorts of inclusions and exclusions, which define the terms of debate over the meaning and purpose of sports. The hope is to better understand sports in this particular historical context, while also sketching out a genealogy of the South's current sports culture. At the very least, the cynics among us might become slightly more empathetic toward those crazy fans whose collect and cherish random hunks of metal from Oxford, Mississippi.

Notes

1. Steven Godfrey, "Ole Miss Beats Alabama," *SB Nation*, October 6, 2014, http://www.sbnation.com/college-football/2014/10/6/6909457/ole-miss-alabama-game-2014-oxford-celebration-goalposts (accessed April 15, 2016).

2. Am Kramer, "The Anatomy of a Field Storming," *Bleacher Report*, October 8, 2014, http://bleacherreport.com/articles/2224630-the-anatomy-of-a-field-storming-the-fantastic-saga-of-the-ole-miss-goalposts (accessed April 15, 2016).

3. Warren St. John, *Rammer Jammer Yellow Hammer: A Road Trip into the Heart of Fan Mania* (New York: Three Rivers Press, 2004), 162–63. See also "The Grove," http://www.olemisssports.com/trads/the-grove.html (accessed April 15, 2016).

4. Kramer, "The Anatomy of a Field Storming."

5. Hugh Kellenberger, "The Ole Miss Goalpost," *Clarion-Ledger*, October 8, 2014, http://www.clarionledger.com/story/news/2014/10/07/ole-miss-goalpost-went/16892931/ (accessed April 15, 2016).

6. James Dator, "'Football Celebration Saturday,'" *SBNation.com*, October 6, 2014, http://www.sbnation.com/lookit/2014/10/6/6925189/mississippi-governor-football-celebration-saturday-ole-miss-mississippi-state (accessed April 15, 2016).

7. Andrew Cooper, *Playing in the Zone: Exploring the Spiritual Dimensions of Sports* (Boston, MA: Shambhala Publications, 1998), 50–51.

8. Charles Reagan Wilson, *Flashes of a Southern Spirit: Meanings of the Spirit in the US South* (Athens: University of Georgia Press, 2011).

9. S. Brent Plate, *A History of Religion in 5 ½ Objects: Bringing the Spiritual to Its Senses* (Boston, MA: Beacon Press, 2014).

10. David Chidester, *Authentic Fakes: Religion and American Popular Culture* (Berkeley: University of California Press, 2005), 2.

11. Gary Laderman, *Sacred Matters: Celebrity Worship, Sexual Ecstasies, the Living Dead, and Other Signs of Religious Life in the United States* (New York: The New Press, 2009), 43, 62.

12. William J. Baker, *Playing with God: Religion and Modern Sport* (Cambridge, MA: Harvard University Press, 2007), 85.

13. Ibid., 102.

14. Ibid., 194–95.

15. Patton Dodd, "Tim Tebow: God's Quarterback," *Wall Street Journal*, December 10, 2011.

16. Richard Broome, "The Australian Reaction to Jack Johnson, Black Pugilist, 1907–09," in *The Best Ever Australian Sports Writing: A 200 Year Collection*, ed. David John Headon (Melbourne Victoria: Black Inc., 2001), 536, 542–43.

17. Barak Y. Orbach, "The Johnson-Jeffries Fight and Censorship of Black Supremacy," *New York University Journal of Law and Liberty* 5, no. 2 (2010): 270–346.

18. "The Moving Picture Sensation" and "Much Ado About Nothing," *Richmond Times Dispatch*, July 7 and 8, 1910.

19. Baker, *Playing With God*, 85–107. See also Patrick B. Miller, ed., *The Sporting World of the Modern South* (Urbana: University of Illinois Press, 2002), 1–125. For the New South's interconnectedness to other American regions, see Edward L. Ayers, *The Promise of the New South: Life after Reconstruction* (New York: Oxford University Press, 1992); Beth Barton Schweiger, *The Gospel Working Up: Progress and the Pulpit in Nineteenth-Century Virginia, Religion in the South* (New York: Oxford University Press, 2000); Arthur Remillard, *Southern Civil Religions: Imagining the Good Society in the Post-Reconstruction Era* (Athens: University of Georgia Press, 2011).

20. "The Coming Fistic Battle," *New Orleans Daily Picayune*, July 3, 1910.

21. Arthur Remillard, "Between Faith and Fistic Battles: Moralists, Enthusiasts, and the Idea of Jack Johnson in the New South," *Perspectives in Religious Studies* 39, no. 3 (2012).

22. "Muscle and Brain," *Wilmington Post*, July 15, 1869.

23 Andrew J. Schiff, *"The Father of Baseball": A Biography of Henry Chadwick* (Jefferson, NC: McFarland & Company, 2008).

24. Henry Chadwick, "Baseball in the South," *Outing* (1888): 538–39. Originally printed in an 1871 edition of *DeWitt's Baseball Guide*.

25. "Base-Ball," *Memphis Daily Appeal*, May 12, 1876.

26. "The Cause," *Tar Heel*, December 7, 1893.

27. "The Carolina Spirit," *Tar Heel*, November 22, 1918

28. "Ethics of Outdoor Sports," *Miami Herald*, January 13, 1920.

29. "Centre Saves South," *Atlanta Constitution*, October 30, 1921.

30. "Center College Man Makes Talk on Faith," *Tar Heel*, March 17, 1922; "Football Starts at Trinity 'Hit Trail' At Revival," *Atlanta Constitution*, December 4, 1921.

31. Fuzzy Woodruff, *A History of Southern Football: 1890–1928*, vol. 2 (Atlanta: Walter M. Brown Publishing Company 1928), 123, 48.

32 Natalie Pierre, "A Look Back at 'The Game that Changed the South,'" *AL.com*, January 1, 2015, http://www.al.com/sports/index.ssf/2015/01/a_look_back_at_the_game_that_c.html (accessed April 15, 2016).

33. Fuzzy Woodruff, *A History of Southern Football: 1890–1928*, vol. 1, (Atlanta: Walter M. Brown Publishing Company, 1928), 137.

34. Bill Traughber, "Indians Attack Vanderbilt in 1906," *VUCommodores.com*, November 8, 2006, http://www.vucommodores.com/genrel/110806aaa.html (accessed April 15, 2016).

35. Peter Finney, "The 1908 LSU Football Team," *Times-Picayune*, November 22, 2008, http://blog.nola.com/lsusports/2008/11/the_1908_lsu_football_team_the.html (accessed April 15, 2016); "LSU Leaves to Look for Laurels against Teams in Cuba," *New Orleans Times-Picayune*, December 22, 1907.

36. Patrick B. Miller, "To 'Bring the Race along Rapidly': Sport, Student Culture, and Educational Mission at Historically Black Colleges during the Interwar Years," *History of Education Quarterly* 35, no. 2 (Summer, 1995): 111.

37. Dale A. Somers, *The Rise of Sports in New Orleans: 1850–1900* (Baton Rouge: Louisiana State University Press, 1972); Edward Hotaling, *The Great Black Jockeys: The Lives and Times of the Men Who Dominated America's First National Sport* (Rocklin, CA: Forum, 1999).

The Land of Misfit Relics

Southern Protestants and the Sacred Play of Cultural Objects

CHAD SEALES

Cultural objects can do things to people. They can make them act violently. Baseball fans notoriously scrap over homerun balls in the stands, especially those hit with the promise of cash value historical significance, as they did for Mark McGwire's bombs in 1998, or Barry Bond's 756th career homer in 2007.[1] They can make them behave stupidly. An Illinois woman, shopping for a Christmas present in the late 1990s, stole a Furby from a thirteen-year-old girl at a retail store by biting her hand and snatching the talking furball when she dropped it.[2] They can make them react ecstatically. When Oprah Winfrey gave gifts to her studio audience, from cars to books, they jumped up and down with her, waving their arms and screaming, overwhelmed with excitement. And objects can make Americans respond reverentially. When professional athletes throw headbands, wristbands, or jerseys into the stands after a game, fans reach to catch them. They would never do the same for an ordinary person's sweat.

What do we make of the agency of objects in American culture? Can we classify at least some of them as religious relics? Of those four examples, the first and the last most closely approximate Western and English usages of a relic as "something left behind."[3] Game-worn Rawlings and sweaty swooshes are the material remains of an athletic performance. Both types of sports artifacts were touched by the players and carry with them the memory of their game. But there is a slight problem with calling those objects relics. The figures they connect their holders to, those athletes, are still alive. Even if they left it all on the field or the court, as they say, they lived to play on. A Western relic typically references the dead and not the living. "In the West," historian of religion Gregory Schopen writes, "death—and usually burial—produces remains, remaining fragments; surviving parts," or "the body, or parts of the body, of a dead person."[4] The cultural objects of American celebrity, like those of athletes or TV icons, are made, oftentimes, prior to death. Those cultural objects that conjure the absent presence of a sacred person not yet dead do not fit within the definitional limits of a Western relic. Surveying the American cultural landscape in the late twentieth and early twenty-first centuries, the types of cultural objects that connect a fan or a consumer to the sacred bodily presence of McGwire, Bonds, or Oprah circulate more regularly, and out in the open, than relics of a traditionally religious kind—that is, a sacred object produced through personal death. To qualify this statement, however, it is important to recognize that relics do persist in the US to the present but remain within the bounds of Catholic parish practice (see, for example, the National Shrine of St. Francis of Assisi) or popular domestic devotion (think, for example, of Elvis's shrines at Graceland or Graceland Too). Rarely, though, do we find relics publicly circulating within Protestant popular culture.

In this essay, I am interested in locating relics in relation to American Protestantism, with the interpretive assumption that Protestant Christianity has historically shaped popular culture in the United States. Or, to put it another way, I assume that Protestant Christians have historically dominated American public religious life. And Protestant Christians, as I note below, have often denied having an institutional tradition of religious relics. Yet, as the opening examples suggest, cultural objects definitely can do things to many Americans. Given these observable phenomena, where, then, do relics fit within the material relationship between Protestant Christianity and American culture? To that question, this essay proposes that if we try to find relics within the ecclesial boundaries of Protestant church spaces, then we find very few. But if we look outside the church, as Charles Reagan Wilson did for southern civil religion, and into the realm of southern popular culture, then we find them quite readily in two cases: Civil War reenactments and mob lynchings.

In this essay, I argue that Protestants in the United States, focusing on those of southern varieties, have circulated religious relics in their popular cultural practices, despite theological claims to the contrary. Protestants have long dismissed the agency of relics and mistrusted those, particularly Catholics, who grant them sacred power. As Gregory Schopen puts it, the "reformers were no friends of relics," noting John Calvin dismissed relics as "frivolities," "superstition," and evidence of "the stupidity of men."[5] Protestants sought to purify their beliefs from what they considered idolatry. Obsessed with the empty tomb, they fixed their gaze on the immaterial, on the spirit of resurrection. By their self-understanding, it was impossible for them to have relics.

Yet, they did. Methodists, for example, made a "death mask" of founder John Wesley, which is now property of the archival collection at Drew University along with the thumb of evangelist George Whitefield. But unlike Catholics, who would not be surprised in the least if someone told them their churches contain relics of saints, those eighteenth-century findings are shocking to a twenty-first-century Protestant flock. Most Methodists have no idea that their denomination keeps facial molds and bodily remains of deceased clergy. In response to a query about those holdings, one commentator wrote on Drew University's "U-Know" collaborative website, designed to share information about the school's institutional knowledge, "It *is* true that the Methodist Center contains what purports to be the desiccated thumb of famous Methodist evangelist George Whitefield."[6] In contrast to Catholicism, blatant Protestant relics are rare, and rarer still is the Protestant believer who recognizes them as such. Protestants tend to kill lively things like relics.[7] Wesley's mask and Whitefield's thumb are, to that point, displayed in a library and not a church. Those material markers of sacred history, those things that would make Methodist tradition, have been detached from the place where its believers experience divine presence.

We could leave it at that. Protestants say they don't have relics. And while the ones they have are significant, there are not enough of them to comprise a Protestant tradition of devotional use of relics. But then there are southern Protestants who have had two major sources of relics as understood as the sacred remains of the dead: those produced by death in the Civil War and those made through the lynching deaths of African Americans. Both of these types of objects can be classified as a Western relic, because they are produced through death and are set apart as sacred. And in both cases, southern white Protestants have circulated these objects as relics. In terms of Civil War relics, southerners collect them, and trade them, using references like *Warman's Civil War Collectibles Identification and Price Guide*. And for relics associated with lynching deaths, up until the mid-twentieth century, southerners circulated those objects among family and friends, particularly in postcards of lynchings.

In Civil War reenactments, the authenticity of the objects and their representation is of utmost concern to some participants, who use them to mark the performative text of their historical tradition. Reenactors set apart authentic performers from those who are not. The ones who are not, Ira Glass explained on *This American Life*, are called "farbs," which he claimed is "short for 'far be it from me,' as in 'far be it from me to judge what that person is doing right over there.'" When asked about farbs, a reenactor says, "A farb? A farb is someone who is not as authentic as you think of yourself. That's the easiest way I put it. A farb is anyone who would wear tennis shoes or would wear modern eyeglasses or would wear cotton instead of wool. When I see someone in line and he's got modern glasses, that takes away from my event. It might not affect his event, but it takes away from mine."[8]

I find this distinction of farbs fascinating. Questions of authenticity and sincerity are hallmarks of Protestantism.[9] In terms of measuring or articulating "true" religious belief and "right" practice, the Protestant questions often are, "Did they mean it? Were they sincere?" In the case of farbs, the performers were concerned with the culturally orthodox manner in which a ritual event, the reenactments, should relate to the material objects that connect them to the death of a soldier on a Civil War battlefield. These were the standards of those who distinguish themselves more devout by not wearing underwear or carrying bananas, by those who eat raw meat and infect themselves with fleas. What is a farb to them? It is someone who detracts from the sincerity of the reenactors and the authenticity of their objects. In doing so, the farb, according to the ritual purists, threatens the material power of the objects as relics, by making death less real.

Contrasting that striving for authenticity, the farb willingly accepts the present-age, human-made objects of eyeglasses and tennis shoes, objects not forged in the crucible of war, and is content to wear materials not buried in its death, such as cotton and not wool. In short, the farb is a problem for the religious authentic trucking in sacred relics because the farb does not buffer against—indeed, seems careless to prevent—the invasion of modern life into sacred space. And here, perhaps, in this sectarian clash between the self-identified "authentics" and the pejoratively labeled "farbs," the Lost Cause performers reveal an inner longing for a medieval America, replete with relics forged through death past.

Reflecting on the reenactors, Ira Glass closes the segment with a few thoughts. He says, "You know, it is hard to imagine people in other countries—English and French citizens reenacting the Norman Conquest or North and South Vietnamese recreating their bloody civil war. The question here is why do Americans devote so much emotional energy to restaging the past?" To engage that question from another angle, Glass follows that segment by turning to the simulated worlds that Americans create, from wax museums to imitation coal mines to fake ethnic restaurants. And he opens the next part of the discussion with reference to an essay by Umberto Eco, who upon seeing Disneyland, Las Vegas, and the full, life-size re-creation of the Oval Office in the LBJ Presidential Library on the University of Texas-Austin campus, asked, "Is this the taste of America? Certainly it is not the taste of Frank Lloyd Wright, of the Seagram Building.... But the American imagination demands the real thing and, to attain it, must fabricate the absolute fake." Eco ultimately decides that Americans do such things like reenact the Civil War because they "don't have as strong a sense of history as Europeans have."[10] Lacking history of a certain kind, with the Civil War the only modern war fought on US soil, some Americans turn to the material artifacts of the popular religious culture of the Lost Cause, to mark sacred time and recreate a sacrificial past.

While southerners continue to publically display Civil War relics in battle reenactments, most now hide what was once another tradition of relic practice in the region, the circulation of objects produced through the deaths of lynched African Americans. In the late nineteenth and early twentieth centuries, southern whites used the ritual practice of primitive human sacrifice to reinforce a modern social order built upon what they considered a divinely sanctioned racial hierarchy. Lynchings defined a modern South filled with religious fervor, practiced most prominently during the region's heaviest periods of industrialization in the late nineteenth and early twentieth centuries. According to historian Donald Mathews, lynchings were a southern religious rite. At the 1899 lynching of Thomas Wilkes, who was burned alive, a white observer among the frenzied crowd screamed, "Glory be to God!" as he jumped up and down to imitate the "writhing of the tortured black man." He continued, shouting, "God bless every man who had a hand in this. Thank God for vengeance."[11] Mathews notes that lynchings were more likely to occur in counties with higher church affiliation. And many white southerners considered lynch law, as one commentator put it in the *Sparta (Georgia) Ishmaelite* in 1901, "part of the religion of our people."[12]

From lynchings, many white southerners took relics. They took bones and teeth of burned victims, as well as pieces of noose rope. They circulated pictures and postcards of the human sacrifices they attended, sending them to friends and family.[13] Almost none of these relics continue to circulate in the present, at least not in the public manner in which Civil War relics are bought, sold, and traded. They remain hidden in attic boxes or dresser drawers, buried deep within the family furniture, or have been tossed out by the generations that clean the clutter of the deceased. But as with all relics, their sacred power defies collective repression. In 2000, collector James Allen published *Without Sanctuary: Lynching Photography in America*, which curated photographs and postcards of lynchings that were sold, mailed, and distributed as souvenirs.[14] The collection also circulated in public galleries, including exhibitions at the Chicago Historical Society and the Andy Warhol Museum, and it received significant public attention for its attempt to resurface the artifacts with the pedagogical purpose of witnessing the past.[15] Allen's curatorial work and its display in museum exhibitions publicize the oft-forgotten fact that photographs and postcards of lynchings widely circulated throughout the United States, during the historical period extending from the 1890s through the 1960s.

During the early part of this period, southern progressives who promoted industrialization and championed social progress, sought to civilize the region and reform its primitive practices, including those of lynching. For some, such as lay Methodist W. D. Weatherford, that meant ridding the nation of lynching entirely. Though, it should be noted, such reforming rhetoric served elite white political and economic interests more so than it reduced the number of lynchings, and the persistent work of African American political activists was ultimately responsible for an actual decline in those numbers. For other southern whites, such as Methodist bishop Atticus G. Haygood, modern reform merely meant halting certain primitive forms of lynching. Haygood still defended lynching but denounced the practice of burning someone alive because it was "so much of the Dark Ages surviving in modern and civilized life."[16] Haygood offers an example of how southern Protestants manufactured modern religion in relation to what they identified as primitive practices. The modernizers of relics in this case were also its primitivizers. In his progressive march to Zion, Haygood eliminated a perceived primitive source of relics, but he retained its sacrificial essence. For Haygood, the violence of lynching was a foundation for his history and his civilization. Violence that served the Kingdom of God was not only acceptable behavior; it was requisite action for its realization. Later progressive southerners distanced themselves from Haygood and those like him, denouncing lynching of any kind, as Weatherford had done. Distinguishing themselves from primitive southerners, elite whites vowed to protect southern blacks from the violence of the Klan and radical white supremacists. Their self-identification as "moderns" was based on their professed civility, evidenced in their political ability to claim the end of lynching.[17]

As lynchings declined, however, prominent southern white citizens and their children continued to perform blackface minstrel shows, dressed in blackface, and walked the city streets on civic holidays, particularly Halloween and the Fourth of July. As southerners pursued the modern by reforming the primitive rite of lynching and its relics, they still celebrated the sacred play of racial drama. Blackface performers superseded lynched black bodies, with the smell of burnt cork substituting for the stench of smoldering flesh. In this process, southern whites sought to perform a racialized death without a public killing. Blackface was, in the context of its white usages, the cultural inheritor of religious lynchings. But like Haygood, its period of prominence eventually passed, as the civil rights movement successfully halted performances of blackface formerly considered publically acceptable. But southern whites did not stop killing blacks. Southern progressives removed death and its relics from public view, only to relocate violent death elsewhere, to the nighttime patrol and the state prison. As they reinscribed primitive violence in modern forms, they replaced lynching as the means of killing with the institutional mechanism of police shootings, which have persisted with startling regularity from mid-century to the present, despite continued attempts of social reform.[18]

What, then, does the historical arc of southern relics tell us about the cultural practices of American Protestants? It suggests three possible options for the presence and persistence of religious relics in popular culture. The first, as evidenced in Civil War reenactments, is the importance of religious relics to subcultural memory. The second, as illustrated in lynching relics, is the significance of religious relics to the cultural production and ritual construction of racial difference. And the third, as demonstrated in James Allen's work, is the power of those relics to resurface and strain against historical amnesia, to resist that cultural desire to repress memories of death. For there is a vast difference between death remembered in Civil War reenactments, of white soldiers, and death forgotten in mob lynching, of African Americans. Allen intentionally recovers a collective memory of lynching in order to recognize the haunting capacity of whites for racial violence. Death remembered, in that context, is not celebratory or worthy of reenactment. Rather, it speaks to the human fragility of religious violence. If relics are the remains of death, then the manner and context in which we evoke them speaks to how we imagine and remember ourselves in relation to the past. And, in a national context in which death is a cultural elision, expressed as consumer desire for celebrity connection, southern subcultures may carry forth, into the present moment, the religious fragments of American history.

Notes

1. Phillip Mahony, *Baseball Explained* (Jefferson, NC: McFarland & Company, 2014), 22.

2. Ellen Sandbeck, *Green Barbarians: How to Live Bravely on Your Home Planet* (New York: Scribner, 2010), 8.

3. Gregory Schopen, "Relic," in *Critical Terms for Religious Studies*, ed. Mark C. Taylor (Chicago: University of Chicago Press, 1998), 256.

4. Ibid.

5. Schopen, 257.

6. "U-Know," Drew University History, Drew University, https://uknow.drew.edu/confluence/display/DrewHistory/Whitefield%27s+thumb (accessed August 18, 2015).

7. Annabel Jane Wharton, "Relics, Protestants, Things," *Material Religion* 10, no. 4 (December 2014): 412–30.

8. Ira Glass, *This American Life*, "38: Simulated Worlds Transcript," October 11, 1996, http://www.thisamericanlife.org/radio-archives/episode/38/transcript (accessed April 15, 2016). For a detailed discussion of "farb" as the "worst insult" in the world of Confederate reenactors, see Tony Horwitz, *Confederates in the Attic* (New York: Random House, 1998), 10–12, 125–44.

9. Webb Keane, *Christian Moderns: Freedom and Fetish in the Mission Encounter* (Berkley: University of California Press, 2007).

10. Glass, "38."

11. Donald G. Mathews, "Lynching Is Part of the Religion of Our People: Faith in the Christian South," in *Religion in the American South: Protestants and Others in History and Culture*, eds. Beth Barton Schweiger and Donald G Mathews (Chapel Hill: University of North Carolina Press, 2004), 161.

12. Ibid., 166.

13. Edward J. Blum and W. Scott Poole, *Vale of Tears: New Essays on Religion And Reconstruction* (Macon, GA: Mercer University Press, 2005), 50.

14. James Allen, *Without Sanctuary: Lynching Photography in America* (Santa Fe, NM: Twin Palms, 2000).

15. Roger I. Simon, *A Pedagogy of Witnessing: Curatorial Practice and the Pursuit of Social Justice* (Albany: State University of New York Press, 2014), 41–74.

16. Mary Beth Swetnam Mathews, *Rethinking Zion: How the Print Media Placed Fundamentalism in the South* (Knoxville: University of Tennessee Press, 2006), 18.

17. Chad E. Seales, *The Secular Spectacle: Performing Religion in a Southern Town* (New York: Oxford University Press, 2013), 69–76.

18. Michelle Alexander, *The New Jim Crow: Mass Incarceration in the Age of Colorblindness* (New York: The New Press, 2010); Douglas Blackmon, *Slavery By Another Name: The Re-Enslavement of Black Americans from the Civil War to World War II* (New York: Anchor Books, 2008); Bryan Stevenson, *Just Mercy: A Story of Justice and Redemption* (New York: Spiegel and Grau, 2014).

Afterword

Charles Reagan Wilson as Scholar, Editor, Innovator, and Resonator

TED OWNBY

I write about the work of Charles Reagan Wilson as a friend and, for more than twenty-five years, a colleague in the History Department and the southern studies program at the University of Mississippi. Charles created and taught classes in southern religious history and regionalism, taught seminars on numerous topics related to southern history and cultural life, and collaborated with colleagues in teaching interdisciplinary southern studies classes. He frequently taught southern studies seminars through the lens of community and creativity, and he consistently reshaped classes to meet new developments in the American South and new movements among scholars. He directed numerous dissertations in southern history, often in southern religious history, and served on dozens of MA thesis committees in both southern studies and history, looking always to understand the author's goals and to encourage the author to build on strengths. This short essay, instead of trying to offer a critical perspective on the work of a friend we were honoring with the conference that produced these essays, points to a few of the features of Charles's scholarship that led so many people to gather to talk about southern religion and southern culture.

Of the several ways Charles's scholarship was doing work that later gained a name of a scholarly movement, one stands out. Charles was studying historical memory—a concept that today seems an essential, respected, and utterly normal part of scholarship—before the field of memory studies existed. When, in 1980, Charles published *Baptized in Blood*, studies of the uses of memory probably belonged more to anthropologists than historians. And to be more specific, Wilson linked the study of memory to the study of religion. A great deal of Charles's work analyzed roles religion played throughout southern history, especially beyond the churches and religious organizations.

Baptized in Blood began with some dramatic language: "This is a study of the afterlife of a Redeemer Nation that died. The nation was never resurrected, but it survived as a sacred presence, a holy ghost haunting the spirits and action of post–Civil War southerners."[1] Those two sentences set up some of the intriguing approaches that Charles takes in his work, with its intertwining emphases on redemption, nationhood, the sacred, and spirituality. *Baptized in Blood* asked what happened to people who lost what they believed was a holy war. Above all, it argues that the Lost Cause *became* a form of religion, with its own organizations, rituals, heroes, myths, language, and theology.

It is intriguing that *Baptized in Blood* rarely cited historians of the Civil War and postwar South. Instead, the scholarly inspirations for the book come from works of civil religion, anthropology, and ritual studies. So, Robert Bellah and his work on shared religious commitments to national ideals, Clifford Geertz and his analysis on complicated and overlapping webs of meanings, and Mircea Eliade and his studies of how communities understand symbols provided far more of the intellectual inspiration for *Baptized in Blood* than did scholars of the Civil War and postbellum South. With that unique intellectual apparatus, Wilson made some of his more significant contributions, arguing that ex-Confederates came to see the Civil War and military defeat as a period of religious testing, in which people responded to fears about their own materialism, or challenges to political control, or the possibilities of new definitions of race by calls to keep the faith. In intriguing ways, Charles used Perry Miller's work on Puritan identity more than the work of southern religious historians in order to argue that many white southerners in the late 1800s, like Puritans in the 1600s, understood themselves as a chosen people with a mission. The Lost Cause critique of materialism and embrace of righteous expressions of white supremacy set up twentieth-century movements like the Vanderbilt Agrarians and the second Ku Klux Klan. Charles himself wrote the best description and critique of Lost Cause scholarship in the new preface to *Baptized in Blood*, published in 2009, describing those who agreed with his work, disagreed with it, and took the topic in new directions.[2]

After *Baptized in Blood*, much of Charles's scholarship has appeared in essays. *Judgment and Grace in Dixie: Southern Faiths from Faulkner to Elvis* (1995, with a new preface in 2007) collected essays divided into the study of civil religion (thus continuing his focus from *Baptized in Blood*), then expressive culture, and finally "icons and spaces."[3] Some essays began as journal articles and encyclopedia pieces, some as public lectures, some as presentations to scholarly groups in settings from Mississippi to Europe. *Flashes of a Southern Spirit* (2011), also a collection of essays is, to use a reviewer's cliché, a *tour de force* in the way it brings together regional studies and religious studies.[4]

Charles's essays address many of the biggest issues about the cultural history of the American South, but they do not simply follow questions of previous major scholars. It can be tempting to offer intellectually easy generalizations about the South and southern culture. In many circles, for a long time, expectations asked for generalizations or "central themes" that concluded, for example, the South was poor but proud, or backward but full of creativity, or divided but full of potential, or obsessed with the past or tragedy or maintaining divisions based on ideas of white supremacy, or had a limited-options culture or limited-options politics or suffered from underdeveloped resources, or had traditions of storytelling or a sense of place or history or family or other things.

Looking for central themes could be exciting, but in an age in which we look for multiple stories and overlapping meanings, scholars rarely try to do that. It is important that Charles has used the most ambitious arguments from past southern studies scholars but has not adopted the practice of agreeing or disagreeing with them. How did he respond to C. Vann Woodward's concept of the Burden of Southern History, with white southerners carrying the weight of poverty, the shame of race, the sting of defeat, and the burdens but potential of history?[5] Charles uses the idea to explore what Bear Bryant meant to so many people in the South.[6] How about Samuel S. Hill's argument that the issue of conversion was the central feature of southern religious life, limiting theological possibilities and helping to quiet potential political applications?[7] Charles uses Hill's ideas to help think about Elvis Presley and also southern visionary art.[8] And John Shelton Reed's techniques for measuring regional identity, like the *Yellow Pages* test that mapped the businesses that used "South," "Southern," and "Dixie" in their titles?[9] Wilson uses those techniques not as models to follow but as inspiration and as a starting point, for example, in an essay called "Saturated Southerners."[10] Even H. L. Mencken's cranky old critique that southern religious life was too frowning and anti-intellectual to encourage much of an aesthetic side proved to be useful in an essay in which Charles, only implicitly criticizing Mencken, goes into detail analyzing the forms and languages of religious creativity.[11]

Charles's essays about regionalism almost always interpret other people's interpretations of region. What Wilson does *not* do is to offer regional traits in the tradition of W. J. Cash, who ended *The Mind of the South* with a list of ten positive and twelve negative characteristics of the South.[12] Wilson's work, like that of many scholars of his generation, will not allow "the South" to mean the region of white men with power, so he has spent great effort interpreting region from multiple perspectives. There are no essences, not even if one could reduce regional distinctiveness to a list of twenty-two traits. His goal is far less to figure out the meaning of the South than to study the ways different people at different times defined the region and its multiple meanings.

When Charles studies how people thought about regional identity, he most often shows how they made the connections to—or comparisons with—a broader American identity. He has rarely made South vs. North comparisons, or the comparisons people have made over the generations between Cavalier and Yankee (or Puritan), or backward and progressive, or pre-capitalist or anti-capitalist. Instead of making those comparisons, he studies how all sorts of people made them. For example, his two Faulkner essays, "William Faulkner and Southern Religious Culture" and "Our Land, Our Country: Faulkner, the South, and the American Way of Life," analyze how Faulkner understood southern religion and southern identity as part of American life and also in contrast to some of the primary ideals, myths, and directions of American life.[13]

The essays in *Flashes of a Southern Spirit* show Charles's approach to studying region as an ongoing process of studying conflicting interpretations. "The Burden of Southern Culture" is an ambitious response to C. Vann Woodward's much earlier argument about southern history. Wilson raises the problems of defining key terms like "culture," "South," and "region," and refers to Clifford Geertz's concept of webs of meaning to suggest that he ultimately wants to study "the connection between history and the sense of identity among southerners as a distinct social group."[14] The essay moves through a series of ways people have claimed and interpreted southern identity. First were pastoral visions of an Arcadian South. Next were the upper-class efforts during the antebellum period to claim the South as a paternalist and anti-materialist counterpoint to the industrial, capitalist, and faux-egalitarian Northeast. Third, the rise of evangelical religion in the early 1800s "injected new passions into southern identity that carried it far beyond Jefferson's vision, rooting it in vernacular fears, resentments, and aspirations truly emerging out of the frontier."[15] Fourth, secession and the Civil War inspired "a full-fledged sense of southern mission," and, fifth, the Lost Cause movement embodied "a new model of the South's destiny."[16] Sixth, the numerous writers and other artists of the early decades of the twentieth century created a series of intense works questioning whether the South offered America's crucible for addressing issues of race, rural life, and government. In the civil rights movement, the seventh in Charles's story of interpretations of southern meaning, important voices in the South called for justice and redemptive sacrifice while other voices opposed, by offering meanings of the South rooted in patriarchy and white supremacy. Part of southern self-identification in the post–civil rights period was, the article's eighth point, "the public acknowledgment that blacks were southerners too."[17] To summarize, Charles moved through eight meanings of southern identity, all of them contested, many of them coming from different groups, and all of them emerging from specific issues of their day.

C. Vann Woodward's "The Search for Southern Identity," written in the 1950s, found its only reason for optimism in the idea that recognizing past pain and past failures might discourage an overconfident America from assuming its own decisions were always right and just.[18] Charles, writing decades later, addressed the possibility for optimism in "The Myth of a Biracial South." That myth emerged, again, through multiple interpretations as African American and white southerners thought about new political and economic developments after the civil rights movement, confronted possibilities of shared religious perspective even without many shared religious experiences, thought about tourism, civil rights commemorations, music, North-to-South migrations, media portrayals, and other issues of regional identity. Calling the biracial South a myth meant biracialism was not a clear and easy direction toward which all things were moving, as made clear by various right-wing responses to the biracial South. The essay ended not by declaring success and not by pointing out the limits and possible hypocrisies of the notion of a biracial South. Instead, it ended with words of caution from Albert Murray in 1976: "As a southerner, my main response is through the blues. The nature of the blues is improvisation. . . . You must be ready for all eventualities."[19]

Charles has investigated the role religion played in all sorts of topics in the South—the Million Dollar Quartet, for example, and beauty pageants, and the popularity or unpopularity of books, and Richard Wright's thinking about Spanish popular religion. *Judgment and Grace in Dixie* includes two essays emerging from Charles's interest in understandings of death in southern culture. "Digging Up Bones" asks whether parts of southern culture developed "what can best be categorized as a culture of death."[20] Using the lyrics of country songs, the essay analyzed numerous musicians who confronted death in direct ways, detailed the relationships between death and romantic love by incorporating biblical perspectives into how the musicians understood human relationships and imagined family life as something that transcended earthly life, and used the deaths of celebrities as moments to reflect on the meaning of life. An essay on the death and funeral services of Bear Bryant contrasts the simplicity of Bryant's funeral services with the ways mourners turned it into a grander drama about southern institutions, vernacular culture, keeping things simple in the midst of success, and, for some, movement toward the possibilities of a biracial South.[21]

One should add a few words about Charles Reagan Wilson as editor, since he spent many years as coeditor, with William Ferris, of the *Encyclopedia of Southern Culture* (1989)[22] and then as the general editor of all twenty-four volumes of the updated collection, *The New Encyclopedia of Southern Culture* (2006–2013).[23] Wilson also served as consulting editor for the updated *Encyclopedia of Religion in the South*, working with Samuel Hill and Charles Lippy. Charles and I coedited the *Mississippi Encyclopedia* (2017).[24] And as if that were not enough, Charles edited or coedited collections of scholarly essays on southern religious history (1985),[25] the South and the Caribbean (with Douglas Sullivan-Gonzalez, 2001),[26] religion and the Civil War (with Randall Miller and Harry Stout, 1998),[27] regionalism in America (1998),[28] and religion and region.[29]

The *Encyclopedia of Southern Culture* was crucial to the life of the Center for the Study of Southern Culture at the University of Mississippi. First, it dramatized on page the effort to study the South as a concept that included everybody in the region, or who moved out of or through the region, or who gave serious thought to the region, with all groups included and all topics eligible for entries. In its own 1,600-page way, it rejected any assumptions that the terms "South" and "southern culture" belonged only to white people, or wealthy white people, white landowning people, famous people, or people with roots deep in the region. Second, editing those pieces meant that a great deal of good scholarship went through the Center for the Study of Southern Culture. Successful encyclopedia work meant upholding high standards of editing, with Ann Abadie, Sue Hart, William Ferris, and James G. Thomas, Jr., as encyclopedia collaborators. Third, it meant that numerous scholars appreciated being called on as experts. Walking with Charles Reagan Wilson through the meetings of the Southern Historical Association meant encountering the authors of dozens of articles who Charles and his colleagues had identified as the leading scholars on their subjects.

Encyclopedias, at least to many people, can seem to be stuffy works, big dusty volumes (or sprawling online projects) that claim serious scholarly authority but almost always take too long to complete and run the risk of becoming obsolete soon after they are completed. But there are far more positive than negative sides to encyclopedia work. Editing an encyclopedia means thinking about a wider range of topics than most scholars ever have reason to consider. By working with section editors and volume editors to identify new topics and new scholars to write about them, and by writing the occasional entry himself, encyclopedia work encouraged Charles to keep up with new scholarship, to consider new topics and even new fields and subfields of scholarship, and to occasionally write on topics that were necessary but whose scholars had not yet emerged. The encyclopedia editor needs to keep thinking about what is new in scholarship. And the fact that he wrote *Encyclopedia of Southern Culture* entries on topics from agribusiness to palm trees, from stoicism to "We Shall Overcome," from funerals to poverty to Clifton Chenier says something about the range of Charles's interests.[30]

That willingness to learn and think well beyond one's specialties has characterized much of Charles's work. Upon reading and listening to scholarship on the Global South—scholarship that has challenged scholars of the South to reconsider their subjects, assumptions, and their questions—Charles turned the concept into a major lecture and publication called *Southern Missions: The Religion of the American South in Global Perspective*.[31] When he recognized that a collection on religion and the Civil War did not have an essay comparing its topic to other nations and other civil wars, he wrote one.[32] And he began the introduction to *Flashes of a Southern Spirit* by suggesting how the scholarship of the new southern studies—another challenging recent movement that has encouraged close attention to the intended or unintended politics behind regional thinking—can benefit by getting a little religion.[33]

In his scholarship and teaching, Charles has shown impressive attention to aesthetic issues.[34] He has studied self-taught artists, and *Flashes of a Southern Spirit* is in part a response to art scholar Robert Ferris Thompson's daring 1984 volume *Flash of the Spirit*.[35] He has collaborated with multiple photographers, including David Wharton,[36] Tom Rankin,[37] and Larry McPherson.[38] Sound, especially music, is crucial to Charles's scholarship in essays on Hank Williams, Elvis Presley, and scholarly discussions of gospel, blues, and country music. And touch? In southern studies circles, Charles is famous for stopping in the middle of lectures to display relevant examples from his impressive collection of southern church fans, thus connecting religion and visual sources to ways people have tried to stay cool.[39]

Friends of Charles know that he frequently uses the expression that a good idea "resonates." As a scholar committed to interdisciplinary approaches in both southern studies and as an encyclopedia editor interested in virtually everything, he needs aesthetic language that goes far beyond conventional scholarly categories. An idea that resonates, in Charles's language, is not only one that is convincing and clear and clearly supported by evidence, though all of those are crucial. An idea that resonates, to use the first dictionary definition of the term, should "continue to produce a loud, clear, deep sound for a long time." As I write these words, Charles Reagan Wilson is working on the final chapters of a book on southern identity and ideas about civilization. I feel certain it will resonate.

TED OWNBY

Notes

1. Charles Reagan Wilson, *Baptized in Blood: The Religion of the Lost Cause, 1865-1920* (Athens: University of Georgia Press, 1980), 1.
2. Charles Reagan Wilson, "Preface to the 2009 Edition: The Lost Cause and Civil Religion in Recent Historiography," in Wilson, *Baptized in Blood: The Religion of the Lost Cause, 1865-1920*, rev. ed. (1980, repr., Athens: University of Georgia Press, 2009), ix-xx.
3. Charles Reagan Wilson, *Judgment and Grace in Dixie: Southern Faiths from Faulkner to Elvis* (1995, repr., Athens: University of Georgia Press, 2007).
4. Charles Reagan Wilson, *Flashes of a Southern Spirit: Meanings of the Spirit in the US South* (Athens: University of Georgia Press, 2011).
5. C. Vann Woodward, "The Search for Southern Identity," in *The Burden of Southern History* (1960, repr., Baton Rouge: Louisiana State University Press, 1968), 3-25.
6. Charles Reagan Wilson, "The Death of Bear Bryant: Myth and Ritual in the Modern South," in *Judgment and Grace*, 37-51.
7. Samuel S. Hill, Jr., *Southern Churches in Crisis* (New York: Holt, Rinehart, and Winston, 1967).
8. Charles Reagan Wilson, "'Just a Little Talk with Jesus': Elvis Presley, Religious Music, and Southern Spirituality," in *Flashes of a Southern Spirit*, 178-92; Charles Reagan Wilson, "Southern Religion and Visionary Art," in *Judgment and Grace in Dixie*, 73-83.
9. John Shelton Reed, "The Heart of Dixie: An Essay in Folk Geography," in *One South: An Ethnic Approach to Regional Culture* (Baton Rouge: Louisiana State University Press, 1982), 61-77.
10. Charles Reagan Wilson, "Saturated Southerners," in *Flashes of a Southern Spirit*, 61-76.
11. Charles Reagan Wilson, "Beyond the Sahara of the Bozart: Creativity and Southern Culture," in *Flashes of a Southern Spirit*, 117-27.
12. W. J. Cash, *The Mind of the South* (New York: Vintage Books, 1941), 439-40.
13. Charles Reagan Wilson, "William Faulkner and the Southern Religious Culture," in *Judgment and Grace*, 55-72; Charles Reagan Wilson, "Our Land, Our Country: Faulkner, the South, and the American Way of Life," in *Flashes of a Southern Spirit*, 77-92.
14. Charles Reagan Wilson, "The Burden of Southern Culture," in *Flashes of a Southern Spirit*, 53.
15. Ibid., 55.
16. Ibid., 56.
17. Ibid., 58.
18. C. Vann Woodward, "The Search for American Identity," in *The Burden of Southern History*, 3-25.
19. Charles Reagan Wilson, "The Myth of the Biracial South," in *Flashes of a Southern Spirit*, 113.
20. Charles Reagan Wilson, "Digging Up Bones: Death in Country Music," in *Judgment and Grace*, 96.
21. Charles Reagan Wilson, "Death of Bear Bryant," in *Judgment and Grace in Dixie*, 37-51.
22. Charles Reagan Wilson and William Ferris, eds., with Ann J. Abadie and Mary L. Hart, associate eds., *Encyclopedia of Southern Culture* (Chapel Hill: University of North Carolina Press, 1989).

23. Charles Reagan Wilson, general ed., James G. Thomas, Jr., managing ed., *The New Encyclopedia of Southern Culture*, vols. 1–24 (Chapel Hill: University of North Carolina Press, 2006–2013).

24. Ted Ownby and Charles Reagan Wilson, eds., Ann Abadie, Odie Lindsey, and James G. Thomas, Jr., associate eds., *The Mississippi Encyclopedia* (Jackson: University Press of Mississippi, 2017).

25. Charles Reagan Wilson, ed., *Religion in the South: Essays* (Jackson: University Press of Mississippi, 1985).

26. Douglass Sullivan-Gonzalez and Charles Reagan Wilson, eds., *The South and the Caribbean* (Jackson: University Press of Mississippi, 2001).

27. Randall M. Miller, Harry S. Stout, and Charles Reagan Wilson, eds., *Religion and the American Civil War* (New York: Oxford University Press, 1998).

28. Charles Reagan Wilson, ed., *The New Regionalism: Essays and Commentaries* (Jackson: University Press of Mississippi, 1998).

29. Charles Reagan Wilson and Mark Silk, eds., *Religion and Public Life in the South: In the Evangelical Mode (Religion and Region)* (Lanham, MD: Alta Mira Press, 2005).

30. All of these entries appear in the *Encyclopedia of Southern Culture*.

31. Charles Reagan Wilson, *Southern Missions: The Religion of the American South in Global Perspective* (Waco, TX: Baylor University Press, 2006).

32. Charles Reagan Wilson, "Religion and the American Civil War in Comparative Perspective," in Miller, Stout, and Wilson, ed., *Religion and the American Civil War*, 385–407.

33. Charles Reagan Wilson, *Flashes of a Southern Spirit*, xiv–xvi.

34. See his "Reimagining Southern Studies: Time and Space, Bodies and Spirits," in Jodi Skipper and Michele Coffey, eds., *Navigating Souths: Transdisciplinary Explorations of a US Region* (Athens: University of Georgia Press, 2017).

35. Robert Farris Thompson, *Flash of the Spirit: African and Afro-American Art and Philosophy* (New York: Vintage, 1984).

36. David Wharton, with an introduction by Charles Reagan Wilson, *The Power of Belief: Spiritual Landscapes from the Rural South* (George F. Thompson, 2016).

37. Tom Rankin, with an introduction by Charles Reagan Wilson, *Sacred Space: Photographs from the Mississippi Delta* (Jackson: University Press of Mississippi, 1993).

38. Larry E. McPherson, with an introduction by Charles Reagan Wilson, *Memphis* (Jackson: University Press of Mississippi, 2002).

39. Charles Reagan Wilson, "Church Fans," in *Judgment and Grace in Dixie*, 84–93.

Contributors

Ryan L. Fletcher is associate professor of history at Oakland City University.

Darren E. Grem is associate professor of history and southern studies at the University of Mississippi. He is author of *The Blessings of Business: How Corporations Shaped Conservative Christianity* and, with Amanda Porterfield and John Corrigan, coeditor of *The Business Turn in American Religious History.*

Paul Harvey is professor of history and Presidential Teaching Scholar at the University of Colorado, Colorado Springs. He is the author of *Christianity and Race in the American South: A History*, and other books.

Alicia Jackson is associate professor of history at Covenant College.

Ted Ownby is director of the Center for the Study of Southern Culture at the University of Mississippi and has a joint appointment in history and southern studies. He is the author of *American Dreams in Mississippi: Consumers, Poverty, and Culture, 1830–1998* and *Subduing Satan: Religion, Recreation and Manhood in the Rural South, 1865–1920*. He is the coeditor, with Charles Reagan Wilson, of the *Mississippi Encyclopedia*.

Otis W. Pickett is assistant professor of history at Mississippi College.

Arthur Remillard is associate professor of religious studies at Saint Francis University. He is author of *Southern Civil Religions: Imagining* *the Good Society in the Post-Reconstruction Era* and is currently writing a religious history of sports in America.

Chad Seales is an associate professor of religious studies at the University of Texas. His research addresses the relationship between religion and culture in American life, as evident in the social expressions of southern evangelicals, the popular religious practices of Latino migrants, and the moral prescriptions of corporate managers and business leaders. He is the author of *The Secular Spectacle: Performing Religion in a Southern Town*.

Randall J. Stephens is associate professor of British and American studies at the University of Oslo. He is the author of *The Devil's Music: How Christians Inspired, Condemned, and Embraced Rock and Roll*, *The Fire Spreads: Holiness and Pentecostalism in the American South*, and *The Anointed: Evangelical Truth in a Secular Age*, co-authored with Karl Giberson. He also edited *Recent Themes in American Religious History, Historians in Conversation Series*.

Index

Abadie, Ann, 126
abortion, 9
Africa, 11
African American Word of Faith, 80
African Methodist Episcopal Church (AME), xvi, 67
African Methodist Episcopal Zion Church (AME Zion), xvi, 67
African Presbyterian Church (Coloured Presbyterian Church), 58; Calhoun St. Congregation, 58
Africans, 12
Alabama, 64; Huntsville, 34; Tuscaloosa, 109
Alaska, 90
Alcorn Agricultural and Mechanical College, 64
AME Church Review, 65
Americanization, southern, 6
Andy Warhol Museum, 117
anti-lynching laws, 57
anti-populism, 34
Applebome, Peter, 79
Appomattox Court House, Battle of, 54
Arcadian South, 124
Arkansas, 19–46, 64, 71, 83; Article VII of the 1836 Arkansas Constitution, 19, 21; Benton County, 30; Chicot County, 19, 20, 21, 32–34, 42n27, 43n36; Christ Church in, 24; constitutional convention (1836), 19, 20; Crittenden County, 32; Delta, 20, 33; Desha County, 32; Episcopalians in, xvi; Fort Smith, 34–35, 37; Helena, 34; Hope, 91; House of Representatives, 22, 40n19; Lawrence County, 24–25; Legislature, 35; Little Rock, 23, 25, 27, 33–37; Marianna, 34; Mountain Spring campground in Dallas County, 27; Osceola, 93; Pay Act (1843), 24; Phillips County, 32, 34; Prairie County, 29, 37; Pulaski County, 26, 29, 33, 40n19, 41n24; Real Estate Bank (REB), 22, 23, 25, 33, 44n36; Senate, 22, 37, 40n19; St. Francis County, 22; Supreme Court, 23; Washington County, 23
Arkansas Baptist State Convention (ABSC), 27
Arkansas River, 27, 34
Ashley, Chester, 28, 41n25
Ashley, William E., 36
Asia, xvi
Associated Mechanics of Little Rock (AMLR), 29
Auburn University football, 108–9

Bacardi Bowl, 109
Bachman, John, 54
Baker, William, 106
Bakker, Jim and Tammy Faye, 79
Baptist Normal School (Holly Springs, Mississippi), 65

Baptists, 22, 24, 25, 27, 37, 80, 87–90, 108; Southern Baptists, 5, 7, 9
Barbee, J. D., 69
baseball, 113
Baseball Hall of Fame, 104
Bayliss, William H., 27
beauty pageants, 125
Bellah, Robert, 122
Bering Sea, 90
Bible, 6, 13, 26, 28, 35
Bible Belt, 8, 82; Norway's, 80
blackface, 118
blackness, xiii
Blackwood Brothers, 93
blues, xiv, 127
Bolton, S. Charles, 20
Bonds, Barry, 113–14
Book of Common Prayer, The, 20, 33, 36
Bowler, Kate, 80
Bray, James, 70
Brazil, 80
Brewer, Billy, 102–3
Brown v. Board of Education, 57
Brown, R. T., 63
Bryant, Bear, xiv, 14, 123, 125
Buchanan, James, 36
Buddhists and Buddhism, 8
Burns, Tommy, 105
Buttrick, Wallace, 66–67

Cadillac, x
California, Los Angeles, 82, 84
Calvin, John, 114
Calvinists and Calvinism, 34, 47–48; Calvinist Presbyterians, 54
camp meetings, 21
Campbell, Alexander, 27–28
Campbell, Heidi, 81
Campbell Movement, 27
Capers, Ellison, 54
capitalism, 4
Carlisle (Pennsylvania) Indians football, 109
Carnegie, Andrew, 70
Cartesian mind/body dualism, 12, 14
Cash, Johnny, vii, 7, 94

Cash, Wilbur J., 3, 7; *The Mind of the South*, 123
Cassels, Louis, 87, 96
Catholics, vii, 4, 7, 8, 87, 114, 115; in Atlanta, 8; in Charleston, 8; in Charlotte, 8; Eucharistic Congress, 8; Latino, 4–5, 7, 94, 114; in Little Rock, 8; Louisiana, 7; in Nashville, 8; in the Research Triangle, 8
Cavalier, 124
Center for the Study of Southern Culture, 126
Central Alabama Institute, 67
Central Tennessee College (Nashville, Tennessee), 65
Centre College Praying Colonels (Kentucky), 108–9; in the Dixie Classic, 108
Chadwick, Henry, 107
Chaplin, Charlie, 82
Charles, Ray, 94
Charles Edmonson Historical Lectures (Baylor University), xv
Chenier, Clifton, 127
Cherokee folktales, 14
Chicago Historical Society, 117
Chick-fil-A, xv
Chidester, David, 104
Christian Index, 63, 70, 72
Christian Right, xv
church fans, 6, 127
Churchill, Thomas J., 36
civil rights movement, xiv, 9, 72, 118, 124–25
Civil War, xiv, xvi, 47–60; reenactments, 114–19
Cobb, James C., xiv
Coca-Cola, x
Cold War, 90
College of Charleston, 59; Randolph Hall, 59
Colored Methodist Episcopal Church (CME Church), 63, 65, 67, 69, 70, 71; schools, 68
Confederacy, xiii, 6; death of, xiii; monuments to, xiii, 51, 54, 55, 57
Confederate Memorial Day, xiii, 48, 49, 51, 53
Cordell, Amelia, 33
Cottrell, Elias, 65–72
Coughlin, Father, 88

country music, 127
Cronwell, John Franklin, 105
Cumberland Presbyterian Church, 30–32

Dabney, Robert Lewis, 50; *A Defense of Virginia and the South*, 48, 53; *Ecclesiastical Equality of Negroes*, 53
Dalton, Georgia, 4
Daniel, Vattel Elbert, 86–87
Davies, Anthony H., 19–23, 33–34, 44; Davies Bill, 22
Davis, Jefferson, xiii
Dawkins, Richard, 81
Democratic Party, 90
Disneyland, 116
Divine, Father, 89, 90
Dodd, Gil, 105
Dogan, M. W., 67
Dram Shop Act, 39n11
Drennen, John, 25, 32
Drew University, 115, "U-Know" collaborative website, 115
Dunlap, William, xi; "hypothetical realism," xi, xii

Early, John, 36
Eco, Umberto, 116
Eliade, Mircea, 122
Ellis Auditorium (Memphis), 93
Elsner, Jás, xviin1
Emory and Henry College, 105
Episcopal Church, 20–21, 34
"Everyday Will Be Sunday By and By" (Dorsey), 93

Fairbanks, Douglas, 82
Falwell, Jerry, 79, 80
Faulkner, Sandford C., 33
Faulkner, William, 7
Ferris, William, 126
Fields, Barbara J., 21
Fifteenth Amendment, 65
Fillmore, Millard, 32
Finster, Howard, 6
Flash of the Spirit (Thompson), 127

Fletcher, Ryan L., xvi
Florida, 7; Cuban Americans in, 8; St. Augustine, 3
Flory, Richard, 94
Fontana, D. J., 94
Fourteenth Amendment, 65
Fourth of July, 118
Franklin, Ben, 88
Freedman's Aid Society, 64
Freedman's Bureau, 64
Freeman, George W., 26, 32, 33, 34, 37
Furby, 113

gay marriage, 9
Geertz, Clifford, 14, 122, 124
General Association of Eastern Arkansas, 22
General Education Board (GEB), 66, 68
Georgia Tech football, 109
Gettysburg, Battle of, 54
Girardeau, John Lafayette, 47–60; Confederate chaplain (Twenty-third Regiment of South Carolina Volunteers), 49; "Ecclesiastical Relations to Freedmen" (*Southern Presbyterian Review*), 52; "Spurgeon of the South," 51
Glass, Ira, 116
Global South, 80, 127
Godbey, W. B., 83
Gone with the Wind (Mitchell), xiv
gospel, xiv, 127
grace, ix, xiv, 27, 30, 55
Grace, Sweet Daddy, 89, 90
Graham, Billy, 82, 92, 105
Great Awakening, 11
Great Depression, 72, 89
gris-gris, 11
Gustafson, Cloyd V., 85–86

Hackett, Reverend Otis, 34
Hagee, John, 80
Hall, Tom T., 14
Halloween, 118
Hamill, James, 91–93
Hammond, J. D., 69, 70
Hampton Institute, 66

Happy News, 88
Happy News Café, 88
Harris, Sam, 81
Hart, Sue, 126
Harvard Crimson football, 108–9
Harvey, Paul, xvi, 84
Havana, Cuba, 109
Haygood, Atticus G., 118
Haygood Seminary, 65
Heisman, John, 109
Heyrman, Christine Leigh, 36
High Church Christianity, 7
Hill, James, 64
Hill, Samuel S., 123, 126
Hindus and Hinduism, 8
History of Religion in 5 1/2 Objects, A (Plate), 104
Hitchens, Christopher, 81
Holden, George, 32
Holly Springs School, 64
Holsey, Lucius, 68–70
Holy Table of Episcopalians, 32
Homer Seminary (Louisiana), 65
Horowitz, Tony, xiv
"How Happy Are They Who Their Savior Obey," 25
Howard, Perry W., 67
Howard University, 109–10
Hurricane Katrina, 3, 7

"Idol with the Golden Head, The" (Coasters), 83
Illinois, Chicago, 86
immigrants and immigration, 4, 7, 8; Asian, 7, 8; Jewish, 7; Latino/Mexican, 7, 8, 84
Indian Territory, 35
Islam, Southeast Asian, 8
Izard, Mark W., 22, 39n11

Jackson, Alicia, xvi
Jackson, Andrew, 23
Jackson, Stonewall, xiii, 57
Jacksonian Democrats, 22
Jamestown, Virginia, 3, 7
jazz, xiv

Jeffries, Jim, 106
Jesus Christ, ix, 6, 52, 82, 83, 84, 88, 92, 93
Jim Crow, xiii, 4, 9, 49, 59, 60, 64, 68, 72, 84, 110; in Memphis, ix; voter restriction, xiii. *See also* segregation and segregationists
Johnson, Jack, 105–6, 110; Johnson-Jeffries match, 106
Johnston, John T., 27
Jones, John T., 34
Jordan River (Israel), 90

Kansas: Topeka, 82; Wichita, 82
Kennedy, John F., 90, 96
Kentucky, xiii, 83; Louisville, 69
King, B. B., 94
King, Martin Luther, Jr., xiv, xv, 14
Kings River (Arkansas), 25
Klingo, John, 105
Kuhlman, Kathryn, 84

Laderman, Gary, 104
Ladies' Memorial Association of Charleston, 54
Lakey, Othal, 70
Lane, Isaac, 68, 70
Lane College (Lane Institute), 70
Latin America, xvi
Lawless, Elaine J., 96
Lay, Henry C., 34–35
Lee, Robert E., xiii
Leigh, Vivian, xiv
Lewis, Jerry Lee, vii, 94
LGBTQ activism, xv
Lippy, Charles, 126
Little Rock Bible Society (LRBS), 29
Livets Ord Theological Seminary (Uppsala, Sweden), 80
Llwellyn, John, 33, 44n36
Long, McKendree, 14
Lorraine Motel, xiv, xv
Lost Cause, xiii, xvi, 47–60, 116–17, 122, 124
Louisiana, 5, 7, 64, 106, 109; New Orleans, 3, 110; Spiritualists in New Orleans, 4
Louisiana State University football, 109

Lucy, Autherine, 71–72
Luter, Fred, 9
lynching, xiii, 114–19; lynch law, 117; relics, 119
Lyndon Baines Johnson Presidential Library (University of Texas-Austin), 116
Lynn, Loretta, 7

MacLeod, Elvis Aaron Presley, x
MacLeod, Paul, ix–x; death, x; Graceland Too, ix–x, xiii
Magnolia Cemetery (Charleston, South Carolina), 54
Mandrell, Barbara, 4
Martin, David, 94, 95
Maryland, 7
mass media, 79–96; ABC Radio, 92; Apollo Records, 90; *Arkansas State Gazette*, 27; *Atlanta Constitution*, 84, 108; *Baltimore Afro American*, 91; Broadcast and Film Commission of the National Council of Churches, 95; *Christ Is the Answer*, 92; *Christianity Today*, 87; Daystar Television, 80; Decca Records, 90; *Directory of Religious Broadcasters*, 79; electronic church, 79; Fox Movietone, 89; *Hartford Courant*, 91; *Hour of Power* (Schuller), 79; *Memphis Mirror*; 92; *New York Times*, x, 79; Nielson ratings, 79; *Radio Church of God*, 88; *Revivaltime* (Springfield, Missouri), 92; *Richmond Times-Dispatch*, 106; *Sparta (Georgia) Ishmaelite*, 117; *Sporting News*, 103; *This American Life*, 115; *Time* magazine, 89; Trinity Broadcasting Network, 80; *Washington Post*, 88; WJSB Radio Church of God, 90; WJSV (Alexandria, Virginia), 88; WMPS (Memphis), 93; *Words of Life*, 92
Mathews, Donald, xiii, 117
McGwire, Mark, 113–14
McMillin, Bo, 108
McPherson, Larry, 127
McPherson, Sister Aimee Semple, 84, 87–88, 90
Meltzer, Françoise, xviin1

Memphis First Assembly, 91, 93; *Grace and Truth*, 91
Mencken, H. L., 123
Methodism and Methodists, 5, 7, 22, 87, 105, 115, 118
Methodist Episcopal Church (MEC), 22–23, 26–27, 29, 64
Methodist Episcopal Church-South, 36; Arkansas Annual Conference, 36–37
Methodist Manual Labor School, 35
Meyer, Birgit, 80, 81
Michaux, Elder Lightfoot Solomon, 88–90, 92–93; "Happy Am I," 89
Miles, Edward R., 54
Miles, Henry, 68
Miles, W. H., 69
Miles Memorial College (Alabama), 65, 71–72
Miller, Perry, 122
Miller, Randall, 126
Million Dollar Quartet, 125
minstrel shows, 118
mission work, 51
Mississippi, 64, 71, 72; Columbus, 58; Football Celebration Saturday, 103; Hattiesburg, 91; Holly Springs, xi, 63–72; legislature, 64; Marshall County, 64, 68; Old Hudsonville, 65; Oxford, 102, 110; Philadelphia, 70; Pugh's Hill, 91; Sardis, 69; Tupelo, 91; Wall Hill, 67
Mississippi Conference, 68
Mississippi Episcopal Church South (MECS), 68, 69, 70
Mississippi Industrial College (MI), 63–72; Catherine Cottrell Hall, 63, 65, 71, 72; Hammond Hall, 69; Washington Hall, 63, 65
Mississippi State University football, 103
Mississippi Theological and Industrial Seminary, 65
Mitchell, Margaret, xiv
Moor, Annelies, 81
Moore, Scotty, 94
Moravians (North Carolina), 4
More Than Belief (Vasquez), 10, 12

Morgan, Gertrude, 14
Morrison, Jacky, 53
movement of mechanics (MM), 35–37, 45n44
Murray, Albert, 125
Muskogees (Alabama), 12
Muslims, 8, 10

National Association for the Advancement of Colored People (NAACP), 72
National Civil Rights Museum, xiv
National Negro Business League (Mississippi Chapter), 65
National Shrine of St. Francis of Assisi, 114
Nevada: Las Vegas, 116; Reno, 106
Never Surrender: Confederate Memory and Conservatism in the South Carolina Upcountry (Poole), 48
New Mind of the South, The (Thompson), 6
New South, xiii, 105–6
new southern studies, 127
Newton, Thomas W., 25–26, 28–33, 40n19, 41n24, 42n27, 43n36
Nigeria, 80
Nixon, Richard, 96
Norman Conquest, 116
North Carolina: Charlotte, 105; Dunn, 84; Wilmington, 107

O'Hara, Scarlett, xiv
Oklahoma: Oklahoma City, 8; Okmulgee, 91
Oral Roberts University, 80
Oregon, Portland, 85
Orishas, 11
Orr, David, 24
Otey, James H., 24

Paine College (Georgia), 69, 70; Paine Principle, 69–70
Palmer, Benjamin Morgan, 58
Paschal, George W., 28
Peay, Gordon N., 37
Pentecostalism and Holiness, vii, xiv, xvi, 7, 79–96; Assemblies of God, 84, 85, 91–92; Church of Christ (Holiness), 88; Church of God (Cleveland, Tennessee), 84; Church of God in Christ, 84; FCC (Federal Communications Commission), 94; Gospel Spreading Church of God, 88; Higher Life movement, 82; Oneness Pentecostals, 84; Pentecostal Holiness Church, 84
Philippines, 80
Phillips, Pearlie, 67–68
Pickett, L. L., 83
Pickett, Otis W., xvi
Pinson, M. M., 91
Playing with God (Baker), 104–5
police shootings, 119
Polk, James K., 42n25
Porter Fortune History Symposium, xvi
Powhatan Confederacy (Virginia), 4
Presbyterian Church in the United States (PCUS), 48, 52, 59; General Assembly, 49
Presley, Elvis, vii, ix, xiv, 6, 14, 91–94, 123, 127; death of, xii; Graceland, xi; "Hound Dog," 83; "Jailhouse Rock," x; NBC '68 Comeback Special, 94; relics, x; sacred figure, xi, xii, xvi, xviin1
Presley, Vernon and Gladys, 91
Price, William, 53
Puritan identity, 122

Race and Reunion: The Civil War in American Memory (Blight), 47–48, 60
Rankin, Tom, 127
reconciliation, 9
Reconstruction, 47–51, 53, 56–58, 60
Redeemers, 122
Reed, John Shelton, 123
regionalism and regional identity, 123, 124, 126
relics, religious, 113–19. *See also* lynching
Remillard, Arthur, xvi
revivalists, 21
Revolution, American, 8
Rice, Jamison W., 34
Richard, Little, vii, 94
Ricketts, R. C., 27

Ringo, Daniel W., 23, 32
Roane, John S., 32, 43n34
Robbins, Roger, 95
Roberts, Oral, 91
Robertson, Pat, 79
Robinson, Samuel, 53
rock and roll, xiv, 82, 94
"Rock around the Clock" (Richard [sic]), 83
Rockefeller, John D., Sr., 66
Rodgers, H. G., 91
Roosevelt, Franklin Delano, 90
Rose Bowl, 109
Rosenthal, Michele, 95
Rotary Club, 95
Rust College (Holly Springs, Mississippi), 64, 67–68, 72

Sabbath Breaking Act, 39n11
Sargeant, Kimon, 94
Saunders, T. F., 70
Schopen, Gregory, 114
Seagram Building (New York), 116
Seales, Chad, xvi
Second Presbyterian Church (Charleston, South Carolina), 50
sectionalism, 49
secularism, 10
segregation and segregationists, xiii, xiv, 49, 53, 57, 60, 72. *See also* Jim Crow
Shaw, J. B. F., 67
Shaw, William M., 106
Shroud of Memphis, The (Dunlap), vii, viii, xi, xii
Silk, Mark, 8; *Religion and Public Life in the South: In the Evangelical Mode* (Wilson and Silk), 9
slaves and slavery, xiii, xvi, 3, 4, 5, 6, 9, 11, 12, 13, 19–23, 26–29, 31–45, 47–53, 55, 58–60, 68, 70; African, 11; Christmas presents for, 33; slave revolts, 12
Smith, Jacqueline, xv
Smith, Lillian, 7
social justice, 10
Solid South, 4, 6, 7
Songfellows Quartet, 93

South Carolina, 83; Charleston, 6, 47, 49, 50, 52, 54, 56, 58; white Charlestonians, 59
South Korea, 80
Southern Baptist Convention (SBC), 9; Asians in, 9; blacks in, 9; Latinos in, 9
Southern Historical Association, 126
Southern Intercollegiate Athletic Association, 109
Southern Presbyterian Church, 53, 59
southern studies, xi, 123, 127
Spencer, William, 53
sports, college, 102–10
Spring River Baptist Association (Arkansas), 24
Spurious Liquors Act, 39n11
St. Francis Baptist Association (Arkansas), 22
Stamps Quartet, 93
State Normal School (Holly Springs, Mississippi), 64–65
states' rights, 57
Stein, Stephen, 95
Stephens, Randall, xvi
Stout, Harry, 126
Stout, William C., 35
"Strange Fruit" (Holiday), xiii
Student Nonviolent Coordinating Committee, 72
Stueck, William, xiv
Styron, William, 89
sugar plantations, 11
Sullivan-Gonzalez, Douglas, 126
Sunday, Billy, 82, 88, 90
Sunday school, 51
Swaggart, Jimmy Lee, 79; *Gospel Hour*, 79
Sydney (Australia) Anglican Synod, 105

Tara, xiv
Taylor, David Dwight, Jr., x, xiii
Taylor, Zachary, 32
Tebow, Tim, 105
technology, xvi
Teen-agers for Christ, 93
Tennessee, 71; Columbia, 91; Jackson, 64; Memphis, 64, 72, 91, 93, 107

Texas, 7, 64, 83; Dallas, 92; Mexican Americans in, 7–8
Texas A&M football, 103, 108–9
Thom, Sandy David, 59
Thomas, James G., Jr., 126
Thornwell, James Henley, 48
Tomlinson, A. J., 95
Trapnall, Frederick W., 25, 26, 29, 32–33, 40n19, 42n27, 43n36
Trescot, Paul, 51, 53
Trinity College (Duke University), 105, 108
Tweed, Thomas, 12

Ulster Scots, 13
United Society of Christian Endeavor, 106
United States House of Representatives, 25, 27
United States Senate, 42n27
University of Alabama, 71; Crimson Tide football, 102, 109
University of Chicago, 85
University of Florida, 105
University of Mississippi (Ole Miss), vii, 102–3, 121; Barnard Observatory, vii, xi; Center for the Study of Southern Culture, 126; football, 104, 105; Grove, 102, 104; History Department, 121; southern studies program, 121; Tupelo Room, vii, xi; Vaught-Hemingway Stadium, 102
University of North Carolina, student newspaper, 108

Vanderbilt Agrarians, 122
Vanderbilt University football, 108, 109
Vardaman, James K., 64–65, 66, 72
Vietnam War, 116
Vietnamese, 8
Virginia, 8; Little Boat Harbor (Newport News), 89; Newport News, 88; Richmond, 107

Wacker, Grant, 92
Wake Forest University, 105
Walker, David, 25
Wallace, George, 72
Walmart, xv
Ward, A. J., 45n48
Ward, Clara Mae, 90
Ward, C. M., 92
Warman's Civil War Collectibles Identification and Price Guide, 115
Warner, Pop, 109
Warren, John, 53
Washburn, Cephas, 30
Washington, Booker T., 66; Tuskegee Institute, 65, 66
Washington, DC, 88; Griffith Stadium, 89, 90
Washington Huskies football, 109
Waugh, Bishop Beverly, 23
Weatherford, W. D., 118
Welch, Gillian, xi
Wells, Ida B., 64
Wesley, John, 115
Westminster Confession of Faith, 54
Wharton, David, 127
Whig Party and Whiggish Episcopalians, 21, 25, 26, 28–33, 41n24, 43n36
White River Presbytery, 31
white supremacy and supremacists, xii–ix, 21–23, 35, 37, 45n44, 49, 57, 118, 122–24; Ku Klux Klan, 118, 122
Whitefield, George, 115
whiteness, xii–xiii
Wiley College, 67
Wiley College (Texas), 86
Wilkes, Thomas, 117
Williams, Daniel, 80
Williams, Edwin M., 37
Williams, Hank, xi, 127
Williamson, Joel, ix
Wilmot Proviso, 28
Wilson, Charles Reagan, xi, xii, xv, xvi, 4, 6, 8, 14, 79, 104, 114, 121; *Baptized in Blood: The Religion of the Lost Cause, 1865–1920*, xii, 14, 48, 122; "The Burden of Southern Culture," 124; as editor, 126; *Encyclopedia of Religion in the South*, 126; *Encyclopedia of Southern Culture*, 126, 127; *Flashes of a Southern Spirit:*

Meanings of the Spirit in the US South, xv, 14, 123, 124, 127; *Judgment and Grace in Dixie: Southern Faiths from Faulkner to Elvis*, xiv, 122, 125; Lost Cause, xiii; *The Mississippi Encyclopedia*, 126; "The Myth of a Biracial South," 125; *The New Encyclopedia of Southern Culture*, 126; "Our Land, Our Country: Faulkner, the South, and the American Way of Life," 124; *Religion and Public Life in the South: In the Evangelical Mode* (Wilson and Silk), 9; *Southern Missions: The Religion of the American South in Global Perspective*, 127; "William Faulkner and Southern Religious Culture," 124

Wilson, Cyrus W., 29–30, 32, 33, 43n34
Winfrey, Oprah, 113–14
Wisconsin Appropriations Bill (WAB), 28, 41n25
Without Sanctuary: Lynching Photography in America (Allen), 117
Woodruff, Fuzzy, 108–9
Woodward, C. Vann, 4, 7; Burden of Southern History concept, 123; "Search for Southern Identity," 125
World War I, 88
World War II, 83
Worley, Ted, 22
Wright, Frank Lloyd, 116
Wright, Richard, 14, 125

Yale University, 105
Yankee, 124
Yell, Archibald, 23–25, 28, 40n19
Yellow Pages, 123
Youth for Christ, 93

Zion Presbyterian Church (Glebe Street), 49, 50, 51, 53
Zion-Olivet Church, 59

www.ingramcontent.com/pod-product-compliance
Lightning Source LLC
Chambersburg PA
CBHW030556230426
43661CB00054B/2156